THE ILLUSTRATED ENCYCLOPEDIA OF
GUiTAR HEROES

Publisher and Creative Director: Nick Wells
Project Editor and Picture Research: Sara Robson
Art Director and Layout Design: Mike Spender
Digital Design and Production: Jake Jackson

Special thanks to: Chelsea Edwards, Anna Groves, Chris Herbert,
Victoria Lyle, Geoffrey Meadon, Fiana Mulberger,
Polly Prior, Julia Rolf, Catherine Taylor and Claire Walker

First published 2008
This edition published 2010 by
FLAME TREE PUBLISHING
Crabtree Hall, Crabtree Lane
Fulham, London SW6 6TY
United Kingdom

www.flametreepublishing.com

Music information site: www.flametreemusic.com

12 11

5 7 9 10 8 6 4

Flame Tree is part of the Foundry Creative Media Company Ltd

The CIP record for this book is available from the British Library.

ISBN: 978-1-84786-218-1

Printed in China

THE ILLUSTRATED ENCYCLOPEDIA OF

GUITAR HEROES

Rusty Cutchin • Hugh Fielder • Mike Gent • Michael Mueller • Dave Simons

consultant editor · Rusty Cutchin

foreword by Brian May

PUBLISHER'S NOTE

You only need to look to the internet and the hundreds of guitarist websites out there to realize that music fans have strong opinions on who the world's best guitarists are. Once you've seen a few of them it's hard to imagine another subject as hotly debated. Anyone who remembers the reaction of seething Van Halen fans after *Rolling Stone* magazine published their list of the 100 greatest guitarists of all time, in which Jack White featured higher than Eddie, will understand what we mean.

We knew that creating our very own definitive guide to the world's greatest legends of the sonic axe would be no easy task, and we were right. Aside from the buzz and excitement of producing such an ambitious book, deciding on our final list of heroes was a very long and drawn-out process. After all, getting a group of passionate music fans together to come up with our list of greats was bound to throw up a few arguments. One thing we came to understand is that if we polled every guitarist we have written about here to ask them who their favourites were, then we probably would have ended up with a book that was well over 1,000 pages long.

All this aside, after expert advice from our wonderful and noted authors, and of course Dr Brian May, our very own Guitar Hero, we have come up with a book that we hope will satisfy even the most die-hard of music fans. We believe it is the sheer scope of this book that will appeal to all, and we hope you agree!

There are many guitarists who narrowly missed out on a spot in this edition. Apologies must be given to Joe Bonamassa, Doyle Dykes, Guthrie Govan, Shawn Lane, Jeff Loomis, Brent Mason and George Van Eps, each of whom came very close to being included. We also want to give a special mention to Vivian Campbell, Steve Clark, Phil Collen, Jeff Healey, Tony Hicks, Steve Jones, John Mayer, Mick Ralphs, Brian Setzer, Laurie Wisefield and Link Wray, who would also have made it if we had had the space. A final apology must go out to the girls, especially Joan Jett, Joni Mitchell and Nancy Wilson. Where are all the guitar heroines? The list goes on and on.

One thing we can all agree on is that a book like this will never be complete. No doubt we will continue to revise and update it, so if we've missed out any of your personal favourites, please email us with your suggestions at guitarheroes@flametreepublishing.com. We can't promise to agree with you, but we would love to hear from you. Let the debate rage on!

Our 181 heroes have been grouped into seven chapters based on the genre of music they are most closely associated with. Each chapter is then organized chronologically according to the guitarists' birth dates. Whilst we resisted the temptation to rank our heroes according to their talents, we have hinted at our personal favourites by kicking things off with a special Virtuosos chapter, covering a range of genres.

CONTENTS

contents

alternative and indie

soft rock and pop

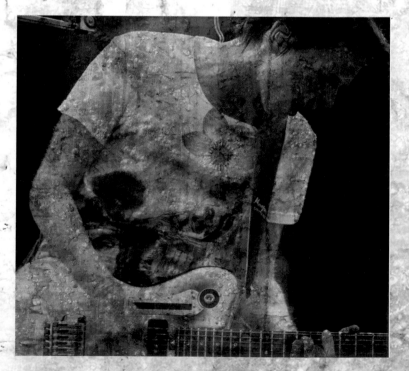

contents

beyond rock

FOREWORD

There have been many books about guitarists, but none quite like this one. When I was asked to provide a foreword for this new project, I, was in the beginning, happy to be included in such auspicious company at all, but then, humbled by the task of introducing such an ambitious work. Following their huge success with *The Definitive Illustrated Encyclopedia of Rock*, Flame Tree decided to take up the challenge of producing a truly encyclopedic work on, not just guitarists, but Guitar Heroes.

I have always felt that the supreme joy of the guitar is that it is a voice, a vehicle for expressing emotion, for every kid, of any age, who picks it up. We are all still kids with a guitar in our hands, and there is little point in debating 'who's best' ... we are all outputting our passions in a way which is somehow defined by the passion inside us. So what is it that makes a guitarist into a hero? It has to be simply the passion he elicits in others. Flick through the huge catalogue of guitarists here, covering a wide spectrum of styles ... and you will be reminded, on every page, of great moments in guitar music, when the players not only thrilled their audience, but inspired those who followed to reach inside themselves and make new great moments.

Here you will find the inspiration for almost every known kind of guitar-speak, from pivotal pioneers like Chet Atkins and Les Paul to rock giants like Beck, Van Halen, Page, Townshend and Hendrix. But here also you will find tantalizing tastes of all kinds of greatness, from Segovia to Satriani, from Marvin to Malmsteen, from Reinhardt and Burton to Rundgren and Syd Barrett, and beyond. Almost by definition, no catalogue of Guitar Heroes could ever be complete ... beauty is in the eye of the beholder, and heroism must surely be in the ears and eyes of those who 'were there'. So there will inevitably be cries of 'shame' from those who witnessed, for instance, a superb player in Nashville breaking five strings in one song and still managing to finish the piece sounding like an orchestra – I'm sorry – you have to be there! Yes, truly there are many great and inspiring players the compilers (not my gig, I'm happy to say!) could not squeeze in. But if you want to have at your bedside, or on your coffee-table (or bar) a genuine attempt to collate an across-the-board collection of some of the greatest Guitar Heroes who ever spanked a plank, look no further – this is the encyclopedia for you.

Rock!

Brian May

ViRtuosos

The guitar hero is the iconic image of rock'n'roll. Beyond image, the rock-guitar virtuoso is about the playing – the talent, the technique and, above all, the dedication. The dedication involves practising for hours every day, cultivating the talent and the technique, obsessing over sounds and how to create and control them and then putting it all into the context of a performance as part of a rock band onstage. But while the guitar hero inspires the audience, the guitar virtuoso also inspires and influences other guitarists, who can see beyond the image to the dedication and details in the music and the performance.

FRANK ZAPPA

FATHER OF HARMONY

Renowned as the leader of avant-garde satirical group the Mothers Of Invention in the Sixties, Frank Zappa (1940–93) developed a singular guitar prowess that emerged in the Seventies as his band became increasingly adventurous, drawing on a wide variety of classical, jazz and rock forms while maintaining their razor-sharp wit. His approach to playing influenced many guitarists, including band members Steve Vai and Adrian Belew.

Zappa's guitar style was unique – based more around harmony than melody – because he approached the instrument as a composer and arranger rather than as a player only. 'There are plenty of people who play faster than I do, never play a wrong note and have a lovely sound,' Zappa told an interviewer in 1984. 'But there isn't anyone else who will take the chances that I will take with a composition onstage in front of an audience.'

Born in 1940, Zappa grew up in Los Angeles and wrote film scores in the early Sixties before forming the Mothers Of Invention in 1965. His guitar playing on *Freak Out!* (1966), *Absolutely Free* (1967) and *We're Only In It For The Money* (1968) was succinct, but he began stretching out on solo albums like *Hot Rats* (1969), *Apostrophe (')* (1974), *One Size Fits All* (1975) and *Zoot Allures* (1978). Zappa's reputation was enhanced by extended guitar solos on a succession of live albums through the Seventies – *Live At The Fillmore East* (1971), *Roxy & Elsewhere* (1974), *Live In New York* (1977) and *Sheik Yerbouti* (1979).

In 1981 Zappa encouraged his guitar fan club with a triple album set called *Shut Up And Play Your Guitar* that featured 'solos and nothing else'. And he continued to push his own boundaries with the rock musical *Joe's Garage Acts I, II & III* (1979), *Ship Arriving Too Late To Save A Drowning Witch* (1982) – featuring 'Valley Girl', the closest he came to a hit single – and *Jazz From Hell* (1987), which won a Grammy for Best Rock Instrumental Performance.

By the time of his death from prostate cancer in 1993, Zappa had amassed a catalogue of over 60 albums.

JIMI HENDRIX
THE GUITAR EXPERIENCE

Jimi Hendrix (1942–70) remains the most innovative and influential rock guitarist in the world. He changed the way the guitar was played, transforming its possibilities and its image. Other guitarists had toyed with feedback and distortion but Hendrix turned these and other effects into a controlled, personalized sound that generations of guitarists since have emulated and embellished.

He was left-handed and played his favourite guitar, a right-handed Fender Stratocaster, upside down and re-strung, giving him a different perspective on the Fender's tremolo arm and enabling him to bend notes and chords without the strings going out of tune. He never stopped looking for ways to get new sounds out of the guitar, from electronic gadgets he could plug into it, to the experimental techniques he employed in the studio.

Hendrix's career was remarkably brief. He was born in Seattle in 1942 but there was no hint of success before he moved to England in 1966 after being spotted in a New York club by Chas Chandler, bassist with the recently disbanded Animals. Hendrix had started playing guitar in 1958, three years before he joined the army. He was discharged because of a broken ankle in 1962 and spent the next four years as a touring musician with, among others, Little Richard, the Isley Brothers and Curtis Knight.

Arriving in England, Hendrix formed the Jimi Hendrix Experience with bassist Noel Redding and drummer Mitch Mitchell. He recorded a version of 'Hey Joe', creating a buzz that launched his career. His second single, 'Purple Haze', early in 1967, galvanized the music scene. *Are You Experienced* (1967) was an audacious debut album, drawing on a whole range of styles and influences and opening up a new world of guitar sounds that included flanging, double tracking and variable recording speeds.

Hendrix returned to America in the summer of 1967 to play the Monterey Pop Festival, a stunning debut that was captured on film. Before he returned to England he recorded 'Burning Of The Midnight Lamp', which showcased the recently introduced wah-wah pedal, making it another weapon in the Hendrix arsenal.

Barely six months after his first album, *Axis Bold As Love* (1967) pushed the sonic innovations, particularly the phasing technique, still further and fused his rhythm and blues influences with the music he had heard in England. An instant hit album in the UK, the album also spent a year on the American charts, and Hendrix spent much of 1968 touring his home country.

Electric Ladyland (1968) was his most ambitious and successful record, with 16 songs spread across a double album, ranging from the futuristic funk of 'Crosstown Traffic' to the emblematic style of 'Voodoo Child (Slight Return)'. But if Hendrix's music was peaking, tensions were growing within his band. As Hendrix jammed with a widening circle of musicians in the studio, Redding in particular became irritated. In June 1969 Hendrix disbanded the Experience and formed a new band called Gypsy Sun And Rainbow that included bassist Billy Cox and guitarist Larry Lee, with whom Hendrix had played before heading to England in 1966.

With Mitchell reinstated as drummer, Gypsy Sun And Rainbow made a tentative debut at the Woodstock Festival in August, notable for Hendrix's unaccompanied rendition of 'The Star Spangled Banner', performed against a sustained wall of feedback. In fact he had been playing it regularly for the past year.

Within a month the band had disintegrated and little was heard from Hendrix until the end of 1969, when he played two nights at New York's Fillmore East with a new trio called the Band Of Gypsys, featuring Cox and drummer Buddy Miles. *Band Of Gypsys* (1970) was the last Hendrix album released before he died.

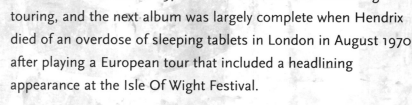

The Band Of Gypsys lasted no longer than Gypsy Sun And Rainbow, and Hendrix reverted to the Experience with Cox and Mitchell. The first half of 1970 was divided between recording and touring, and the next album was largely complete when Hendrix died of an overdose of sleeping tablets in London in August 1970 after playing a European tour that included a headlining appearance at the Isle Of Wight Festival.

In the aftermath of his death, unreleased studio recordings were hurriedly released, bearing no relation to the album he had been planning. It wasn't until 1997 that *First Rays Of The New Rising Sun*, roughly corresponding to a suggested track listing Hendrix had scrawled on a tape box, was released. In the meantime over a hundred studio and live albums of varying quality and provenance had come out. It is a tribute to Hendrix's genius that his status as the ultimate guitar hero remains undiminished.

JIMMY PAGE

YARDBIRDS TO LED ZEPPELIN

The last of the triumvirate of guitar legends who played with the Yardbirds, Jimmy Page (b. 1944) became an icon of rock guitarists in the Seventies with Led Zeppelin. Elements of his playing style have been copied to the point of cliché in the years since Led Zeppelin dominated the rock world, but as the originator Page developed the heavy-metal blueprint for all the guitarists who followed.

Jimmy Page was born and grew up in Epsom, south of London. His first electric guitar was a 1949 Gibson Les Paul, the guitar with which he became associated throughout his career. After leaving school at 16 he briefly played with Neil Christian & the Crusaders before becoming an in-demand session musician.

Between 1962 and 1968 Page played on hundreds of recording sessions for a variety of bands including the Rolling Stones, the Who, the Kinks, Donovan, Them, Cliff Richard and Burt Bacharach. He was often hired as an insurance policy in case the band's guitarist couldn't cut it in the studio. He played on Jet Harris & Tony Meeham's 'Diamonds', a No. 1 in 1962, and Joe Cocker's 'With A Little Help From My Friends', a No. 1 in 1968.

The joy of sessions was already fading by 1966 when Page joined the Yardbirds, for whom Jeff Beck was lead guitarist. A short but exciting experiment with Beck and Page as twin lead guitarists ended when Beck abruptly left the band. Page soon found himself carrying an increasingly disillusioned band, and after the commercial failure of *Little Games* (1967), he started planning a new band, encouraged by Yardbirds' road manager Peter Grant.

Page, Robert Plant, John Paul Jones and John Bonham came together as the Yardbirds were disintegrating in 1968, and recorded *Led Zeppelin I* (1969) before manager Peter Grant secured a record contract with Atlantic. The album's raw sound and Page's dynamic range, along with innovative techniques like playing his guitar with a violin bow, made a resounding impact. *Led Zeppelin I* It spent 18 months in the charts in the US and UK.

Led Zeppelin II (1969) maintained the same high energy level and topped the charts on both sides of the Atlantic, propelled by Page's signature riff on 'Whole Lotta Love'. With more time to prepare *Led Zeppelin III* (1970), the band broadened their scope, adding more folk-influenced acoustic songs and putting more emphasis on the arrangements. This approach paid off spectacularly on *Led Zeppelin IV* (1971), which featured the bombastic 'Black Dog' and 'Rock And Roll', the more restrained 'Misty Mountain Hop' and 'Going To California', and the monumental 'Stairway To Heaven', which drew on elements of both. The band's refusal to release singles or appear on TV did not prevent 'Stairway To Heaven' from becoming the most-played album track on radio.

Through the mid-Seventies Led Zeppelin swept all before them with *Houses Of The Holy* (1973), *Physical Graffiti* (1975), *Presence* (1976), and an epic live show that was captured in all its rock-god glory on the film and soundtrack album *The Song Remains The Same* (1976). But in the summer of 1977 the band's career came to a sudden halt when Plant's son died suddenly during yet another successful American tour. They returned in 1979 with two major British shows at the Knebworth Festival, but the following year, while rehearsing for a US tour, Bonham died after a drinking binge and Led Zeppelin was at an end.

During the Eighties Page occupied himself with the film soundtracks *Death Wish II* (1982) and *Lucifer Rising* (1987), a solo album *Outrider* (1988), the Robert Plant collaboration *The Honeydrippers Volume One* (1984), and *The Firm* project with singer Paul Rodgers. In the Nineties he worked with former Deep Purple singer David Coverdale on *Coverdale Page* (1993) before reuniting with Plant for *No Quarter* (1994) and *Walking Into Clarksdale* (1998). In 2000 he worked with the Black Crowes on *Live At The Greek*.

One-off Led Zeppelin reunions at Live Aid (1985) and Atlantic Records' twenty-fifth anniversary (1988) proved unsatisfactory, but towards the end of 2007 the band reformed with Bonham's son Jason on drums to play a spectacular show at London's O2 Arena to benefit the late Atlantic founder Ahmet Ertegun's charitable trust.

At the closing ceremonies of the 2008 Olympics, Jimmy Page represented Britain in a performance marking the change in Olympic venue to London in 2012. The same year he co-produced a documentary film on the history of the electric guitar, entitled *It Might Get Loud*. In January 2010, Page announced the publication of a limited-edition autobiography.

JEFF BECK

YARDBIRDS TO PIONEER

The most mercurial guitarist of his generation, Jeff Beck (b. 1944) has never conformed to the conventional image of a guitar hero. He has repeatedly left or broken up bands before their commercial potential could be realized. He restlessly changes style from one album to the next, refusing to be tied down musically. And his live appearances are intermittent. 'I just can't stand endless nights playing,' he told an interviewer in 1990. 'The pitch that I play at is so intense that I just can't do it every night.' But despite these idiosyncrasies, he is widely acclaimed as a genius.

These virtuoso qualities became apparent soon after he joined the Yardbirds in 1965 as a 20-year-old unknown to replace Eric Clapton. His vibrant, fearless playing – using distortion, bottleneck and Indian influences – was a major element of the band's biggest hits: 'Heart Full Of Soul', 'Evil Hearted You', 'Shapes Of Things' and 'Over Under Sideways Down'. But towards the end of 1966 he abruptly quit the band, which had recently added guitarist Jimmy Page, at the start of an American tour.

Early in 1967 Beck scored a solo hit single with 'Hi Ho Silver Lining', an unabashed pop song that he has disowned ever since. But the instrumental flip side, 'Beck's Bolero', a riotous swirl of feedback, overdubbing and backwards guitar, has become something of a signature tune.

He then formed the Jeff Beck Group with Rod Stewart on vocals and Ron Wood on bass. *Truth* (1968) is arguably a template for Led Zeppelin's first album a year later with Beck taking the blues to excess. But internal tensions broke apart the group after they recorded their second album, *Beck-Ola* (1969), and Stewart and Wood decamped to form the Faces.

Beck had been planning to form a band with bassist Tim Bogert and drummer Carmine Appice from Vanilla Fudge when he cracked his skull in a car crash in 1969, putting his career on hold for 18 months. He returned with a new group of his own that included Bobby Tench (vocals), Max Middleton (keyboards) and Cozy Powell (drums), blending rock with funk on *Rough And Ready* (1972). When *Beck Bogert & Appice* finally got recorded

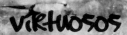

in 1973, it was suitably bombastic but lacked a singer to match the instrumental pyrotechnics and by early 1974 Beck was on his own again.

After another hiatus Beck re-emerged with the all-instrumental, funk-infused jazz-rock of *Blow By Blow* (1975), his most successful album. Recorded as a quartet with Max Middleton, Phil Chenn (bass) and Richard Bailey (drums), the album was produced by former Beatles producer George Martin. For the follow up, *Wired* (1976), Beck brought in Mahavishnu Orchestra keyboard player Jan Hammer and drummer Narada Michael Walden. Hammer also was featured on *There And Back* (1980), which included contributions from UK musicians Tony Hymas (keyboards) and Simon Phillips (drums).

While Beck's solo career was becoming less prolific, he was making guest appearances on Stevie Wonder's *Talking Book* (1972), Stanley Clarke's *Journey To Love* (1975) and *Modern Man* (1978), Rod Stewart's *Camouflage* (1984), Robert Plant's *The Honeydrippers Volume One* (1984), Mick Jagger's *She's The Boss* (1985), Roger Waters' *Amused To Death* (1992) and Kate Bush's *The Red Shows* (1993). He also took part in the 1993 ARMS benefit shows for multiple sclerosis research with Eric Clapton and Jimmy Page – the only time all three legendary Yardbirds guitarists have appeared on the same stage together.

His own albums have taken bold and diverse directions. *Flash* (1985), produced by Nile Rodgers, confronted the Eighties style of rock guitar as well as disco. *Guitar Shop* (1989) won a Grammy for Best Instrumental Rock Album. *Crazy Legs* (1993) was a tribute to Gene Vincent's guitarist Cliff Gallup. *Who Else!* (1999), *You Had It Coming* (2001) and *Jeff* (2003) all set Beck's guitar against a varying backdrop of techno beats and electronica. *Live Beck!* (2006), recorded in 2003, and *Live Bootleg USA 06* (2006), faithfully captured his concert performances.

In recent years Beck has opened for B.B. King and appeared at Eric Clapton's Crossroads Guitar Festival (2004) and the Grammy Awards (2010). He has performed with artists as diverse as Kelly Clarkson (for charity) and the young bassist Tal Wilkenfeld. Beck announced a world tour in early 2009 and critically acclaimed *Emotion & Commotion* was released in 2010.

Beck's preferred guitar is a Fender Telecaster, although in the Yardbirds he played a Fender Esquire. He gets his distinctive sound by using his fingers rather than a plectrum and using the tremolo arm and a wah-wah pedal.

ERIC CLAPTON

YARDBIRDS TO LEGEND

The most famous living guitarist in the world, Eric Clapton's (b. 1945) career has passed through an extraordinary series of highs and lows during his five decades as a guitar hero. He has also experimented with numerous stylistic changes but has always returned to his first love, the blues.

A love child born in 1945, Clapton was brought up by his grandparents, whom he believed were his parents until he was nine. He started playing guitar at the age of 13 and in 1963, after playing in a couple of south London bands, joined the Yardbirds, establishing his reputation on the rough and ready *Five Live Yardbirds* (1964). He quit the Yardbirds in 1965 after recording their first hit, 'For Your Love', and joined John Mayall's Bluesbreakers. *Bluesbreakers With Eric Clapton* (1966) is still regarded as one of the seminal blues guitar albums, characterized by the fierce, sustained notes that Clapton created by controlled feedback.

Before the album was released, Clapton left to form Cream with fellow virtuoso musicians Jack Bruce (bass) and Ginger Baker (drums). Their jazz background was the perfect foil for Clapton's blues and the band became superstars as a result of three albums – *Fresh Cream* (1966), *Disraeli Gears* (1967) and *Wheels Of Fire* (1968) – and a series of American tours. But within two years the band was worn out and Clapton subsequently hooked up with another virtuoso, ex-Spencer Davis Group and Traffic keyboard player and singer Steve Winwood, to form Blind Faith, which also included Baker. Unfortunately, *Blind Faith* (1969) could not live up to the hype surrounding the group, and they split after one American tour.

Clapton sought refuge in Blind Faith's support group, Delaney & Bonnie, who helped him record his first solo album, *Eric Clapton* (1970) and then provided him with the musicians for his next group. Derek & the Dominos recorded one incandescent album dealing with pain and unrequited love, *Layla And Other Assorted Love Songs* (1970). Here Clapton was joined by guitarist Duane Allman, and the band toured Britain and America before imploding in a maelstrom of drug use.

Clapton was left with a heroin dependency, and after appearing – just – at George Harrison's *Concert For Bangladesh* (1971) he retreated from view for the next three years, apart from one shaky show at London's Rainbow Theatre. He returned, clean and rejuvenated, with *461 Ocean Boulevard* (1974), a major worldwide hit album that introduced the then unknown Bob Marley through Clapton's version of 'I Shot The Sheriff', a No. 1 hit in the US. He also broadened his skills from guitar hero to songwriter, notably on *Slowhand* (1977) with 'Wonderful Tonight' and 'Lay Down Sally'. Extensive worldwide touring helped maintain his popularity, but by the end of the decade another dependency, alcohol, was hampering his playing.

By 1983 he was sober again, and *Money And Cigarettes* (1983) and *Behind The Sun* (1985) confirmed his return to form. His appearance at Live Aid in 1985 and his duet with Tina Turner on 'Tearing Us Apart' in 1987 raised his profile further. *Crossroads* (1988), a four-CD box set, went triple platinum in America, setting new standards in the reissue market, while *Journeyman* (1989) was his most successful contemporary rock album to date.

But it was the blues that set the seal on Clapton's career. In 1992 he played the first Unplugged show for MTV, performing an acoustic version of 'Layla', 'Tears In Heaven' (written after the death of his son Conor) and a selection of blues songs. *MTV Unplugged* (1992) sold over 12 million copies. *From The Cradle* (1994), an electric blues album, topped the UK and US charts, selling 10 million copies.

Since then Clapton has balanced contemporary albums, such as *Pilgrim* (1998) and *Reptile* (2001), with the blues albums *Riding With The King* (2001) – recorded with B.B. King – and *Me And Mr Johnson* (2004) – featuring songs by Clapton's hero Robert Johnson. Clapton also revisited his past, joining John Mayall for his seventieth birthday concert in 2003, reuniting with Cream in 2005 and teaming up with Winwood for shows throughout 2008 and 2009.

In March, 2009, Clapton performed with The Allman Brothers Band for their 40th anniversary but cancelled a spot at the Rock and Roll Hall of Fame's 25th anniversary show in October 2009 because of gallstone surgery. Clapton teamed again separately with Jeff Beck and Steve Winwood for shows during the first half of 2010.

In his early years Clapton favoured Gibson guitars, starting with a Les Paul Sunburst, and followed by a Gibson Firebird, a Gibson ES-335 and a Gibson SG (painted in psychedelic design), before moving to Fender Stratocasters in 1969. His most famous Stratocaster, 'Blackie', was sold at auction for $959,500 in 2004 to raise money for his Crossroads Centre for drug and alcohol addictions. In 1988 Fender inaugurated their signature range of guitars with an Eric Clapton Stratocaster model.

DAVID GILMOUR

PINK FLOYD PIONEER

As the guitarist in Pink Floyd, David Gilmour's (b. 1946) place in the pantheon of guitar heroes is guaranteed. But it's not simply his playing on albums like *The Dark Side Of The Moon* that has assured his status. His meticulous attention to the sound and tone of his guitar in the studio and in concert has earned the universal admiration of guitarists, as well as millions of Pink Floyd fans.

Gilmour was born in Cambridge in 1946 and as a teenager he was friends with Syd Barrett, with whom he learned to play guitar, and Roger Waters. When Barrett and Waters moved to London in the early Sixties, where they formed Pink Floyd with Richard Wright and Nick Mason, Gilmour stayed in Cambridge and played with local band Joker's Wild.

At the beginning of 1968 Gilmour was asked by Waters to join Pink Floyd as an additional guitarist to cover for Barrett, whose performances and behaviour were becoming increasingly erratic. Within weeks Barrett left the group and Gilmour became lead guitarist. The band had already started work on their second album, *A Saucerful Of Secrets* (1968), and Gilmour helped to structure the title track. Gilmour played an important instrumental and vocal role in the band compositions that formed the major part of *Atom Heart Mother* (1970) and *Meddle* (1971), as well as contributing songs of his own. And although Waters was responsible for the underlying concept behind the band's defining album, *The Dark Side Of The Moon* (1973), Gilmour's carefully constructed guitar parts and solos, particularly on 'Time' and 'Money', were a distinctive element of the Pink Floyd sound. While most guitarists created their sound from overdriven distortion, Gilmour focused on getting a strong, clean tone from his guitar that he then blended with a variety of effects pedals.

He developed his sound further on *Wish You Were Here* (1975). His evocative, melancholic playing on 'Shine On You Crazy Diamond' set the atmosphere for the album's centrepiece. He also co-wrote the acoustic 'Wish You Were Here' with Waters. While Waters tightened his grip on the band for *Animals* (1977), Gilmour's guitar continued to characterize lengthy tracks like 'Dogs' and 'Sheep', as Gilmour shared much of the production work with Waters.

By the time of *The Wall* (1979) Waters had assumed complete control over Pink Floyd (pictured below) and Gilmour's expressive scope was becoming limited. Nevertheless, his guitar break on 'Another Brick In The Wall Part 2' is often cited as the best example of his 'clean' tone, and his monumental solo on 'Comfortably Numb' (which he co-wrote) was voted the finest guitar solo of all time by listeners to digital radio station Planet Rock in 2006. Gilmour's dissatisfaction with the recording of *The Final Cut* (1983) was such that he had his production credit removed. He had released his first solo album, *David Gilmour*, in 1978 and in 1984 released his second, *About Face*, which was accompanied by a tour of Europe and America.

In 1986 Waters quit Pink Floyd, declaring the band 'a spent force creatively', but Gilmour and the others decided to continue, releasing *A Momentary Lapse Of Reason* in 1987 with Gilmour writing songs with producer Bob Ezrin and guitarist Gary Moore, among others. They embarked on a world tour that eventually ran for three years and yielded the live *Delicate Sound Of Thunder* (1988).

The Division Bell (1994) and the subsequent world tour produced another live album and video, *Pulse* (1995), reissued on DVD in 2006. Gilmour then resumed his solo career, playing acoustic shows that were subsequently released on DVD as *David Gilmour In Concert* (2003).

In 2005 Waters rejoined Gilmour, Mason and Wright for a 20-minute set at the climax of the Live 8 concert in London's Hyde Park. The following year he released his third solo album, *On An Island* (2006), and toured Europe and North America.

A video recording of a show from Gilmour's solo tour, entitled *Remember That Night - Live At The Royal Albert Hall* was released in 2007. The final show of David Gilmour's 'On an Island' tour was held at the Gdansk Shipyard on 26 August 2006.

before a crowd of 50,000. In 2009, he participated in a concert as part of the 'Hidden Gigs' campaign against homelessness. On 4 July 2009, he joined Jeff Beck onstage at the Royal Albert Hall, and in August he released an online single, 'Chicago – Change the World,' produced by long-time Pink Floyd collaborator Chris Thomas, to promote awareness of the plight of computer hacker Gary McKinnon.

Throughout his career Gilmour has generally played a Fender Stratocaster. He also has an extensive collection of guitars that have been used on various occasions, including a Gibson Les Paul, a Gretsch Duo-Jet and a Gibson EH1 50 lap steel guitar. His acoustic guitars include models by Gibson, Ovation and Martin.

STEVE HOWE

THE YES MAN

As the guitarist in Yes throughout their heyday in the Seventies, Steve Howe's (b. 1947) tasteful, eclectic playing helped to define a new style of rock music. Despite occasional absences during Yes's convoluted history during the Eighties and Nineties, Howe remained a pivotal member of the group and has been a permanent member since 1996. He was also a founding member of progressive supergroup Asia in the Eighties and has released more than a dozen solo albums.

Howe was born in 1947 in north London and started playing guitar at the age of 12, incorporating a wide variety of interests including classical, jazz, pop, and rhythm and blues. He joined his first professional band, the Syndicate, aged 16, and during the latter half of the Sixties played with Tomorrow (who were popular on the London underground scene with their hippy anthem, 'My White Bicycle') and Bodast before he was contacted by Yes bassist Chris Squire in 1970 and agreed to join the band.

Yes were redefining their style for their third album, *The Yes Album* (1971), and Howe made an immediate impact with his jangling, jazzy/country playing, adding an atmospheric dimension to tracks like 'Starship Trooper' and 'I've Seen All Good People' and contributing his virtuoso acoustic piece, 'The Clap'.

Fragile (1972) brought together the classic Yes line-up with keyboard player Rick Wakeman joining Howe, Squire, vocalist Jon Anderson and drummer Bill Bruford. The album marked their commercial breakthrough as the group's combined chemistry brought a new dynamic to their furious riffs, tight harmonies and anthemic refrains on lengthy tracks like 'Roundabout' and 'Long Distance Runaround'. *Close To The Edge* later the same year spread the same verve across even longer songs, and *Yessongs* (1973) demonstrated their live prowess with Howe revealing himself as more of a rock guitarist than he had in the studio.

By the release of *Tales From Topographic Oceans* (1974) Bruford had departed. (He was replaced by Alan White.) Howe and Anderson constructed a double-album concept (based on an Indian philosophy) that succeeded musically but lacked the band's earlier discipline. Wakeman left

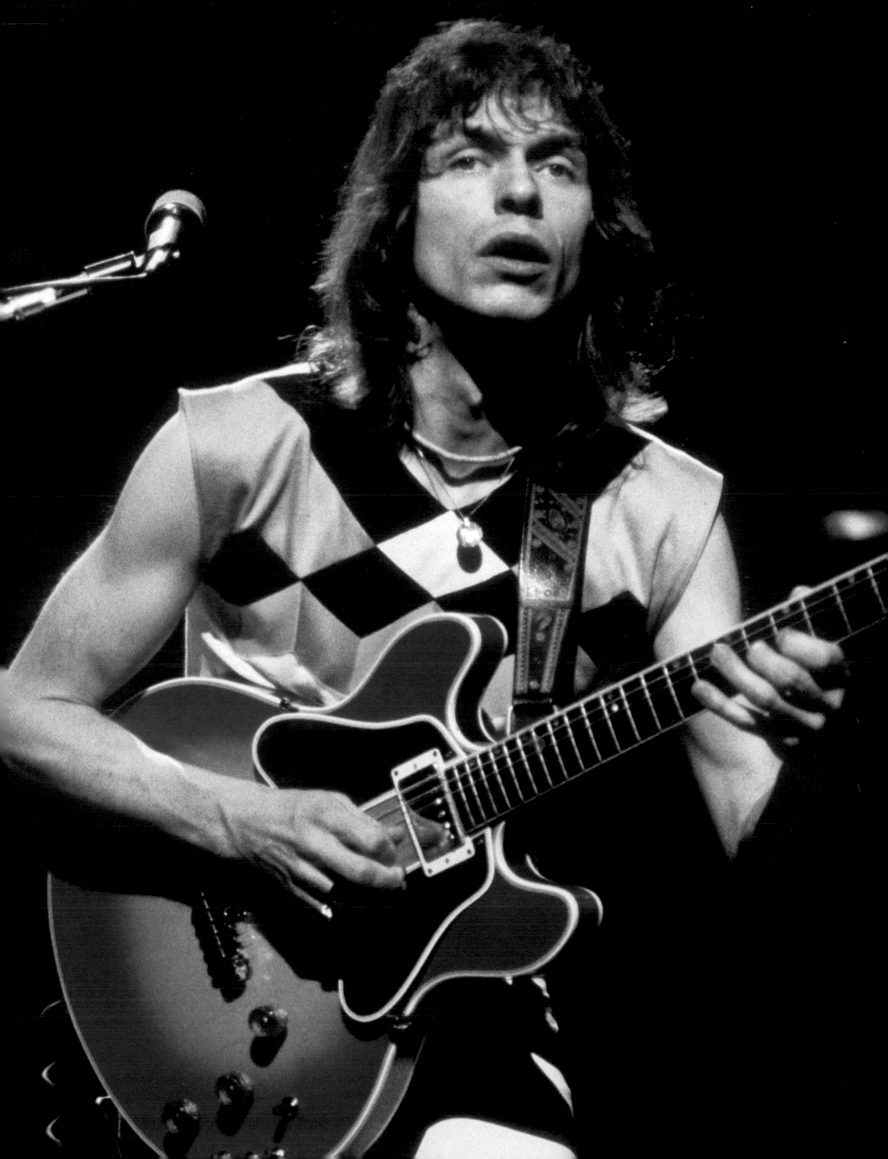

before *Relayer* (1974), was replaced by Patrick Moraz, and the music became more dissonant, enhanced by frequent tempo changes. Howe released his first solo album, *Beginnings*, in 1975, showcasing a broader range of instruments as well as his own vocals.

The return of Wakeman for *Going For The One* (1977) revived his fruitful partnership with Howe, but it was getting harder to maintain the cohesion within the band and, after another spate of line-up changes, Yes split in 1981. Howe, who had released his second solo album, *The Steve Howe Album* in 1979, teamed up with ex-King Crimson bassist/vocalist John Wetton, ex-ELP drummer Carl Palmer and keyboardist Geoff Downes (who had been in the final Yes line-up) to form Asia. Their self-titled debut, released in 1982, repackaged the progressive rock sound for the Eighties and became a worldwide hit.

Soon after the follow-up, *Alpha* (1983), Asia was beset by personnel problems and Howe left in 1984 before the next album. For his next project he teamed up with former Genesis guitarist Steve Hackett and singer Max Bacon for GTR. They released their self-titled album in 1986. It charted in America, and the group undertook a world tour before disbanding.

In 1989, Howe released *Anderson Bruford Wakeman Howe* with former Yes members. An attempt to combine ABWH with the Squire-led Yes on *Union* (1991) was an unsatisfactory compromise, and Howe was not involved in the subsequent Yes line-up. Instead he focused on his solo career, releasing *Turbulence* (1991), *The Grand Scheme Of Things* (1993), *Not Necessarily Acoustic* (1994) and *Homebrew* (1996), as well as contributing to the Asia album, *Aqua* (1992).

In 1995 Howe was involved in another attempt to reunite the Seventies Yes line-up. They played low-key dates the following year and the resulting live album, *Keys To Ascension* (1996), which included additional studio material, encouraged the band to continue recording new material with *The Ladder* (1999). Howe has contributed to every Yes album since then while also participating in Asia reunions and maintaining his solo career. Howe rejoined the three founding members of Asia in a 25th anniversary reunion tour in late 2006. In the ensuing years Asia released a DVD, *Fantasia*, and a new CD entitled *Phoenix* in 2008.

Throughout his career Howe has favoured the Gibson ES-175 guitar (he has a treasured 1964 model) and Gibson have made a signature model. His extensive guitar collection has been the subject of a book and several of his instruments have been exhibited in museums.

BRIAN MAY

QUEEN'S GUITAR KING

Queen guitarist Brian May (b. 1947) is among the most recognizable players in the world. His distinctive tones, created by the homemade guitar he built when he was 16 and has used throughout his career, are integral to the sound of Queen. Many of the sounds he produced were so innovative that the first seven Queen albums pointedly stated that no synthesizers had been used on their records. May has also written some of Queen's most famous hits.

May grew up in Hampton, south-west London. He started playing guitar at the age of seven. Academically gifted, particularly in physics, he made his own guitar with help from his father when he was unable to afford the Fender Stratocaster he wanted. The Red Special (also known as the Fireplace Guitar, because the mahogany neck was carved from a 200-year-old fireplace) took 18 months to build at a cost of £18, and he played it with a sixpence rather than a plectrum.

May formed 1984 with bassist friend Tim Staffels prior to entering Imperial College, London in 1965. After 1984 broke up, May and Staffels formed the trio Smile with drummer Roger Taylor. After one failed single, 'Earth', in 1969, Staffels left. Staffels' flatmate Freddie Mercury (pictured below) approached May and Taylor about forming another band. In 1971, bassist John Deacon joined them, completing the Queen line-up. Their debut album, *Queen* (1973), featured a variety of styles and included their first May-composed single, 'Keep Yourself Alive'. *Queen II* (1974) reached No. 5 in the UK charts thanks to extensive touring.

Sheer Heart Attack (1974), recorded while May was suffering from hepatitis and a duodenal ulcer, brought their stylish hard rock into focus, exemplified by the 'Killer Queen' single that, like the album, reached No. 2 in the charts. May's guitar was also showcased on the opening 'Brighton Rock'. With *A Night At The Opera* (1975) Queen moved beyond conventional rock labels into a category of their own, a theatrical pop dominated by multi-layered guitars and vocals. The operatic 'Bohemian Rhapsody', with May's memorable solo, became a global hit.

A Day At The Races (1976) kept to the formula, with May drawing on Queen's hard roots for 'Tie Your Mother Down' and contributing one

of his finest solos to Mercury's flamboyant 'Somebody To Love'. There was a rockier edge to *News Of The World* (1977), opening with May's anthemic 'We Will Rock You', and a broader sweep to *Jazz* (1978), which featured the May-penned 'Fat Bottomed Girls'. This trend continued on *The Game* (1980), the first Queen album to use synthesizers. May contributed two ballads, 'Sail Away Sweet Sister'and 'Save Me'.

Queen explored a more rhythmic direction on *Hot Space* (1982). May's guitar parts were more succinct, and he wrote three tracks on the album, including the single 'Las Palabras de Amor'. The band took an extended break in 1983, and May recorded a solo project with guitarist Eddie Van Halen that was released as a mini-album, *Star Fleet Project*, later that year. Queen reconvened to record *The Works* (1984), which was pop-oriented, although May's two songs, 'Hammer To Fall' and 'Tear It Up', maintained the band's hard-rock stance.

A Kind Of Magic (1986) followed Queen's show-stopping appearance at Live Aid in 1985 with May writing and arranging the orchestra parts for 'Who Wants To Live Forever', a single that was also featured in *Highlander*. *The Miracle* (1989) and *Innuendo* (1991) saw all tracks credited to the band, although May was largely responsible for 'Scandal' and 'I Want It All' on the former and 'Headlong' and 'I Can't Live With You' on the latter. In 1991 the band continued recording until Mercury's death from AIDS at the end of that year.

May completed his first solo album, *Back To The Light* (1992), which featured the hit singles 'Too Much Love Will Kill You' and 'Driven By You', and embarked on a world tour. He then worked with Deacon and Taylor, completing songs for which Mercury had already recorded vocals, on *Made In Heaven* (1995). Second solo album, *Another World* (1998), was followed by a world tour.

In 2004 May and Taylor began working with former Free and Bad Company vocalist Paul Rodgers, making their debut at Nelson Mandela's 46664 AIDS Awareness Concert in South Africa in 2005 as Queen + Paul Rodgers. They toured Europe, North America and Japan later in 2005 and 2006. In 2007 the band entered the studio and began recording an album of new material with Rodgers as lead vocalist.

Brian May was appointed Chancellor of Liverpool John Moores University in 2007. Since then he has produced and played on albums for Kerry Ellis and performed on Meat Loaf's *Hang Cool Teddy Bear* (2010). In 2009, May appeared on the reality TV show *The X Factor* with Queen band mate Roger Taylor.

MARK KNOPFLER

DIRE STRAITS TO MASTER

From the unlikeliest of beginnings in the British new wave of the late Seventies, Dire Straits became one of the biggest bands of the Eighties, due in large part to Mark Knopfler's (b. 1949) fingerpicking guitar style, which has continued to define the sound of his solo work.

Born in Glasgow in 1949, Knopfler spent his teenage years in Newcastle, playing in a number of local schoolboy bands. After attending college he came to London and formed Dire Straits in 1977 with his brother David on rhythm guitar, bassist John Illsley and drummer Pick Withers, and took to playing the pub circuit. A demo tape of 'Sultans Of Swing' sent to DJ Charlie Gillett stirred up interest and the band secured a contract with Vertigo Records.

Dire Straits (1978) attracted little attention in Britain but took off in Europe, followed by America, where 'Sultans Of Swing' was a hit. *Communiqué* (1979) maintained the stripped-down sound, while *Making Movies* (1980) and *Love Over Gold* (1982) stretched out their country-rock groove. But it was 1985's *Brothers In Arms* that hit the zeitgeist, becoming the first-ever million-selling CD, propelled by the hit 'Money For Nothing' and a massive world tour. Afterwards Knopfler switched to solo projects, including soundtracks (having had success with *Local Hero* in 1983) and the low-key Notting Hillbillies. Dire Straits appearaed at the Nelson Mandela Tribute Concert in 1988.

Dire Straits reformed for *On Every Street* (1991) and played another world tour that produced a live album, *On The Night* (1993), before Knopfler dissolved the band for good and pursued a solo career that has included *Golden Heart* (1996), *Sailing To Philadelphia* (2000), *The Ragpicker's Dream* (2002) and *Shangri-La* (2006).

Knopfler released his fifth solo album *Kill To Get Crimson* in 2007. A tour of Europe and North America followed in 2008. *Get Lucky* was released in 2009; Knopfler embarked on a world tour in 2010.

Although Knopfler is left-handed, he plays right-handed guitars, usually Fender Stratocasters and Telecasters. He used a National Steel Resonator Guitar on 'Romeo & Juliet' (pictured on the cover of *Brothers In Arms*).

STEVE HACKETT

GUITAR GENIUS AND GENESIS

The guitarist in Genesis from 1970–77, Steve Hackett (b. 1950) developed a technical skill and tone control that was a vital factor in shaping the band's music. He also helped to steer the post-Peter Gabriel Genesis towards a new style before leaving to pursue a solo career. An undemonstrative performer, Hackett has been a major influence on guitarists looking beyond the blues tradition.

Hackett was born in 1950 and grew up in Pimlico, London, teaching himself guitar as a teenager. Leaving school at 16, he started placing classified advertisements in music paper *Melody Maker* seeking 'receptive musicians determined to strive beyond existing stagnant music forms'. In 1970 he was approached by Genesis, who were looking for a new guitarist. He joined singer Peter Gabriel, keyboard player Tony Banks, bassist Mike Rutherford and newly recruited drummer Phil Collins.

His introspective manner suited Genesis' style on *Nursery Cryme* (1971), adding an extra dynamic to 'The Musical Box' and the dominant theme to 'The Fountain Of Salmarcis'. The line-up gelled more effectively on *Foxtrot* (1972), with Hackett's acoustic and electric guitars blending with the tight arrangements and tempo changes on the 23-minute 'Supper's Ready'.

On *Selling England By The Pound* (1973) Genesis reverted to shorter, self-contained songs, and Hackett made some of his strongest contributions with controlled guitar effects on 'Dancing With The Moonlit Knight' and his epic solo on 'Firth Of Fifth'. *The Lamb Lies Down On Broadway* (1974) was a complex concept album and Hackett's guitar, fed through a range of distortion devices, was an evocative part of the musical tapestry on 'In The Cage', 'The Carpet Crawlers' and 'The Lamia'.

When Gabriel left in 1975 the rest of Genesis decided to stay together as Hackett took the opportunity to record his first solo album, *Voyage Of The Acolyte* (1975), expanding on areas he had touched on in Genesis. The next Genesis album, *A Trick Of The Tail* (1976), with Collins handling the vocals, marked a new beginning for the band and Hackett contributed some strident playing on 'Squonk', 'Dance On A Volcano' and 'Los Endos' as well as atmospheric

effects on 'Ripples'. He also co-wrote 'Entangled With Banks'. But despite several co-writing credits on *Wind And Wuthering* (1977), he was dissatisfied with the level of his contribution and left Genesis while they were preparing the live *Seconds Out* (1977).

Hackett's second solo album, *Please Don't Touch* (1978) was deliberately diverse, using different guest vocalists as Hackett ventured towards folk and soul, while giving a fresh twist to his progressive style on the vibrant 'Narnia'. *Spectral Mornings* (1979) focused on Hackett's own identity with powerful guitar playing on 'Every Day', balanced by the ambient atmospherics of the title track. *Defector* (1980) maintained the same direction, using Hackett's touring band.

Cured (1981) and *Highly Strung* (1983) moved closer to the pop mainstream, and the former gave him a Top 50 UK album while the latter brought him a minor UK hit with 'Cell 151'. Throughout the Eighties Hackett consciously varied the style of his albums. *Bay Of Kings* (1983) focused on his acoustic playing; *Till We Have Faces* (1984) was recorded in Brazil with Latin percussionists while Hackett also introduced oriental themes. *Momentum* (1988) was another acoustic album, exploring flamenco themes and classical pieces.

In 1986 Hackett took part in the GTR project, forming a group with Yes and Asia guitarist Steve Howe. GTR undertook a world tour but disbanded soon afterwards. Hackett released his first live album, *Timelapse*, in 1992, taken from concerts in 1981 and 1990. Since then his albums have switched between acoustic and electric: *Guitar Noir* (1993) was a contemporary album; *Blues With A Feeling* (1994) revisited the rhythm and blues he had grown up with; *A Midsummer Night's Dream* (1998), based on Shakespeare's play, featured the Royal Philharmonic Orchestra; *Darktown* (1999) was a personal album; *Sketches Of Satie* (2000) featured arrangements for guitar and flute played by Hackett's brother John, who has appeared on most of his solo albums.

Hackett's prolific solo career continued in the Noughties, with electric and acoustic based albums, including *Feedback 86* (2000), *To Watch the Storms* (2003), *Metamorpheus* (2005), *Wild Orchids* (2006), *Tribute* (2008), and *Out of the Tunnel's Mouth* (2009). In 2009, his official biography, *Sketches Of Hackett*, was published.

Hackett's favourite guitar is a 1957 Gibson Les Paul Goldtop. He also plays a Fernandes Monterey Elite, an Ovation UK2, a Yairi Classical and a 1975 Zemaitis acoustic 12-string.

STEVE MORSE

DIXIE DREGS TO DEEP PURPLE

A consummate guitarist in an extraordinary variety of styles, including jazz, classical, country, rock and heavy metal, Steve Morse (b. 1954) also has the compositional skills and the improvising genius to match. He has played with, among others, Dixie Dregs, Kansas and Deep Purple while also maintaining his own band.

Morse was born in 1954 into a musical family and learned piano, clarinet and violin before picking up the guitar He met bassist Andy West at high school and formed Dixie Grit, a heavy-metal covers band, in the late Sixties. Morse and West went on to the University of Miami, where they took part in a musical lab project called Rock Ensemble II, which became the Dixie Dregs, playing a mixture of jazz rock and Southern rock.

Free Fall (1977), *What If* (1978) and *Dregs Of The Earth* (1980) were critically praised, but even Grammy nominations couldn't generate commercial sales, and the group disbanded in 1983. Morse formed his own trio out of the Dixie Dregs and released *The Introduction* (1984) and *Stand Up* (1985) before he joined the reformed Kansas for *Power* (1986) and *In The Spirit Of Things* (1988). Resuming his solo career, Morse expanded his own parameters on *High Tension Wires* (1989), *Southern Steel* (1991) and *Coast To Coast* (1992), while participating in the Dixie Dregs revival on *Bring 'Em Back Alive* (1992) and *Full Circle* (1994).

In 1994 Morse joined Deep Purple, replacing Ritchie Blackmore for *Purpendicular* (1996). He has remained their guitarist ever since, consolidating his role on *Abandon* (1998), *Total Abandon* (1999), *Bananas* (2003) and *Raptures Of The Deep* (2005). Live releases include *They All Came Down to Montreux* (2007). Morse has also maintained his solo career with *Major Impacts* (2000), featuring his own compositions that pay tribute to his own guitar heroes, *Split Decision* (2002) and *Major Impacts II* (2004). Morse returned solo with 2009's *Out Standing In Their Field*.

During his time with the Dixie Dregs, Morse played a customized Fender Stratocaster with a Telecaster neck that he assembled himself. He now has a signature model made by Ernie Ball Music Man.

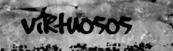

ERIC JOHNSON

INSTRUMENTAL IDEAL

Defying categorization with his blend of rock, blues, country and melodic pop styles, Eric Johnson (b. 1954) is highly revered by guitarists of all genres for his skill and perfectionism on stage and in the studio, and for his uniquely rich, overdriven tone.

Born in 1954, Johnson grew up in Austin, Texas. Encouraged by his parents, he started playing piano aged five and guitar at the age of 11. After hearing Jimi Hendrix's *Are You Experienced* (1967) he began experimenting with new sounds on the guitar. He formed a fusion band, the Electromagnetics, building a reputation around Texas in the mid-Seventies, but his prospects were badly damaged when he signed a six-year contract with a production company that failed to release his album, *Seven Worlds*, recorded in 1977.

Playing local gigs and recording sessions with Cat Stevens, Carole King and Christopher Cross, Johnson resumed his career in 1984, signing to Warner Brothers (reportedly recommended by Prince) and releasing his first album, *Tones* (1986). Despite critical praise for his range of playing, the album did not sell commercially.

Johnson's next album, *Ah Via Musicom* (1990), saw sales that matched the reviews. He won a Grammy for Best Instrumental with 'White Cliffs Of Dover'. *Venus Isle* (1996) featured rock instrumentals, blues and jazz. In 1996 he was part of the first G3 guitarists tour of North America with Joe Satriani and Steve Vai (both pictured above). Johnson has since taken part in G3 tours of Asia (2000) and South America (2006). In 2006, Johnson took part in a theatrical production titled 'Primal Twang: The Legacy of the Guitar,' an examination of the guitar's history. This was followed in 2007 by 'Love In: A Musical Celebration,' in which Johnson performed a set of Jimi Hendrix songs.

Johnson's quest for perfection has enhanced his cult status. *Live & Beyond* (2000), recorded with power trio Alien Love Child, was blues-oriented. *Bloom* (2005) was a reflection of his nomadic musical styles. Johnson mostly plays a Stratocaster, although he also plays vintage Gibson guitars and a Flying V. 'I like them all,' he told a journalist. 'They're all just different.'

EDDIE VAN HALEN

HAIL TO HEAVY METAL

Eddie Van Halen (b. 1955) redefined the sound of heavy metal at the end of the Seventies. His high-velocity solos, distinguished by his fingertapping technique and tremolo bar effects, on Van Halen's 1978 debut album heralded a new era in hard-rock guitar, that rejected the clichés of a jaded genre. His solo on Michael Jackson's 'Beat It' in 1982, which effectively compressed his style into one 30-second explosive burst, took Van Halen's guitar sound into the mainstream.

Born in Holland in 1955, Van Halen moved to Pasadena, California, with his family and older brother Alex in 1962. His father had played clarinet and saxophone in Dutch jazz bands, and both sons studied classical piano before Alex took up drums and Eddie started playing guitar at the age of 12. They formed a band in 1972, recruiting bassist Michael Anthony and singer David Lee Roth (pictured below). They played the competitive Los Angeles rock scene as Mammoth until they changed their name to Van Halen.

The album *Van Halen* (1978) made an immediate impact on the heavy metal scene. Eddie poured 10 years of obsessive practising into his solo instrumental, 'Eruption', with its innovative use of two-handed tapping, high-speed fretwork, vibrato and tremolo picking. His 'Frankenstrat' guitar (pictured on the album cover), made from a Charvel body and neck with a modified

Gibson humbucker pickup and Fender tremolo arm, provided his distinctive tone. The band's swaggering, high-energy rock style was vigorously displayed on 'Running With The Devil', 'Ain't Talkin' 'Bout Love' and a cover of the Kinks' 'You Really Got Me', and the album went platinum by the end of the year, turning Eddie into an instant guitar hero.

Van Halen II (1979) capitalized on their initial success with Eddie's singular riff providing the compelling component to 'Dance The Night Away' – their first hit single – while his acoustic playing on the instrumental 'Spanish Fly' and use of harmonics on the introduction to 'Women In Love' broadened his scope. *Women And Children First* (1980) and *Fair Warning* (1981) consolidated Van Halen's position as a guaranteed Top 10

album band in America – as well as a stadium-filling live act – and *Diver Down* (1982) brought them another hit single with a cover of Roy Orbison's '(Oh) Pretty Woman', while Eddie refined and developed his own style on the instrumentals 'Cathedral' and 'Intruder'.

Following Eddie's groundbreaking solo on Michael Jackson's 'Beat It', the album *1984* (1984) propelled Van Halen to superstardom with their No. 1 hit 'Jump'. He also expanded his repertoire of riffs and runs on 'Panama' and 'Hot For Teacher'. Ironically, *1984* was kept off the top of the US album charts by Michael Jackson's *Thriller*, and the simmering competitive tension that had been growing between Eddie and Roth led to the singer's departure in 1985.

Van Halen's success continued with new vocalist Sammy Hagar. The album *5150* (1986) finally gave them a No. 1 album. The band overhauled their sound mix, and the chemistry between Eddie's riffs and Hagar's vocals was evident on 'Best Of Both Worlds' and the hit singles 'Why Can't This Be Love', 'Dreams' and 'Love Walks In'. The discs *OU812* (1988) and *For Unlawful Carnal Knowledge* (1991) also hit No. 1, along with the live *Right Here, Right Now* (1993). The studio rapport between Eddie and Hagar was still strong on *Balance* (1995), but personality clashes over recording a song for the film soundtrack to *Twister* led to Hagar's departure.

Roth was recalled to sing two new tracks for a Greatest Hits collection (1996), but the band then replaced him with Extreme vocalist Gary Cherone for *Van Halen III* (1998) amid controversy, and the reaction to the longer songs and less bombastic style was mixed. The album also featured Eddie taking lead vocals on one track, 'How Many Say I'. The band played a world tour with Cherone, but he left the band amicably during recording for the next (unreleased) album. Eddie had a hip replacement operation and was also treated for tongue cancer.

Van Halen stayed dormant until 2004 when Hagar rejoined to record three tracks for another Greatest Hits compilation (2004) and toured North America with the band. Afterwards he resumed his solo career. In March 2007 Van Halen were inducted into the Rock And Roll Hall Of Fame but neither Van Halen brother attended the ceremony. Eddie announced that he was in rehab for alcohol addiction. In September 2007 Van Halen with Roth (but without Anthony, who was replaced by Eddie's son Wolfgang) began an American tour, which continued into 2008.

In 2009 Eddie guest-starred as himself in an episode of the American television series *Two And A Half Men*, in a scene in which he was shown playing his guitar in a mens' room.

JOE SATRIANI

GUITAR GIANT

American guitarist Joe Satriani (b. 1956) is widely credited with pioneering the rock-instrumental style in the Eighties, opening up the genre for guitarists like Steve Vai, Eric Johnson and Yngwie Malmsteen. His talent for creating highly evolved music, using a pop-song structure with tuneful melodies before applying his own virtuoso skills, has made him one of the most successful guitar instrumentalists.

Satriani was born in 1956 and brought up in Westbury, New York, the youngest of five siblings who all played musical instruments. He played piano and drums until he first heard Jimi Hendrix's 'Purple Haze' and picked up the guitar. Three years later, he was told of Hendrix's death, and the hobby became a compulsion. 'I went home and played my Hendrix records,' he told the *Los Angeles Times*. 'Then I had to play.'

He acquired a Hagstrom III solid-body guitar and, although he never had any formal lessons, he studied music theory at high school. By the age of 17 he was giving guitar lessons to students, one of whom was his classmate Steve Vai. In the mid-Seventies he was on a Rolling Stones list of possible replacements for Mick Taylor before they opted for Ron Wood. Unsure what musical direction to take, Satriani spent two months studying with jazz pianist Lennie Tristano and six months living alone in Japan, practising constantly. In 1977 he returned to America, settled in Berkeley, California, and resumed teaching. Among his students were Vai (again), Kirk Hammett (Metallica), David Bryson (Counting Crows), Larry Lalonde (Primus, Possessed), Alex Skolnick (Testament) and Charlie Hunter.

In 1986 he released his first, self-financed album, *Not Of This Earth*, focusing on sound textures rather than technique. *Surfing With The Alien* (1987) was his major breakthrough, highlighting his composing, production and playing talents, including two-handed tapping, sweep picking, whammy bar effects, frenetic legato runs and volume swell. The album became the most successful rock instrumental

album since Jeff Beck's *Wired* a decade earlier, with 'Satch Boogie' and 'Always With Me, Always With You' getting extensive airplay. On the back of his new profile Satriani was recruited by Mick Jagger for his solo tour of Japan and Australasia in 1988.

Flying In A Blue Dream (1989) felt more experimental, introducing Satriani's vocals and displaying a sense of humour on 'The Phone Call'. *The Extremist* (1992) put more emphasis on melodic rock with catchy hooks on 'Friends', 'Why' and the stirring 'Cryin''.

In the early Nineties Satriani guested on albums by Alice Cooper and Spinal Tap, and in 1993 he joined Deep Purple at short notice when Ritchie Blackmore quit the band in the middle of a tour. But he turned down the offer to join them permanently. *Time Machine* (1993) consisted of studio tracks from earlier EPs together with recent live material while *Joe Satriani* (1995), produced by Glyn Johns, took a more relaxed, bluesier approach.

In 1996 Satriani set up the first G3 tour of North America with Steve Vai (pictured above) and Eric Johnson, putting three guitarists on the same bill, performing separately and together. The success of the tour and subsequent CD/DVD *G3: Live In Concert* (1997) ensured that G3 became a regular event, with Satriani and (usually) Vai choosing a third guitarist (Robert Fripp, Yngwie Malmsteen, John Petrucci, Uli Jon Roth and Paul Gilbert have all taken part). The tours have also expanded into Europe, Asia and South America.

Meanwhile Satriani continued his own career. *Crystal Planet* (1998) evoked comparisons with *Surfing With The Alien*, with its signature power ballads, anthems and rockers. *Engines Of Creation* (2000) was more experimental, incorporating techno and electronica. *Strange Beautiful Music* (2002), *Is There Love In Space* (2004) and *Super Colossal* (2006) have all brought the guitar back to the fore, showing that the Hendrix flame still burns, and that Satriani's flair for great hooks is intact.

Satriani's album *Professor Satchafunkilus And The Musterion Of Rock* was released in 2008. He released the *Live In Paris: I Just Wanna Rock* DVD and a companion two-CD set in 2010. The same year, Satriani joined other guitarists in the Experience Hendrix Tribute Tour, performing music written and inspired by Jimi Hendrix.

Satriani has had a long association with Ibanez guitars (with DiMarzio pick-ups) and Peavey amplifiers, and both companies have made customized equipment for him.

RANDY RHOADS

QUIET RIOT TO OZZY

Randy Rhoads (1956–82) had a career that lasted only six years. He played with Quiet Riot and Ozzy Osbourne before dying in a plane crash in 1982. But his guitar style, which included classical influences, opened up new directions in heavy metal, and he was an acknowledged influence on a subsequent generation of guitarists, including Zakk Wylde. Rhoads also played with Warren Di Martini (Ratt), George Lynch (Dokken) and Alex Skolnick (Testament).

William Randall Rhoads, born in Santa Monica, California, grew up with a strong musical background. His mother owned a music school in Hollywood. Rhoads was learning acoustic guitar by the age of seven and played in various bands from the age of 14. He formed Quiet Riot in 1976 with friend and bassist Kelly Garni and vocalist Kevin DuBrow. The band gained a strong following in Los Angeles, but they were unable to get a US record deal, signing instead with Columbia in Japan. Neither *Quiet Riot* (1977) nor *Quiet Riot II* (1978) was released in America. In 1979 Rhoads successfully auditioned for Ozzy Osbourne, who was recruiting a new band, and came to the UK to record *Blizzard Of Ozz* (1980). Rhoads co-wrote seven tracks including 'Mr Crowley' with its 'neo-classical' guitar solo, and 'Crazy Train', with a guitar riff that has been regularly used on American sports programmes. He also wrote the intricate acoustic solo, 'Dee'.

The band toured Britain, where the album went Top 10. Rhoads co-wrote every track on their second album *Diary Of A Madman* (1981), including 'Flying High Again', on which his compact solo ushered in a new style of Eighties metal guitar. The band toured the US tour during the summer of 1981 and commenced another four-month schedule at the end of the year as sales of both albums took off. On 19 March 1982 Rhoads was killed when a plane in which he was a passenger clipped the tour bus and crashed in Leesburg, Florida. A live album, *Tribute*, recorded in 1981, was released in 1987.

During his career Rhoads had three guitars custom-made for him. The first was a black and white polka dot Flying V made by Karl Sandoval, the second was a white Flying V made by Grover Jackson of Charvel Guitars, the third was a variation of the first Jackson guitar in black. As a tribute to Rhoads, Marshall Amplification released the 1959RR in 2008. The amp is a limited-edition, all-white Marshall Super Lead 100-watt head modeled after Randy's own Super Lead amp.

STEVE VAI
LEGEND AMONG LEGENDS

Schooled by Joe Satriani, trained by Frank Zappa and turned into a guitar hero by David Lee Roth, Steve Vai (b. 1960) has combined an energetic technique with a distinctive and often unusual sense of tone.

Born and raised in North Hempstead, New York, Vai began taking guitar lessons from his schoolmate Satriani when he was 14. He attended the Berklee College of Music in Boston, where he developed an obsession with transcribing Frank Zappa guitar solos. Zappa hired him in 1979, and he appeared on *Tinsel Town Rebellion* (1981), *Shut Up 'N Play Your Guitar* (1981), *You Are What You Is* (1981), *Ship Too Late To Save A Drowning Witch* (1982) and *The Man From Utopia* (1983).

He left Zappa's band in 1982 and recorded his first solo album, *Flex-Able* (1984). That year he joined Alcatrazz, replacing Yngwie Malmsteen. After *Disturbing The Peace* (1985) Vai accepted an offer to join Roth's post-Van Halen band. *Eat 'Em And Smile* (1986) and *Skyscraper* (1988) combined the band's fire with Roth's showmanship, and both albums went platinum. Vai left Roth's band in 1989 and temporarily joined Whitesnake before recording a solo album, *Passion And Warfare* (1990), which went gold. He formed a conventional rock band for *Sex & Religion* (1993) but returned to his standard format for *Alien Love Secrets* (1995) and *Fire Garden* (1996). In 1996 he also took part in the first G3 tour with Satriani and Eric Johnson and has played on almost every tour since.

Vai has continued to release studio albums like *Real Illusions: And Reflections* (2005); live albums like *Alive In An Ultra World* (2001); and compilations like *Elusive Light And Sound* (2002), which featured his film work for *Crossroads*, *PCU*, and *Bill And Ted's Excellent Adventure*. He has taken part in classical projects with the Netherlands Metropole Orchestra and the Tokyo Metropolitan Symphony Orchestra and been active in creating music for the video game *Halo 2*, which also became available as downloadable tracks for the game *Guitar Hero 3*.

Like Satriani, Vai favours Ibanez guitars with a DiMarzio pick-up. In the Nineties he pioneered the use of seven-string guitar, which was used by Korn and other bands to create the nu-metal sound.

YNGWIE MALMSTEEN

A GUITAR FORCE

A leading figure of Eighties 'neo-classical' rock guitarists, Yngwie Malmsteen (b. 1963) learned his breakneck arpeggios and baroque composing style from classical composers and performers as well as rock artists. His own sweep-picking technique, his use of harmonic scales and pedal tones and his aggressive playing have helped create his distinctive style.

Born in Stockholm, Sweden, Malmsteen's interest in the guitar started, like many of his contemporaries, with the death of Jimi Hendrix in 1970. Also influenced by Ritchie Blackmore's style, which was influenced by the classics, Malmsteen studied classical composers like Bach and flamboyant nineteenth-century violinist Niccolò Paganini. Malmsteen practised intently and by the age of 18 was playing in various bands around Sweden.

A demo tape that Malmsteen unsuccessfully sent around to Swedish record companies was picked up by US label Shrapnel, and he was invited over to join metal band Steeler. He played on their self-titled debut album (1983) before moving on to Alcatrazz, where he had more input, recording *No Parole For Rock & Roll* (1984) and *Live Sentence* (1984). However, he still felt stifled, so he formed his own band, Rising Force, with keyboard player Jens Johansson. *Rising Force* (1984) showcased Malmsteen's writing and playing abilities and charted in the US. The band released *Marching Out* (1985), *Trilogy* (1986) and *Odyssey* (1988), which featured 'Heaven Tonight'. Malmsteen disbanded the group and recruited Swedish musicians for his next band. *Eclipse* (1990), *Fire & Ice* (1992), *The Seventh Sign* (1994) and *Magnum Opus* (1995) were major successes in Japan. *Inspiration* (1996) featured covers of songs by Deep Purple, Hendrix and Rush. In 1998 he recorded the 'Concerto Suite For Electric Guitar And Orchestra' with the Czech Philharmonic Orchestra. He also revived Rising Force for *Unleash The Fury* (2005). Malmsteen added singer Tim Owens for *Perpetual Flame* (2008). In 2009, Malmsteen released *Angels Of Love*, featuring acoustic arrangements of some of his best-known ballads.

Malmsteen's best-known guitar is his 1972 blond Fender Stratocaster. Bought when he was a teenager, he has used it throughout his career. In 2009 *Time* magazine named him number 9 on their list of the 10 best electric guitar players of all-time.

JOHN PETRUCCI

DREAM THEATRE TO G3

The guitarist in Dream Theater, John Petrucci (b. 1967) brought his virtuoso style – lengthy syncopated lines, complex rhythmic variations and grinding tone – into the progressive-metal scene. In the past decade he has been involved in several extra-curricular projects, often with other members of Dream Theater.

Raised in Long Island, New York, Petrucci started played guitar at the age of 12 and assiduously practised and emulated his heroes, working his way through the acknowledged masters from Steve Howe to Randy Rhoads. At 18 he attended Berklee College of Music in Boston with his school friend, bassist John Myung. There they met drummer Mike Portnoy and formed the basis of Dream Theater.

Recruiting keyboard player Kevin Moore and singer Charlie Dominici, they released *When Dream And Day Unite* (1989). *Images And Words* (1992) with new singer James LaBrie broke them to the MTV audience with the epic 'Pull Me Under'. *Live At The Marquee* (1993) and *Awake* (1994) consolidated their following with an emphasis on lengthy but concisely written pieces. *Metropolis Part 2: Scenes From A Memory* (1999) was a concept album that featured new keyboard player Jordan Rudess. *Six Degrees Of Inner Turbulence* (2002) balanced heavy, experimental songs with progressive pieces. *Train Of Thought* (2003) had an underlying theme of anger, *Octavarium* (2005) was fixated around the number eight, and *Systematic Chaos* (2006) was dramatic and aggressive.

Petrucci's first side project was *Liquid Tension Experiment* (1998) with Portnoy, Rudess and bassist Tony Levin. Its success resulted in *Liquid Tension Experiment 2* (1999). In 2001 Petrucci joined the G3 tour of North America with guitarists Joe Satriani and Steve Vai (both pictured left). He toured with them in 2005, playing music from his solo album *Suspended Animation* (2005).

Dream Theater signed with Roadrunner Records in 2006, and their releases since then include *Systematic Chaos* (2007) and tenth studio album, *Black Clouds & Silver Linings* (2009)

Petrucci mainly plays Ernie Ball/Music Man guitars and has two signature models; he also plays a seven-string guitar. His complex stage rig is based around Mesa Boogie amps and speakers.

JONNY GREENWOOD

RADIOHEAD TO GUITAR HERO

The lead guitarist in Radiohead, Jonny Greenwood (b. 1971) has straddled the line between dissonance and resonance, noise and melody. His arsenal of effects, virtuosity and unconventional phrasing have been key features in this very English band's development. No wonder Pink Floyd's David Gilmour is a fan. 'They've done some very good things. I can see why people make the connection,' he told the *Guardian* in 2003. In fact Greenwood is a multi-instrumentalist, playing synthesizers, keyboards, xylophone, ondes martenot (an early electronic instrument) and viola (on which he was classically trained) with Radiohead.

Born in Oxford in 1971, Greenwood met the other members of Radiohead in 1986 through his older brother Colin at the nearby Abingdon public school. Singer Thom Yorke, guitarist Ed O'Brien and drummer Phil Selway were all older than Greenwood. Originally called On A Friday, they gigged around Oxford and continued to play after Greenwood's bandmates had left for university and when they returned in 1991. The band changed their name to Radiohead after signing a record deal with EMI.

Pablo Honey (1993) blended guitar-led anthemic rock with atmospheric instrumental passages, veering from thoughtful to angst, often in the same song, such as 'Creep', a slow-burning hit

around the world with Yorke's self-loathing lyrics contrasting with Greenwood's scratchy, grunge guitar. *The Bends* (1995) refused to conform to the expected follow-up and was instead a low-key album of melancholic grandeur with Yorke's vocals set against dense guitar arrangements. But they had built up a loyal following; 'High And Dry', 'Fake Plastic Trees', 'Just' and 'Street Spirit' were not pop songs but they were all UK hit singles. MTV and American radio were less keen on the singles, however, and *The Bends* barely made the US charts, even though Radiohead supported REM on their Monster world tour and built up a broader audience.

OK Computer (1997) was a minimalist art-rock album with structured guitar riffs, mechanical rhythms, pop melodies and the band's trademark production with its cold, emotional

feel that changed the face of Nineties rock. Greenwood (pictured below with Thom Yorke) used a wide range of sounds and effects to enhance the songs: an evocative solo on 'Airbag'; smooth, sliding tones and a squealing solo on 'Paranoid Android'; complex, spacey sounds on 'Subterranean Homesick Alien'; eerie, Pink Floyd-style playing on 'Exit Music'; wailing jangly riffs on 'Electioneering'; droning sounds on 'Climbing Up The Walls'; and melodic textures on 'Lucky'. *OK Computer* topped the UK charts, reached No. 21 in the US, and was a major worldwide success.

Kid A (2000) was a reaction to the success of *OK Computer*, deliberately moving away from conventional melodies or commercial sounds. Guitars were less in evidence although Greenwood's guitar was prominent on 'Optimistic', and was sparsely but effectively used on 'Motion Picture Soundtrack'. Greenwood also played the Theremin-like ondes martenot on two tracks and arranged the string orchestra on 'How To Disappear Completely'. Despite its radical nature, *Kid A* topped the US and UK charts.

Recorded at the same time as *Kid A*, *Amnesiac* (2001) had a lighter feel, but the guitars were mostly used for ambient textures, apart from Greenwood's catchy hook on 'I Might Be Wrong'. While the songs on *Hail To The Thief* (2003) remained complex, some of Radiohead's earlier energy returned. After a lengthy hiatus, *In Rainbows* (2007) restored the passion in the studio that Radiohead had never lost on stage, with guitars coming back into favour and making a telling contribution.

Meanwhile Greenwood had become the first member of Radiohead to release a solo album, *Bodysong* (2003), a film soundtrack that featured guitars on just two tracks, as he focused on his multi-instrument and arranging skills. In 2004 he was appointed composer in residence at the BBC and composed several pieces for orchestra, piano and ondes martenot. Some of this work later appeared in his *There Will Be Blood* (2007) soundtrack album, which had critical acclaim and was named Best Film Score in the Evening Standard British Film Awards for 2007. Greenwood and Radiohead worked on various projects in 2008/09, releasing singles from sessions on their website in anticipation of a new studio album in 2010.

Greenwood has generally favoured Fender Telecaster guitars that have been customized and rewired, although he also has a number of Gibson electric and acoustic guitars as well as a Gretsch. He uses a Vox AC30 amplifier for clean tones. For distorted tones he uses effects pedals and a Fender Deluxe 85.

blues pioneers

As Muddy Waters put it,
'The Blues Had A Baby And They Named It Rock'n'Roll'.

The blues continued to be a driving force as rock'n'roll matured into rock music, with American rhythm and blues influencing the Rolling Stones and the Animals. Heavy metal began as the bone-rattling blues of Led Zeppelin and others, and punk was in some ways a musical throwback to raw blues. The sound of the blues and its messengers also evolved – from the solo singer-guitarist to the electrified wailer fronting a band – but the primal 12-bar structure and the raw emotion of the singers and players remained the bedrock of the blues.

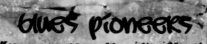
CHARLEY PATTON

DELTA BLUES PIONEER

The first great Delta-blues singer, Charley Patton (1887?–1934) developed a raw, driving and percussive kind of guitar playing that was a seminal influence on the following generation of Mississippi blues singers, including Robert Johnson, Muddy Waters, Howlin' Wolf and John Lee Hooker. All the elements that became integral to the Delta blues – different guitar tunings and picking techniques along with the bottleneck slide – were developed by Patton, who sang in a heavily accentuated growl that made his words hard to decipher but compelling to listen to.

Born near Edwards, Mississippi, in 1887 or 1891 (accounts vary), Patton moved north with his family to Dockery Farms plantation and grew up listening to field hollers and levee-camp moans as well as gospel, ragtime, country folk and novelty songs. He learned guitar in his late teens from itinerant musicians such as Willie Brown and Henry Sloan, who travelled around the plantations.

By the early Twenties Patton had several distinctive songs in his repertoire including 'Pea Vine Blues' (about a local railway line), 'Spoonful Blues' (extolling the pleasures of cocaine), 'Tom Rushen Blues' (chronicling his run-ins with a local sheriff), 'Mississippi Boweavil Blues' (a humorous take on the scourge of the cotton plantations) and his signature tune, the socially aspiring 'Pony Blues'. He was an extrovert showman, playing his guitar behind his back or with his teeth and hitting the guitar body for rhythmic emphasis.

He was already a local legend by the time he made his first recordings, including his first and most successful, 'Pony Blues', in Richmond, Indiana, in 1929. It was backed by 'Banty Rooster Blues', a description that could have applied to Patton himself, a snappy dresser who had several wives. A second session later that year produced 'High Water Everywhere', a vivid commentary on the devastating Mississippi floods of 1927.

By his final recording session early in 1934 in New York, Patton's lifestyle was beginning to catch up with him. His voice had deteriorated after his throat was slashed (reportedly in a fight over a woman) the previous year, and the songs included two religious numbers performed with his then wife, Bertha Lee. Patton died later that year from a heart attack in Holly Ridge, Mississippi.

BLIND LEMON JEFFERSON

A COUNTRY BLUESMAN

Blind Lemon Jefferson (1893–1929) opened up the market for blues records in 1926 when 'Got The Blues', backed with 'Long Lonesome Blues', became the biggest-selling record by a black male artist. It brought him the trappings of success, including a car and chauffeur, and he released nearly a hundred songs over the next four years before his death in 1929.

Jefferson played country blues, a style he customized by listening to the flamenco intonations of local Mexican guitarists in Texas, where he grew up, as well as cotton-field songs. He developed a fast, complex guitar technique that, unlike that of most blues legends, has never been duplicated.

He was a direct influence on Leadbelly, Lightnin' Hopkins and T-Bone Walker, who all played and travelled with him. The full range of his shifting rhythms, boogie-woogie bass runs and rippling tremolos can be heard on 'Match Box Blues', a song that had a major impact on the rock'n'roll scene in the Fifties after Carl Perkins recorded it.

Little is known about Jefferson before 1926. He was reportedly born blind (although the only known photograph shows him wearing glasses), probably in 1893. He was playing house parties, brothels and drinking dens around Wortham, Texas, in his late teens before travelling widely around Oklahoma, Louisiana, Mississippi, Alabama and Virginia. He was eventually contacted by Paramount Records, who recorded him in Chicago. He would make most of his records there, although he remained settled in Dallas. Songs like 'Black Snake Moan', one of his biggest 'hits', had a blatant sexual theme, albeit couched in humour and double-entendre. Cheating women were also a concern on 'Eagle Eyed Mama', but titles like 'One Dime Blues', 'Prison Cell Blues' and 'See That My Grave Is Kept Clean' (which Bob Dylan recorded on his first album) hint at deeper fears. He could cut a desolate sound, and while his instrumental style was hard to copy, his lyrics were widely appropriated by other performers for their own songs.

Confusion even surrounds Jefferson's death in Chicago in 1929. It was said that he froze to death, but a heart attack in the back of his car seems more likely.

T-BONE WALKER

TURNING BLUES ELECTRIC

The first bluesman to record with an electric guitar, T-Bone Walker (1910–75) shaped the course of post-war blues, influencing everyone from B.B. King and Chuck Berry to Jimi Hendrix and beyond. B.B. King acknowledges that the first time he heard Walker he knew he had to get an electric guitar, and Berry and Hendrix took as much notice of Walker's showmanship – playing his guitar behind his head and generally thrilling the ladies – as his soulful playing. Even today Walker's style remains an essential element of lead-guitar playing.

Born in Linden, Texas, in 1910, Walker grew up in a musical household in Dallas, learning guitar, ukulele, banjo, violin and piano. Blind Lemon Jefferson was a family friend and Lonnie Johnson played nearby. By the age of 16 Walker was earning a living as a musician, playing local shows. In 1929 he won a talent contest to join Cab Calloway's band and made his first recordings. He also started a band with another local guitarist, Charlie Christian. He began touring a wider region and in 1934 moved to California, where he played and sang in various big bands.

Walker started playing amplified guitar in order to be heard, and his defining moment came in 1942 at a recording session with Freddie Slack's Big Band when he got the chance to take the spotlight for a couple of blues songs. 'Mean Old World' was arguably the first electric blues record and he followed it with 'Call It Stormy Monday', which became his signature tune and a blues classic. Before long he was leading his own band and scoring blues hits with 'T-Bone Shuffle', 'Glamour Girl', 'The Hustle Is On' and 'Cold Cold Feeling'.

Walker's big-band background and the jazz musicians who played with him gave his blues a sophistication that was in marked contrast to the raw blues coming out of Chicago and the rock'n'roll coming out of Memphis. Ironically, this made him unfashionable for a while, although his reputation as a live performer never dipped. After a car accident in the early Seventies his health deteriorated and he died of bronchial pneumonia following a stroke in 1975.

ROBERT JOHNSON

BLUES MYTH MAKER

The hold that the legend of Robert Johnson (1911–38) exerts on the blues is out of all proportion to his career and output. He died relatively unknown at the age of 27 and recorded just 29 songs. But those songs of dreams and nightmares, crossroads and hellhounds revealed a darkness at the heart of Johnson's blues, expressed with a chilling eloquence that has never been matched.

The legend was fostered by the Sixties generation of British blues guitarists, led by Eric Clapton and Keith Richards, who were in thrall to *King Of The Delta Blues Singers* (1962), a collection of Johnson's songs that personified the iconic image of a blues singer. The fact that there were more myths than facts about Johnson's life – no picture was known of at that time – only intensified the iconography. Clapton recorded 'Rambling On My Mind' with John Mayall and merged 'Cross Road Blues' and 'Travelling Riverside Blues' into 'Crossroads', a cornerstone of Cream's career, while the Rolling Stones' version of 'Love In Vain' was a crucial part of their late Sixties reinvention.

In fact the legend – and myths – had started before Johnson even made a record. Born in Hazlehurst, Mississippi, in 1911, he moved north to Robinsonville as a teenager and learned guitar and harmonica, hanging around with Charley Patton, Son House and Willie Brown. He disappeared for two years, and when he returned the dramatic improvement in his playing led to speculation that he had sold his soul to the devil. Songs like 'Cross Road Blues', 'Preaching Blues (Up Jumped The Devil)', 'Stones In My Passway', 'Hellhound On My Trail' and 'Me And The Devil Blues' did nothing to dispel those notions. Even today, guitarists struggle to master Johnson's technique. The two photographs of Johnson since discovered show he had particularly long fingers, but this doesn't explain where the inspiration came from.

Johnson recorded twice, in 1936 and 1937, and had 11 records released, the most popular of which was the bawdy 'Terraplane Blues'. He was famously poisoned by a jealous husband while playing a juke joint near Greenwood, Mississippi, in 1938. As befits his legend, he has three marked burial sites. While his ardent disciples have left some of his most haunting songs alone, others like 'I Believe I'll Dust My Broom', 'Sweet Home Chicago', 'Come On In My Kitchen' and 'Walking Blues' have become a standard part of the blues repertoire.

MUDDY WATERS

BRIDGING DELTA AND CHICAGO

Muddy Waters (1915–83) is the vital link between the pre-war Delta blues and the post-war Chicago blues. Born in Rolling Fork, Mississippi, he grew up on Stovall's Plantation near Clarksdale and became steeped in the slide-guitar blues of Son House and Robert Johnson. In 1941 he was recorded by archivist Alan Lomax playing 'Country Blues' and 'I's Be Troubled'.

Two years later, Waters moved north to Chicago, following the general migration. While his voice still sounded as if it was coming from the cotton fields on his 1946 recordings, his amplified guitar (necessary if he was to be heard above his band) opened up a whole new dimension for his Delta licks. By 1948, when he had his first local hit with 'I Can't Be Satisfied' (an updated version of 'I's Be Troubled'), his guitar playing had developed a trademark style, bringing a more aggressive quality to his single-note Delta riffs and slide technique.

Waters put together a prime band of musicians he could rely on – guitarist Jimmy Rogers, bassist Willie Dixon, pianist Otis Spann and harmonica player Little Walter – and built a powerful reputation in Chicago's clubs and bars, helped by his own commanding presence. During the mid-Fifties Waters recorded a series of songs that would become anthems of Chicago blues: 'I Just Want To Make Love To You', 'Got My Mojo Working', 'I'm Ready' and 'I'm Your Hoochie Coochie Man'. The last two used a variation on the call-and-response songs from the Delta plantations, with Waters filling in the spaces with moaning vocals or stinging guitar breaks.

By 1960, when he played the Newport Jazz Festival (released as *At Newport*), he was the leading Chicago bluesman. He took advantage of the British blues boom of the Sixties to broaden his audience, touring the UK and Europe and recording *The London Muddy Waters Sessions* (1971) with Rory Gallagher and Georgie Fame. During the Seventies he toured with the Rolling Stones and Eric Clapton and appeared in the Band's 'The Last Waltz' concert and film. His record career was revived in the late Seventies with a trio of Johnny Winter-produced albums: *Hard Again* (1977), *I'm Ready* (1978) and *King Bee* (1981). He died in his sleep from a heart attack in 1983.

JOHN LEE HOOKER

THE BOOGIE MAN

The original boogie man, John Lee Hooker (1917–2001) sustained a career of more than 50 years with his incessant one-chord stomp and half-spoken vocal style. But behind the captivating, hypnotic rhythm Hooker found his own deep blues – one with dark tones and mysterious flurries of notes – as he groped to express, often with a wicked irony, his own feelings of pain and desire. His style was particularly infectious among British blues bands of the Sixties, notably the Animals. In America Canned Heat built a multi-platinum career out of Hooker's boogie.

The youngest of 11 children, Hooker was born in Clarksdale, Mississippi, in 1917 to a family of sharecroppers. After his parents separated he learned guitar from his stepfather before leaving home for Memphis, followed by Cincinnati and Detroit, where he made his first recordings in 1948. 'Boogie Chillen' contained all the basic elements of his style and was a No. 1 rhythm and blues hit. Hooker immediately cashed in, recording for several different labels under a variety of pseudonyms (a laughable ploy given his distinctive style), and had more hits with 'Hobo Blues', 'Crawling Kingsnake' (1949) and 'I'm In The Mood' (1951).

In the mid-Fifties Hooker started recording with an electric band, heightening the rhythmic emphasis of his boogie with songs like 'Dimples' and 'Boom Boom'. When these records became successful in Britain in the Sixties, he toured the UK and Europe regularly. Meanwhile, he was enjoying a parallel career as a solo folk/blues artist in America, although by the end of the decade he was back in the rock fold, thanks to the success of his disciples Canned Heat, who repaid their debt by recruiting him for *Hooker 'N' Heat* (1970).

Further collaborations with Van Morrison and guitarist Elvin Bishop maintained Hooker's profile in the Seventies, but his career sagged in the Eighties before a sudden and unlikely revival in 1989 with *The Healer*, which featured duets with Carlos Santana, Bonnie Raitt, George Thorogood, Los Lobos and the remnants of Canned Heat. The album's success set Hooker up for the Nineties as Van Morrison, Keith Richards, Ry Cooder, Robert Cray and Albert Collins queued up to appear on subsequent albums including *Mr Lucky*, *Boom Boom* and *The Hook*. Hooker died in 2001 at the age of 83.

ELMORE JAMES
THE BOTTLENECK ELECTRIFIED

The swooping, full-octave slide-guitar riff that opened Elmore James's (1918–63) first record, 'Dust My Broom', in 1951 not only electrified the legacy of Robert Johnson, it also established one of the basic riffs of post-war blues. Bottleneck guitar had always been part of the blues, but James was the first to use it in a hard rocking electric-blues context. The fat, distorted sound he got for his primal riff was no accident either; in his day-job James repaired radios, and he customized the components and configurations of his amplifier to get a dirty, sustained tone. These modifications are now a standard option on any modern amplifier.

James cut several versions of 'Dust My Broom', recording a new one every time he switched record labels, which was often. And many of his other songs were close copies, such as 'Dust My Blues', 'I Believe' and 'Wild About You Baby'. But James was no one-trick pony. His version of Tampa Red's 'It Hurts Me Too' and his own interchangeable 'The Sun Is Shining' and 'The Sky Is Crying' each have a slow-burning intensity and desperation that threaten to implode before the song ends.

Born Elmore Brooks in Richland, Mississippi, in 1918, James started learning guitar in his teens and hung out with Sonny Boy Williamson II and Robert Johnson, from whom he learned 'I Believe

I'll Dust My Broom'. He played regularly with Williamson and began playing electric guitar when he formed a band in the early Forties. His first version of 'Dust My Broom' featured Williamson on harmonica. In 1952 he moved to Chicago, where his primal riffs were an instant success. He formed the Broomdusters and soon became one of the most popular attractions on the live scene.

James had always suffered from heart problems that were not helped by his excessive drinking and asthma. There is no evidence of any frailties on his final recordings made in New Orleans in 1961, featuring the frisky 'Look On Yonder Wall' and 'Shake Your Moneymaker', but in 1963 he died from a heart attack in Chicago. His legacy lived on among British blues bands like John Mayall's Bluesbreakers and Fleetwood Mac and American bands like the Paul Butterfield Blues Band and the Allman Brothers.

ALBERT KING

GOT BLUES AND SOUL

Few blues guitarists had more style and presence than Albert King (1923–92). At 6ft 4in (1.93m) and 250lbs (113kg), he cut an imposing figure on stage. Equally distinctive was his Gibson Flying V guitar, a right-handed instrument that King played left-handed and upside down. This gave him an unusual, tormented sound when he bent the strings on his fretboard. He also used his thumb rather than a pick. The master of the single-string solo, King was one of the earliest bluesmen to cross over to soul with his Stax recordings in the Sixties.

Born Albert Nelson in Indianola, Mississippi, the same town as B.B. King, Albert changed his name to King after B.B.'s initial success in the early Fifties. He hadd grown up in Arkansas, playing guitar from the age of 16. But he didn't make his first record, 'Be On Your Merry Way', until 1953 after he had moved to Gary, Indiana. His progress remained slow, and it wasn't until 1964 that he scored a minor hit with 'Don't Throw Your Love On Me So Strong'.

His fortunes changed when he signed to Memphis rhythm and blues-soul label Stax in 1966 and was paired with Booker T & the MGs, whose soulful grooves transformed King's blues in the studio. Their first session produced 'Laundromat Blues', which put the blues into a modern context. His second hit, 'Crosscut Saw', added the Memphis Horns and emphasized how far King had travelled from the Delta. *Born Under A Bad Sign* (1967) with its magnificent title track was acclaimed as one of the most stirring blues albums of the late Sixties. Its influence on Eric Clapton and Jimi Hendrix was soon evident.

King was the first blues artist to play San Francisco's famed Fillmore, opening up a new audience, and the resulting album, *Live Wire/ Blues Power* (1968), was a template for a new generation of blues bands in the American South. In the Seventies King added funk to his bluesy soul on *I'll Play The Blues For You* (1973) and in later years he took to smoking a pipe and wearing a hat on stage. By the late Eighties he was planning to retire but died of a heart attack in 1992, just two days after another farewell performance.

B.B. KING

AMBASSADOR OF BLUES

The bluesman who took the blues into the mainstream, B.B. King (b. 1925) is also its ambassador to the world. His solid, seasoned style is heard around the world. His style draws on the Mississippi blues of Elmore James and Muddy Waters, the Chicago blues of Buddy Guy and Magic Sam, and the West-Coast blues of T-Bone Walker and Lowell Fulsom, all filtered through his distinctive vibrato and the phrases that flow out of his beloved Gibson ES-355, forever named Lucille. His feel for the blues is consummate and instinctive, his licks coming seamlessly out of vocal lines or horn riffs, always with room to breathe within the song.

Born in Itta Bena, Mississippi, King was raised in a farming family and found his voice in a gospel choir. He started playing the guitar in his teens and moved to Memphis in his early twenties, securing a sponsored radio spot. Recruiting a band, he embarked on the 'chitlin' touring circuit around the American South, honing his style and arrangements.

King scored a No. 1 rhythm and blues record with 'Three O'Clock Blues' in 1951 and followed it with a string of hits: 'You Know I Love You' (1952), Please Love Me (1953), 'You Upset Me Baby' (1954), 'Sweet Little Angel' (1956) and 'Sweet Sixteen' (1960). In the Sixties, as his blues waned in favour of soul and Motown, King signed to major label MCA to broaden his audience. *Live At The Regal* (1964) failed in that respect, although it has been acclaimed as one of the greatest blues albums ever recorded. But later in the Sixties he found an appreciative audience in the rock scene, scoring a Top 20 hit with 'The Thrill Is Gone' in 1970.

In subsequent decades, King regularly toured the world, taking on the ambassadorial role that enabled him to survive passing fashions and occasionally hitting the spotlight, as with his collaboration with U2 in 1988 on 'When Love Comes To Town'. In 2006 he undertook a farewell world tour but since then, the performances, and awards and accolades, have mounted. In 2006, President George W. Bush awarded King the Presidential Medal of Freedom. In 2007, King was awarded an honorary doctorate in music by Brown University. In 2009, *Time* named B.B. King number three on its list of the 10 best electric guitarists of all-time.

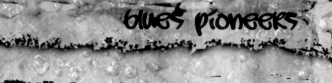

GUITAR SLIM
HIGH-VOLTAGE HERO

In his brief, meteoric career, Guitar Slim (1926–59) electrified the blues in more ways than one. While most bluesmen didn't alter their style as they moved from acoustic to electric guitar in the Forties and Fifties, Slim developed a uniquely electric style, utilizing a 150-ft (46-m) (some say 350-ft/107-m) cable between his guitar and amplifier and creating a sustained whining note that is now a regular practice but was a revelation in Slim's time.

His live shows were equally high-voltage. Often dressed in a cherry-red suit with matching hair and white shoes, he would start by playing offstage before making his entrance on the shoulders of a burly minder. He was usually carried out the same way, often to the street outside where he would continue playing for passers-by. No one who saw him perform will ever forget him, as Buddy Guy will testify.

Born Eddie Jones in Greenwood, Mississippi, in 1926, Slim worked in the cotton fields before he began hanging around juke joints, singing and dancing with local bands. In 1946 he enlisted in the army, and when he returned two years later he had little time for Delta blues, instead developing a fixation on Louisiana guitarist Clarence 'Gatemouth' Brown. He moved down to New Orleans in 1949, forming a band with Huey 'Piano' Smith and working up his flamboyant stage show.

His early recordings made little impression, but he hit the jackpot in 1954 with the swampy, gospel-flavoured 'The Things I Used To Do', featuring Slim's unique guitar sounds and arranged by Ray Charles, who also played piano. It was the best-selling rhythm and blues record for 14 consecutive weeks and reached No. 23 in the pop charts. Slim's career briefly went into overdrive, but none of his attempts at a follow-up, including the soulful 'Sufferin' Mind', 'The Story Of My Life' and 'Something To Remember You By', or the rocking 'Letter To My Girlfriend', 'Quicksand', 'If I Should Lose You' and 'It Hurts To Love Someone', managed any kind of chart success.

Slim was known for his heavy drinking and womanizing, and his lifestyle eventually caught up with him. He died in New York in 1959 after a bout of pneumonia.

FREDDIE KING

BRINGING BLUES TO ROCK

Freddie (sometimes spelled Freddy) King (1934–76) revitalized the Chicago blues scene in the Sixties. His aggressive playing and piercing solos helped set up the blues-rock movement, and he was a major influence on Sixties British guitarists like Eric Clapton, Peter Green and Mick Taylor.

King's mother taught him to play guitar as a child in Gilmer, Texas, where he was born in 1934. In 1950 the family moved to Chicago, and he was soon immersing himself in the thriving blues scene. From guitarist Jimmy Rogers he learnt a thumb-and-index-finger picking technique that he modified by using a plastic thumb pick and a steel fingerpick that added to his keening technique. He also incorporated the country blues stylings he had grown up with, along with a Texas swagger that gave his playing a raucous edge.

But it was hard for King and other young Turks like Buddy Guy and Otis Rush to break into a blues scene dominated by Muddy Waters and Howlin' Wolf, and harder still to get a record deal. When he finally landed one in 1960 he had a stack of material ready, and at his first session he cut 'Have You Ever Loved A Woman' and the instrumental 'Hideaway', which was a Top 5 rhythm and blues hit and even made the pop Top 30. Both songs would be recorded by Eric Clapton (with Derek & the Dominos) and John Mayall's Bluesbreakers.

King's albums of snazzy, catchy instrumentals, *Let's Hide Away And Dance Away With Freddy King* (1961) and *Freddy King Gives You A Bonanza Of Instrumentals* (1965) were highly prized items among British guitarists in search of covers. Clapton's successor in the Bluesbreakers, Peter Green, picked 'The Stumble', and his successor, Mick Taylor, opted for 'Remington Ride' while Chicken Shack's Stan Webb picked 'San-Ho-Zay'.

Not surprisingly King started making regular tours of Britain, where his disciples were happy to sing his praises, and though the hit records had dried up by the mid-Sixties, his guitar prowess continued to develop, courtesy of his stinging vibrato, lyrical lines, and astute phrasing, and he remained a top live attraction on both sides of the Atlantic. Clapton produced *Burglar* (1974), but King was suffering health problems, and in 1976 at the age of 42 he suffered a fatal heart attack, brought on by bleeding ulcers.

JOHNNY 'GUITAR' WATSON
HERO OF ALL GENRES

Few guitarists have gone through as many career changes as Johnny 'Guitar' Watson (1935–96). Rock, blues, jazz, funk, disco – Watson excelled at all of them. He wasn't just a guitarist either. He could, and did, play anything except drums and horns on his records. But it is as a guitarist that he left the most admiration in his wake.

Watson was a pianist when he arrived in Los Angeles, at the age of 15. He had played guitar growing up in Houston, where he was born. He sometimes played with other budding blues maestros Albert Collins and Johnny Copeland. But it wasn't until he saw the flamboyant Guitar Slim perform that he made the guitar his main instrument. In 1954 Watson recorded the instrumental 'Space Guitar', a riot of reverb and feedback, producing sounds from his Stratocaster that no one else would emulate for at least a decade.

During the Fifties Watson switched between blues and rock'n'roll, touring with Little Richard, Johnny Otis, Etta James and B.B. King. He had a rhythm and blues hit with 'These Lonely Lonely Nights' in 1955 and recorded the first of several versions of his theme tune, 'Gangster Of Love'. In the Sixties he had another rhythm and blues hit with the ballad 'Cuttin' In' and recorded a jazz album, misleadingly titled *The Blues Soul Of Johnny Guitar Watson* (1964), before hooking up with rhythm and blues star Larry Williams for the live *Larry Williams Show With Johnny Guitar Watson* (1965) and the soulful *Two For The Price Of One* (1967).

In the early Seventies he took his soul in a funkier direction with *Listen* (1973) and *I Don't Want To Be Alone, Stranger* (1975) before finding a flashy disco connection with the highly successful *Ain't That A Bitch* (1976), *A Real Mother For Ya* (1977), *Funk Beyond The Call Of Duty* (1977) and *Giant* (1978). He largely disappeared from view in the Eighties, returning with the funk/rap *Bow Wow* (1994). He was making a live-performance comeback when he suffered a fatal heart attack during a Japanese tour in 1996.

BUDDY GUY

LEGEND OF LIVE LICKS

One of the young gunslingers that invigorated the blues in the Sixties, Buddy Guy (b. 1936) wowed audiences with high-octane guitar histrionics and energy that were matched by a tortured vocal manner. He was a master of dynamics, allowing a song to drift towards oblivion before suddenly bringing it back to a crescendo of intensity. Jimi Hendrix, Eric Clapton and Jeff Beck were all notable fans. Guy was essentially a live performer who found it hard to channel his unpredictable virtuosity into the confines of a recording studio.

George Guy was born into a sharecropping family in Lettsworth, Louisiana, and started playing in and around Baton Rouge in his teens. It wasn't until 1957 that he moved north to Chicago, where he was encouraged by his idol, Muddy Waters, and developed his own style, a mixture of the showmanship of Guitar Slim and the rapid-fire phrasing of B.B. King.

He signed with Chess, Chicago's premier label, in 1960, and his first session produced the harrowing 'First Time I Met The Blues'. He scored a rhythm and blues hit with 'Stone Crazy' in 1962, but most of his own recordings remained unreleased (possibly due to internecine politics), although he appeared on countless records by Muddy Waters, Willie Dixon, Little Walter, Sonny Boy Williamson II and Koko Taylor. His first British visit in 1965 with the American Folk Blues Festival launched his prestigious fan club. He also started a long-lasting and fruitful relationship with harmonica player and singer Junior Wells. The duo played together on *Hoodoo Man Blues* (1965), *It's My Life Baby!* (1966), *Play The Blues* (1972) and *Drinkin' TNT 'n' Smokin' Dynamite* (1982), recorded at the 1974 Montreux Festival.

The Seventies and Eighties were a lean period for Buddy Guy recordings and it wasn't until *Damn Right I've Got The Blues* (1991), which featured Clapton, Beck and Mark Knopfler, followed by Grammy winning *Feels Like Rain* (1993) and *Slippin' In* (1995) that he started achieving commercial success. In 2003, Guy was awarded the National Medal of Arts. He was inducted into the Rock and Roll Hall of Fame in 2005 and was still touring the world well into 2010.

Guy has had a long relationship with Fender, preferring to play a Stratocaster through a Fender Tweed Bassman (4 x 10).

STEVIE RAY VAUGHAN

REVIVING THE BLUES

Exploding on to a generally lethargic blues scene in 1983 with his *Texas Flood* album, Stevie Ray Vaughan (1954–90) administered a high-voltage charge that revitalized the blues with his stunning, ecstatic playing and imagination. He took his influences from the most stylish of his idols – Jimi Hendrix, Buddy Guy, Howlin' Wolf, Albert King – but it was the wild style of Fifties blues rocker Lonnie Mack that gave him his aggressive swagger.

To accommodate his large hands and thick fingers, Vaughan used heavy duty guitar strings that he tuned down a semitone. This contributed to his distinctive style that included playing simultaneous lead and rhythm parts. He also used his index finger as a pick, which gave him greater tone control.

Vaughan was born in Dallas, Texas, in 1954, and it was his older brother Jimmie who introduced him to the guitar and the blues. When Jimmie left home to form the Fabulous Thunderbirds in 1972, Stevie quit school and followed him to Austin, where he spent the next three years playing in various bar bands. In 1975 he co-founded Triple Threat with singer Lou Ann Barton, and when the band broke up three years later Vaughan took over the vocals and brought in bassist Tommy Shannon to join drummer Chris Layton, renaming the trio Double Trouble.

The band's reputation gradually spread, and in 1982 they played the Montreux Festival in Switzerland, attracting the attention of David Bowie, who recruited Vaughan to play on *Let's Dance* (1983), and Jackson Browne, who offered his studio for recording. *Texas Flood* (1983), recorded in three days, revelled in Vaughan's influences, such as Buddy Guy ('Mary Had A Little Lamb'), Lightnin' Hopkins ('Rude Mood') and Jimi Hendrix ('Lenny'), while spotlighting Vaughan's own powerful 'Pride And Joy' and the slow, intense 'Dirty Pool'.

Couldn't Stand The Weather (1984) confirmed Vaughan's promise. His playing grew in authority with an inspired revival of Hendrix's 'Voodoo Chile'. His blues ranged from the aggressive 'The Things I Used To Do' to the emotionally charged 'Tin Pan Alley'. The title track, featuring Vaughan's brother Jimmie (pictured below right), added a rock beat and a funky feel to his blues.

For *Soul To Soul* (1985) Vaughan added keyboard player Reese Wynans to the band, fattening up the sound. Wynans' Hammond organ swirled around Vaughan's solid riffs on 'Change It', and he complemented Vaughan's jazzy touch on 'Gone Home'. Vaughan covered Hank Ballard's 'Look At Little Sister' and Willie Dixon's 'You'll Be Mine'. But 'Ain't Gone 'n' Give Up On Love' proved that he could write his own tortured blues.

Vaughan was now a global blues star. He was also collaborating with other artists, recording with Albert King on *In Session* (1983), Johnny Copeland on *Texas Twister* (1984) and Lonnie Mack on *Strike Like Lightning* (1985). But Vaughan's health was suffering because of his drug abuse, and in 1986 he collapsed during a European tour. He checked into a rehabilitation centre for treatment and resumed touring in 1988. *In Step* (1989) showed renewed vigour and commitment with Vaughan's impassioned takes on Buddy Guy's 'Leave My Girl Alone', Howlin' Wolf's 'Love Me Darlin'' and Willie Dixon's 'Let Me Love You Baby', plus Vaughan's own hard-rocking 'Scratch 'n' Sniff' and the slow, personal 'Wall Of Denial' and 'Tightrope'. The album won a Grammy for Best Contemporary Blues Album.

In 1990 Vaughan recorded another Grammy-winning album with his brother Jimmie, *Family Style*, but before its released he was killed in a helicopter crash returning from a concert in Wisconsin that had finished with a jam featuring Vaughan, Eric Clapton, Buddy Guy, Robert Cray and Jimmie playing 'Sweet Home Chicago'. He was 35 years old. In 1991 Jimmie compiled another Grammy winning album of unreleased material, *The Sky Is Crying*, featuring Elmore James's title track, Lonnie Mack's 'Wham', jazz guitarist Kenny Burrell's 'Chitlins Con Carne', and an extended version of Hendrix's 'Little Wing'. Since then Vaughan's legacy has continued to grow. In 2000, Vaughan was inducted into the Blues Hall of Fame.

Vaughan generally played Fender Stratocasters. His favourite, made in 1962 with parts from 1959, had a Brazilian rosewood fingerboard and a left-handed tremolo that gave him a specialized sound quality. Fender has released two tribute models, the Stevie Ray Vaughan Signature Stratocaster in 1992 and in 2007 the Lenny, an exact replica of the 1962 Strat given to him by his wife Lenora. He also played a Hamiltone Custom guitar and a semi-hollow Groove Master.

from blues to Rock

In Fifties America, rock'n'roll was the subversive product of black music combined
with white, the blues mixed with country. The guitarists who pioneered rock'n'roll
influenced the next generation, and as the Sixties progressed styles began to
change as pop toughened into rock. For some guitarists in this category the
blues was a jumping-off point from which to develop different approaches like
psychedelia, progressive rock and hard rock. Others preferred to stay closer
to the original spirit of the blues. Meanwhile, the role of lead guitarist was
elevated to even greater heights; the era of the guitar hero had truly arrived.

CHUCK BERRY

ROCK'N'ROLL'S PIONEER

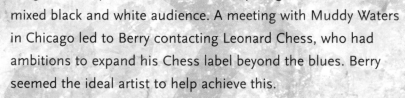

One of the founding fathers of rock'n'roll, Charles Edward (Chuck) Berry (b. 1926) was born in St Louis, Missouri, to a middle-class family. His interest in the blues began in high school, where he gave his first public performance. In 1944, he was convicted of armed robbery and sentenced to three years in an Intermediate Reformatory for Young Men. He was released on his twenty-first birthday. Before his career in music, Berry worked as a hairdresser.

Influenced by the guitar styles of Carl Hogen, T-Bone Walker, Charlie Christian and Elmore James, Berry by 1953 was playing in the Johnnie Johnson Trio. The group mixed the blues with ballads and hillbilly music, and played the songs of Nat King Cole alongside those of Muddy Waters. These combinations, along with Berry's natural showmanship, began to attract a

mixed black and white audience. A meeting with Muddy Waters in Chicago led to Berry contacting Leonard Chess, who had ambitions to expand his Chess label beyond the blues. Berry seemed the ideal artist to help achieve this.

Released in July 1955, Berry's single 'Maybellene', based on an old country song, was one of the first rock'n'roll singles and became a Top 5 hit in America. The string of hits that followed were all self-penned, something that set Berry apart from the majority of his contemporaries. His songs defined rock'n'roll with their teen-oriented themes about cars, girls and dancing. The exciting, driving yet loose guitar sound came courtesy of Berry's Gibson ES 350T. The opening riff of 'Johnny B. Goode' typifies Berry's style and set the template for rock'n'roll for many years to come, exerting a fundamental influence on the Rolling Stones and the Beatles. Even the fledgling Sex Pistols used to practise with the song.

In 1959, Berry was sentenced to a second term in prison, this time under the US Mann Act for transporting a minor across the state line for immoral purposes. The charge involved a hatcheck girl at his nightclub in St Louis. On his release in 1963, Berry's career prospered as the Beatles and the Stones recorded versions of his songs. Berry also inspired surf rock; he

received a co-writing credit on the Beach Boys' 'Surfin' USA' because of its close resemblance to 'Sweet Little Sixteen'. His recording career resumed in 1964, producing more standards, including 'No Particular Place To Go' and 'You Never Can Tell'. Although he remained a popular live draw, Berry's records became less successful as the Sixties progressed.

A return to Chess in 1970 resulted in Berry's only No. 1 single, the suggestive novelty ditty 'My Ding-a-Ling', which was recorded live in England and reached the top of the charts in both the US and the UK. Berry remained unrepentant in the face of criticism, delighted at the money it made for him. The song did rekindle interest in Berry's music and a live version of 'Reelin' and Rockin'', issued shortly afterwards, also charted.

For the rest of the Seventies, hiring a local band to back him at each performance, confident in the expectation that they would be familiar with his material. This led to criticisms of his gigs as slapdash and out-of-tune, although Berry has sometimes been known to deliberately detune his guitar for effect. His insistence on being paid in cash by promoters led to a third stint in prison when he was convicted of tax evasion in 1979.

In 1986, a sixtieth-birthday celebration concert was filmed by Taylor Hackford as *Hail! Hail! Rock'n'Roll*. Berry disciple Keith Richards acted as musical director, finding the curmudgeonly Berry difficult to work with. Amongst those paying homage were Eric Clapton and Robert Cray. The film sees Berry playing a Gibson ES-355, a deluxe version of the guitar he used on his Seventies tours.

The irascible Berry continued managing legal troubles – in 1991 he negotiated a plea bargain for installing a video camera in the woman's restroom of his restaurant – and performing, well into his 80s. He received Kennedy Center Honors in 2000. By 2010 his performances had centered around the Blueberry Hill restaurant's Duck Room in St, Louis, reminiscent of Les Paul's late-career residency at New York's Irridium club. In 2009, *Time* named Berry number seven on its list of the 10 best electric guitar players of all-time.

BO DIDDLEY

INFLUENTIAL RHYTHM MASTER

A pivotal figure in the transition from blues to rock'n'roll, Bo Diddley (1928–2008) was born Elias Bates in McComb, Mississippi. When he was seven the family relocated to Chicago, where he took violin lessons before switching to guitar, inspired by John Lee Hooker. He began by playing on street corners, then in the Hipsters. In 1951, he secured a regular gig at the 708 Club in Chicago's South Side, the cradle of the blues. Here he adopted the stage name Bo Diddley, which was also the title of the first single he recorded for Checker (a subsidiary of Chess) in 1955. The song featured the distinctive jerky rhythm based on the 'patted juba', an African tribal beat adopted by street performers in Chicago, but known subsequently as the 'Bo Diddley beat'.

Diddley was also known for his rectangular-bodied Gretsch, which he adapted himself. Nicknamed 'The Twang Machine', the guitar was at Diddley's side throughout his career, along with similar instruments made by other companies. The modifications made the guitar smaller and less restrictive on stage. Diddley's hard-driving rhythmic style was a major influence on the development of rock'n'roll. Songs such as 'Who Do You Love' and 'Hey Bo Diddley' were based on one chord, de-emphasizing harmony in favour of rhythm. He often used a capo at G to help achieve his staccato sound.

Diddley made 11 albums between 1958 and 1963, while touring relentlessly. In the late Sixties he added funk to his repertoire, and greatly influenced successive generations of musicians. Buddy Holly adapted the Diddley beat for 'Not Fade Away', covered by the Rolling Stones. Diddley was one of the godfathers of the Sixties British rhythm and blues movement. Artists as diverse as George Michael and Guns N' Roses have used the Bo Diddley beat as a basis for songs. The Clash invited him to open for them on their 1979 American tour. He was inducted the Rock and Roll Hall of Fame and the Rockabilly Hall of Fame in 1987 and in 1998 received lifetime achievement awards from the Rhythm and Blues Foundation and NARAS.

In 2008 Diddley died of heart failure at his home in Florida.

SCOTTY MOORE

LEADING THE FIELD

The original rock'n'roll lead guitarist, Scotty Moore (b. 1931) was born near Gadsden, Tennessee. Moore began playing guitar at the age of eight, largely self-taught. Although he aspired to playing jazz like Barney Kessel and Tal Farlow, he was also influenced by country guitarists like Merle Travis and, in particular, Chet Atkins.

After Navy service Moore formed a hillbilly group, the Starlite Wranglers in 1952 with Bill Black on upright bass. After Moore struck up a rapport with Sam Phillips, the proprietor of Sun Records, Phillips suggested that Moore and Black accompany his protégé, Elvis Presley (pictured right). Initially the sessions were unproductive until the trio began playing 'That's All Right (Mama)', which captured the chemistry between them and became Presley's first single in 1954.

Moore and Black, along with drummer D.J. Fontana, backed Elvis on his greatest records. Before Chuck Berry and Bo Diddley, Moore fused various strands of American music to create the language of rock'n'roll lead guitar, establishing it as the main instrument and inspiring countless guitarists. His style was clean, simple and economical, primarily at the insistence of Sam Phillips. Moore favoured Gibson guitars, using the semi-acoustic ES-295 on early Sun recordings with Presley and switching in 1955 to an L5 and later to a Super 400 CES.

Moore continued to back Elvis until 1958. He made his only solo album, the all-instrumental *The Guitar That Changed The World* (1964) and worked with Presley again during the Sixties, appearing with the singer for the last time in the ''68 Comeback Special' television performance. Afterwards, Scotty virtually retired from playing for 23 years, founding his own recording studio in Memphis and concentrating on engineering records and television productions. He was reunited with D.J. Fontana on *All The King's Men* (1997), an all-star celebration of Elvis's music.

Moore has spent most of the last 10 years performing at tribute shows with disciples such as Eric Clapton and Mark Knopfler and accepting awards for his legendary contribution to rock'n'roll. He was inducted into the Rock And Roll Hall of Fame in 2009.

DICK DALE

SURF'S SUPERSTAR

'King of the Surf Guitar' Dick Dale (b. 1937) was born Richard Monsour in Boston, Massachusetts. Dale learned to play drums, ukulele and trumpet before taking up the guitar, inspired by country music. His first break in music was winning an Elvis Presley sound-alike contest. Dale began playing guitar in clubs, solo at first but later backed by the Del-Tones. He was an early enthusiast of the surfing scene that arose on the beaches of southern California in the early Sixties, his family having moved there in 1954.

His recording career began in 1961 with the single 'Let's Go Trippin'', regarded as the first surf-rock song, and he achieved national popularity in the States with *Surfer's Choice* (1962). Diagnosed with cancer in 1966, he was forced to retire, although he made a full recovery. After almost losing a leg to a surfing injury sustained in polluted water, he became an environmental activist. He is best known for 'Misirlou' (1962) which brought him to a new audience when used in the movie *Pulp Fiction* (1994) and led to his comeback.

Dale is left-handed but learned to play on a right-handed guitar without restringing it, effectively playing the instrument upside down. He was notorious for using strings of the heaviest gauge possible but still regularly breaking them and wearing out plectrums because of his forceful playing. This rhythmic, percussive attack was influenced by jazz drummer Gene Krupa.

Dale aimed to recreate the experiences of surfing in his music; his trademark twang was intended to simulate the sound of breaking waves. He is credited with inventing surf music and has been hailed 'the father of heavy metal' due to his work with Leo Fender in increasing the power of amplifiers. He uses a signature-model Stratocaster, given to him by Fender. Dale used the first 100-watt amp. Jimi Hendrix and Stevie Ray Vaughan were among the admirers of his unique style.

In 2008, he was diagnosed with cancer and underwent surgery, but by 2009 he was on tour again. His backup band is anchored by son Jimmy Dale on drums.

DUANE EDDY

THE REBEL ROUSER

Rock'n'roll guitarist Duane Eddy (b. 1938) was born in Corning, New York. His interest in the guitar began when he was five, inspired by singing film-cowboy Gene Autry. In 1951, the family moved to Arizona. While playing guitar in a country duo, Duane met songwriter, producer and disc jockey Lee Hazelwood. The pair embarked on a writing and production partnership, pioneering the rock'n'roll instrumental. 'Movin' 'n' Groovin'' was a minor hit for Eddy in 1958. It was followed by the Top 10 success of 'Rebel Rouser', the first of a string of similar hits.

Eddy achieved his unique twangy guitar sound by bending the bass strings and using a combination of echo chamber and tremolo arm. The twang evoked the sound of hot-rod engines revving up and had echoes of the Wild West. Eddy credited Hazelwood with creating the big sound on his records by mixing them specifically for AM radio. His backing band, the Rebels, consisted of top session players, many of whom became members of Phil Spector's Wrecking Crew in the Sixties. He later introduced female backing vocalists, the Rebelettes, on 'Dance With The Guitar Man'.

Eddy's biggest hit, the theme to the movie *Because They're Young*, brought strings into the repertoire. Eddy was the first rock'n'roll guitarist with a signature model, the Guild DE-400 and deluxe DE-500. For a long time, he was associated with the Gretsch Chet Atkins 6120.

Eddy's chart success started to dry up in 1962, but he remained an innovative performer, recording many albums, including one of instrumental versions of Dylan songs, and branching out into producing and acting. He returned to the British charts in 1975 with 'Play Me Like You Play Your Guitar'; in 1986 he recorded a new version of 'Peter Gunn' with avant-garde outfit Art of Noise. The album *Duane Eddy* (1987) followed. It featured guest appearances by many of the musicians he had influenced, including Paul McCartney, George Harrison, Jeff Lynne, Ry Cooder and John Fogerty. Eddy was inducted into the Rock and Roll Hall of Fame in 1994.

EDDIE COCHRAN

INNOVATION PERSONIFIED

One of rock'n'roll's most influential guitarists, Eddie Cochran (1938–60) was born in Albert Lea, Minnesota. Eddie wanted to join the school band as a drummer but opted for trombone when he was told that he would have to learn piano before being allowed to play drums. When advised that he didn't have the 'lip' for trombone, he asked his brother to show him some chords on guitar and from there taught himself to play.

The family moved to California, where he formed his first group in high school. He later teamed up with Hank Cochran and the duo played country music as the Cochran Brothers, although they were not related, and made some recordings. On seeing Elvis Presley in late 1955, Eddie was inspired to switch to rock'n'roll, and the Cochran Brothers split up soon afterwards.

The year 1956 proved to be pivotal for Cochran. He recorded the Elvis-influenced 'Twenty Flight Rock' and performed it in the classic rock'n'roll movie *The Girl Can't Help It*. The following year, he recorded what would be the only LP issued in his lifetime, *Singin' To My Baby* (1957). He went on to create three seminal and frequently covered rock'n'roll songs 'C'mon Everybody', 'Somethin' Else' and 'Summertime Blues'.

Cochran was hugely popular in Britain. While on tour with Gene Vincent in April 1960, he was killed in car crash in Chippenham, Wiltshire. He was 21 years old. Also in the car were his fiancée and songwriting partner Sharon Sheeley, who was not seriously injured, and Vincent, who was left with a permanent limp. 'Three Steps to Heaven' became a posthumous No. 1 in Britain. Cochran was a fundamental influence on the first generation of British rock'n'rollers. Paul McCartney showed John Lennon how to play 'Twenty Flight Rock' at their first meeting.

Cochran's distinctive rhythmic approach both puzzled and fascinated listeners. One of his innovations was aligning the bass and guitar to equivalent harmonic frequencies. Cochran began by using a Gibson guitar but is most closely associated with a modified 1956 Gretsch 6120 Chet Atkins Western model.

HANK MARVIN

OUT OF THE SHADOWS

Britain's first home-grown guitar hero Hank Marvin (b. 1941) was born Brian Rankin in Newcastle-upon-Tyne. His first instruments were piano and banjo but he switched to guitar upon discovering Buddy Holly. Marvin formed a skiffle band, the Railroaders, with school friend Bruce Welch (pictured below), and they travelled to London in 1958 to compete, unsuccessfully, in a talent contest. Welch and Marvin opted to remain in London and gravitated to the legendary 2i's coffee bar, where they were recruited to play in the Drifters, the backing band for singer Cliff Richard (pictured below).

In addition to working with Richard, the band recorded in its own right. After a change of name to the Shadows, their fourth single, 'Apache', reached No. 1 in 1960, the first of a string of instrumental hits characterized by Marvin's echoing lead lines and manipulation of the tremolo arm. He was the first British guitarist to play a Fender Stratocaster (owned by Cliff Richard) and did so much to popularize the model that in 1961 the company supplied the group with matching red fiesta Stratocasters. Richard and the Shadows' combined output dominated the British pop charts in the period immediately prior to the Beatles, and while the Shadows survived the arrival of Merseybeat, their popularity began to wane in the mid-Sixties.

After the Shadows split up in 1968, Marvin made a self-titled solo album in 1969, and then formed the vocal-harmony trio Marvin, Welch & Farrar, which developed into a revived version of the Shadows. The new line-up's debut, *Rocking With Curly Leads* (1973), saw Marvin experimenting with a vocoder. By the Eighties, the Shadows' output consisted mainly of cover versions. In 1990, Marvin resumed his occasional solo career, and the Shadows reunited for a farewell tour in 2004–05.

Marvin was a melodic guitarist and a tunesmith whose approach remained consistent throughout his career. In addition to his Fender Stratocaster, he worked with Burns of London to develop his signature brand, the Burns Marvin, which he played from 1964 until the Shadows' final tour. Marvin inspired countless guitarists, including Pete Townshend, Neil Young, Carlos Santana, Jeff Beck and Mark Knopfler.

JERRY GARCIA

GRATEFUL'S GREATNESS

A leading figure on America's West-Coast music scene, Jerry Garcia (1942–95) was born in San Francisco. His father was a retired professional musician, his mother a pianist. The musically inclined Jerry began taking piano lessons as a child. The emergence of Chuck Berry, Buddy Holly and Eddie Cochran influenced him to learn guitar at 15, his first instrument being a Danelectro. He took an arts course at San Francisco Institute of Arts, where he encountered the city's Bohemian subculture for the first time. In the early Sixties, he met future Grateful Dead bassist Phil Lesh and lyricist Robert Hunter. Garcia began playing guitar in earnest around this time, also taking up banjo.

Garcia began performing in a bluegrass outfit and subsequently a jug band, which evolved into the Warlocks and ultimately into the Grateful Dead. The band fused such diverse elements as bluegrass, folk, blues, country, Celtic music and jazz, all of which were evident in their long, improvised live jams and in Garcia's extended solos. Rarely captured adequately in the studio, early Dead is best represented on *Live/Dead* (1969). Their commercially successful albums, *Workingman's Dead* and *American Beauty* (both 1970) featured more conventional, country flavoured songwriting and musicianship. Garcia was an accomplished pedal-steel player, and his achievements are all the more remarkable for the fact that he lost two-thirds of his right middle finger in a childhood accident.

Throughout his career, Garcia used a variety of guitars, sometimes favouring the Gibson SG or Les Paul, at other times the Fender Stratocaster. In 1973, he acquired his first custom-built guitar, and later added two more, all from the innovative guitar and bass company Alembic.

Although the Dead gigged relentlessly, Garcia found time for extra-curricular activity, notably the Jerry Garcia Band, some Grateful Dead spin-offs and sessions for other musicians such as Crosby, Stills, Nash & Young, Jefferson Airplane and New Riders of the Purple Sage. After struggling with heroin addiction for many years and surviving a near fatal diabetic coma in 1988, Garcia died of a heart attack in August 1995.

MIKE BLOOMFIELD

BLENDING IN WITH THE BLUES

Blues-rock guitarist Mike Bloomfield (1943–81) was born in Chicago, Illinois, to an affluent Jewish family. He possessed an innate ability on guitar, which he began playing at the age of 13, initially influenced by Scotty Moore. Despite his background, Bloomfield quickly became a devotee of Chicago's indigenous blues scene, frequently visiting clubs on the city's South Side. He often jumped on stage asking to sit in on guitar.

Bloomfield's empathy for blues performers saw him accepted in an area where white faces were rare. He encountered CBS producer John Hammond, who signed him to the label, but Bloomfield's solo work remained unreleased until after his death. An equally important meeting was with harmonica player and singer Paul Butterfield, whose Paul Butterfield Blues Band (pictured below) Bloomfield joined in 1964. Their eponymous 1965 debut was one of the first blues albums to feature a white singer, anticipating the British blues boom of 1968.

East-West (1966) was a groundbreaking work that saw Bloomfield hailed for his fluid lead guitar, particularly on the epic, improvisational title track's blend of blues, psychedelia and Indian raga. Bloomfield switched between Fender Telecaster and Gibson Les Paul on this album, and he would use both guitars throughout his career. His Les Paul work was particularly influential for the way he created long sustained tones on the instrument. He preferred a clean sound with plenty of reverb and vibrato, rarely using distortion or feedback. Bloomfield's session work for CBS was equally groundbreaking as he accompanied Bob Dylan's first, famously controversial steps into electric rock on *Highway 61 Revisited* (1965).

Weary of touring, Bloomfield left Butterfield in 1967 to form the short-lived Electric Flag, which disbanded after one album. He teamed up with Al Kooper, who had played organ with Dylan, and the pair made *Super Session* (1968) with Stephen Stills and *The Live Adventures Of Mike Bloomfield And Al Kooper* (1968). Bloomfield's career in the Seventies was a lower-profile affair. He continued to record and undertake session work, but he had descended into drug addiction and suffered from arthritis in his hands. In February 1981, he died of a heroin overdose.

DICKEY BETTS

THE GOLDIE TOUCH

Southern blues-rock guitarist Dickey Betts (b. 1943) was born in West Palm Beach, Florida. Betts was leading a group called the Second Coming when he met and jammed with the other members of what soon became the Allman Brothers Band. His role as second lead guitarist and his partnership with Duane Allman gave the band their trademark dual-lead sound, which was captured at its most potent on the Allmans' seminal double live album *At Fillmore East* (1971), particularly the side-long epic 'Whipping Post'.

Following Allman's death in 1971, Betts became sole lead guitarist and took on more of the lead vocals. He wrote many of the Allmans' most celebrated songs, including 'In Memory Of Elizabeth Reed', 'Blue Sky', 'Ramblin' Man' – the band's biggest US hit – and 'Jessica', which has served as the theme to British motoring programme Top Gear for many years.

Betts released his first solo album, *Highway Call* (1974), and when the Allmans split in 1976, he resumed his solo career with *Dickey Betts And Great Southern* (1977) and *Atlanta's Burning Down* (1978). The release of a boxed-set retrospective helped rekindle interest in the Allman Brothers Band, leading to a reformation, with a revised line-up, in 1978, which marked the start of a cycle of splits and reunions. The band made three more studio albums and released several live sets, remaining a popular attraction in concert. In the mid-Nineties Betts was suffering problems with alcohol, which necessitated his replacement on some dates. In 2000 he was suspended by his colleagues for 'personal and professional reasons' and, following legal action on his part, the separation became permanent. Betts re-launched his solo career, forming the Dickey Betts Band, which turned into Dickey Betts & Great Southern. His son, Duane, has joined the band on lead guitar. In 2009 Betts announced his retirement from touring and live performances.

Early in his career, Betts played a 1961 Gibson SG, which he subsequently gave to Allman for slide work. He replaced this with a 1957 Gibson Les Paul Goldtop, nicknamed 'Goldie', which became synonymous with him. He has also played Fender Stratocasters and PRS guitars.

KEITH RICHARDS

ICON OF EXCESS

Veteran Rolling Stones guitarist Keith Richards (b. 1943) was born in Dartford, Kent. After being expelled from technical school in 1958, Richards attended Sidcup Art College. The art-school environment was crucial to Richards' development, as it was for many of his generation. He was able to nurture his passion for rhythm and blues, finding many fellow enthusiasts and hearing Big Bill Broonzy and Little Walter for the first time there.

Richards acquired an acoustic guitar and after some help from his grandfather who schooled him in the rudiments, Keith set about mastering the instrument by listening to records. Chuck Berry was a defining influence on the young Richards, who soon graduated to playing a cheap electric guitar. 'To me, Chuck Berry's style is one of the loosest and most exciting to play,' said Richards. 'When I started, I pinched virtually all of his riffs.'

A chance meeting with Mick Jagger revealed a shared interest in the blues. Jagger invited Richards to join the group in which he sang, Little Boy Blue & the Blue Boys. In 1962, Richards successfully auditioned for a rhythm and blues outfit which Brian Jones, a blues fanatic from Cheltenham, was putting together in London and which would ultimately evolve into the Rolling Stones.

Richards took Jagger along, although the singer initially was also working with the Blues Incorporated, led by British blues pioneer Alexis Korner. The foundations for the Rolling Stones were laid by Richards and Jones spending days together practising and trying to figure out how bluesmen like Robert Johnson, Elmore James and Muddy Waters achieved the sounds on their records. 'The Rolling Stones are basically a two-guitar band. That's how we started off. And the whole secret, if there is a secret behind the sound of the Rolling Stones, is the way we work two guitars together,' said Richards. The interlocking lead and

rhythm guitars can be heard to good effect on the first three Stones albums: *Rolling Stones* (1964), *Rolling Stones No.2* (1965) and *Out Of Our Heads* (1965).

The recruitment of Bill Wyman (bass) and Charlie Watts (drums) completed the Stones line-up. Astutely marketed by manager Andrew Loog Oldham as the polar opposites of the wholesome Beatles, the Stones were second only to their Merseyside rivals in the Sixties. Oldham's insistence that Jagger and Richards provide original material for the band changed its dynamic, leading eventually to the marginalization of the increasingly dissolute and unreliable Jones. The first Jagger-Richards A-side, 'The Last Time', featured a menacing, repeated four-note phrase from Richards. Although Oldham was credited as producer on early Stones records, in practical terms it was Richards who carried out the role.

With Jones too out-of-it to contribute, Richards was at his most creative on *Beggars Banquet* (1968), playing almost all the guitar parts on the album, which restored the Stones' fortunes after an unconvincing flirtation with psychedelia. Jones left in 1969, replaced by former Bluesbreakers guitarist Mick Taylor, a skilled blues and jazz player. The high point of Taylor's time in the Stones was *Exile On Main Street* (1972) on which his and Richards' guitars combined and interplayed effortlessly. Former Face Ronnie Wood was recruited after Taylor's departure late in 1974. Wood proved the ideal foil for Richards, both visually and musically. 'We both become one instrument,' said Richards.

Richards was and is an innovative player, claiming the first chart hit to feature a fuzzbox,'(I Can't Get No) Satisfaction', in 1965, while his use of open tunings from the late Sixties became a trademark. He has a collection of over 1,000 guitars and was associated with the Fender Telecaster, although in 1964 he was one of the first stars in Britain to own a Les Paul. In recent years, he has favoured the Gibson ES-345. Richards' look, lifestyle and guitar playing has influenced many musicians, some of whom, like Mick Jones (Clash) and Johnny Thunders (New York Dolls, Heartbreakers), apparently wanted to be Richards, not just sound like him. His longevity, like that of the Stones, remains a source of surprise and delight.

Richards underwent cranial surgery in 2006 after a head injury, but returned to the Stones in 2007. He signed a deal for a biography to be released in 2010.

ALBERT LEE

TRIUMPH ON A TELECASTER

Rock guitarist Albert Lee (b. 1943) was born in Leominster, Herefordshire. The son of a musician, Lee started his musical career on piano, but like many of his generation took up guitar upon the arrival of rock'n'roll, inspired in particular by Buddy Holly. He played in various bands after leaving school at the age of 16, before becoming lead guitarist with Chris Farlowe & the Thunderbirds.

Preferring country to the soul-influenced music of Farlowe, he left in 1968 to join country-rock outfit Head, Hands & Feet. While playing with the band, Lee made his name as a guitarist, gaining a reputation for the amazing speed at which he played his Fender Telecaster. Head, Hands & Feet were a popular live attraction in Britain and Europe, but their critically acclaimed albums failed to reach a mainstream audience.

In 1974, Lee relocated to Los Angeles, where he found himself very much in demand as a session musician but unable to progress his solo career satisfactorily. He joined Emmylou Harris's Hot Band in 1976 as a replacement for one of his idols, James Burton. Two years later he linked up with Eric Clapton, with whom he played for the next five years. Lee has also worked with the Everly Brothers, having masterminded their 1983 reunion concert and served as its musical director. In 1987, he fronted a band for the first time, Hogan's Heroes, with whom he still tours regularly. Although not well-known to the general public, Hogan's Heroes regularly attracted star names to jam with them. Lee has also worked frequently with Bill Wyman's Rhythm Kings.

Because of his long association with the Fender instrument, Lee has become known as 'Mr Telecaster', although he has also played Gibson guitars, an Ernie Ball Music Man and a Stratocaster from time to time. Lee has not been rewarded with great commercial success or fame but is widely admired by his peers and acknowledged as the guitarist's guitarist, particularly renowned for his fingerstyle and hybrid picking techniques. While his trademarks are speed and virtuosity, he is equally adept at slower, melodic passages.

JOHNNY WINTER

BLUES DEVOTION

Blues guitarist Johnny Winter (b. 1944) was born in Beaumont, Texas. Cross-eyed and albino from birth, Johnny showed a precocious talent for music, taking up clarinet at the age of five and switching to guitar after a brief flirtation with the ukulele. Inspired by bluesmen like B.B. King, Muddy Waters and Bobby Bland, he formed his first group, Johnny & the Jammers with brother Edgar. Winter went on to play in several blues bands during the mid- to late Sixties. His break came in 1969 when an album he had recorded as part of a trio came to the attention of two *Rolling Stone* journalists who raved about it in the magazine, leading to its release as *Johnny Winter* (1969) on CBS.

Hailed as the new superstar blues guitarist, Winter played the Woodstock Festival in August 1969. His third album, *Johnny Winter And* (1970), confirmed his success and featured the song that became his signature tune, Rick Derringer's 'Rock'n'Roll Hoochie Koo'. Derringer was added to the band on second guitar as a foil for Johnny on *Live Johnny Winter And* (1971), a milestone in hard-rocking blues. Suffering from drug addiction and depression, Winter took a break, returning for *Still Alive And Well* (1973). He produced two albums for Muddy Waters, *Hard Again* (1977) and Waters' final work *King Bee* (1980). His own *Nothing But The Blues* (1977) was made with members of Muddy's touring band.

Renowned for his fiery style, Winter has used various guitars. In his early days, he played a Gibson ES-125, but switched to an SG for Woodstock, although his first album was made with a Fender Mustang. His early slide work was done on a National Steel Standard but for *Live Johnny Winter And* he used a Gibson Firebird. For the next phase of his career, an Erlewine Lazer was his primary guitar. Johnny has also played an Epiphone Wiltshire extensively. He does not use a flat plectrum, preferring a thumb-pick. In 1995, Smashing Pumpkins paid homage in an instrumental B-side 'Tribute to Johnny'. Still touring despite health problems (he can only play while sitting), Winter concentrates on the blues.

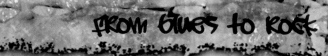

ALVIN LEE

TITAN OF TEN YEARS AFTER

Blues-rock guitarist Alvin Lee (b. 1944) was born Graham Barnes in Nottingham. Inspired by rock'n'roll guitarists Chuck Berry and Scotty Moore, Lee began to play at the age of 13 and formed his first band, Ivan Jay & the Jaymen, in 1960. Lee became lead vocalist in 1962 when the band changed their name to the Jaybirds and played Hamburg's Star Club. They moved to London in 1966, eventually settling on the name Ten Years After. A residency at the Marquee Club led to an invitation to play at the Windsor Jazz and Blues Festival in 1967, which in turn led to a record contract with Deram.

Debut album *Ten Years After* (1967) showcased Lee's soulful, nimble-fingered guitar playing and the band's trail-blazing mix of swing jazz, blues and rock, earning them a cult following in America where they toured for the first of many occasions in 1968. An appearance at the Woodstock Festival in 1969 provided their breakthrough in the States. Lee's virtuoso guitar on what would become his signature tune 'I'm Going Home' was featured in the film and hailed as a highlight of the event. The band also played the Isle of Wight Festival in 1970, the year of their only British hit single, 'Love Like A Man'. After nine studio albums, Lee's dissatisfaction with the group's limitations prompted him to disband Ten Years After in 1974.

Lee's career outside the band had already begun with *On The Road To Freedom* (1973), a country-rock collaboration with Mylon LeFevre that boasted George Harrison, Ronnie Wood and Steve Winwood amongst its superstar guests. In 1978, he put together a new version of Ten Years After, and he toured under the name again in 1989. In between, he worked with Steve Gould of Rare Bird and former Rolling Stone Mick Taylor. In the Nineties, he recorded with rock'n'roll pioneers Scotty Moore and D.J. Fontana. Lee's most recent album, *Saguitar*, was released in 2007.

Lee's favourite guitar is his long-serving Gibson Custom Shop 335, affectionately dubbed 'Big Red'. As it is too valuable to take on the road, the company made him a copy of it.

PETE TOWNSHEND

THE WHO'S WHO OF ROCK

Pioneering guitarist and principal creative force behind the Who, Pete Townshend (b. 1941) was born in Chiswick, London. The Townshends were a musical family – Pete's grandfather was a musician, his father a dance-band saxophonist and his mother a singer. Consequently, a career in music seemed natural for Pete, and his parents encouraged him.

His first instrument was banjo, which he played as a teenager in Dixieland outfit the Confederates with school friend John Entwistle. After leaving school he attended Ealing Art College, where the bohemian atmosphere and emphasis on the exploration of new ideas left an indelible imprint on Townshend. When bassist Entwistle joined the Detours, a rhythm and blues group fronted by singer Roger Daltrey, Townshend, who had switched to guitar at the age of 12, followed him. With the recruitment of drummer Keith Moon, the classic Who line-up was complete.

Townshend's reputation as a destroyer of guitars began by accident in September 1964, when he broke the neck of his guitar on the low ceiling of the Railway Tavern in Harrow, and then smashed the rest of it in frustration. The routine soon became part of the act, with Moon enthusiastically joining in by destroying his drum kit. The other aspects of Townshend's physical approach – the windmilling arm, assaults on the strings and leaps into the air – Townshend claimed to have developed to hide the fact that he could not play the blues properly.

The Who's unique sound was unleashed on their 1965 Kinks-influenced debut single 'I Can't Explain'. The song's signature riff would be widely imitated. The second single, 'Anyway, Anyhow, Anywhere', featured the innovative use of feedback, as Townshend nailed down the rhythm and Moon fired out short drum solos. The Who's first album *My Generation* (1965) was a mix of rhythm and blues and pop, while the follow-up *A Quick One* (1966) was significant in that it contained in the title track Townshend's first conceptual piece.

In Britain, the Who were regarded as a singles band, and they had yet to crack America. After an uncertain year in 1968, the band released *Tommy* (1969), which was hailed as the first rock opera and was a major success in the United States. *Live at Leeds* (1970, reissued with extra tracks in 1995) captured the original line-up at its peak. Townshend's blues riffs and solos on Mose Allison's 'Young Man Blues' and his extended soloing on 'My Generation' are driving forces in the performances.

The Who were established as one of the Seventies' major rock bands, and they consolidated their position with the acclaimed *Who's Next* (1971) and a second rock opera *Quadrophenia* (1973), which looked back to the band's mod roots. In between, Townshend made his first solo album, *Who Came First* (1972). Shortly after the release of *Who Are You* (1978), Moon

died and the future of the Who was thrown into uncertainty, but the band continued with ex-Small Faces and Faces drummer Kenney Jones for two more albums. Townshend pursued a parallel solo career, achieving notable success with *Empty Glass* (1980). In 1983 he declared that the Who were finished, although they reunited for occasional live performances, including Live Aid, during the Eighties. Since 1996, Townshend has worked with various incarnations of the band (not initially billed as the Who), a practice that continued after the death of Entwistle in 2002. With Daltrey, Townshend made the first new Who album in 24 years, *Endless Wire* (2006). The Who continued to perform critically acclaimed sets in the 21st century, including the Concert For New York City (2001), Isle of Wight Festival (2004), Live 8 (2005), Glastonbury Festival (2007), and the 2010 Super Bowl halftime show.

Townshend's early inspirations were John Lee Hooker, Bo Diddley, Eddie Cochran, Link Wray and Hank Marvin. His use of the guitar as a sonic tool as much as a melodic device was influential to many punk guitarists. A prime example of his powerful strumming is the intro to 'Pinball Wizard'. In the Who's early days he played an Emile Grimshaw SS Deluxe, plus 6- and 12-string Rickenbackers. He began using Fender Stratocasters and Telecasters, as these were less expensive to replace. From the late Sixties, he favoured Gibson guitars for live work, using a Gretsch in the studio. Since the late Eighties he has preferred the Fender Eric Clapton Stratocaster to his own signature model.

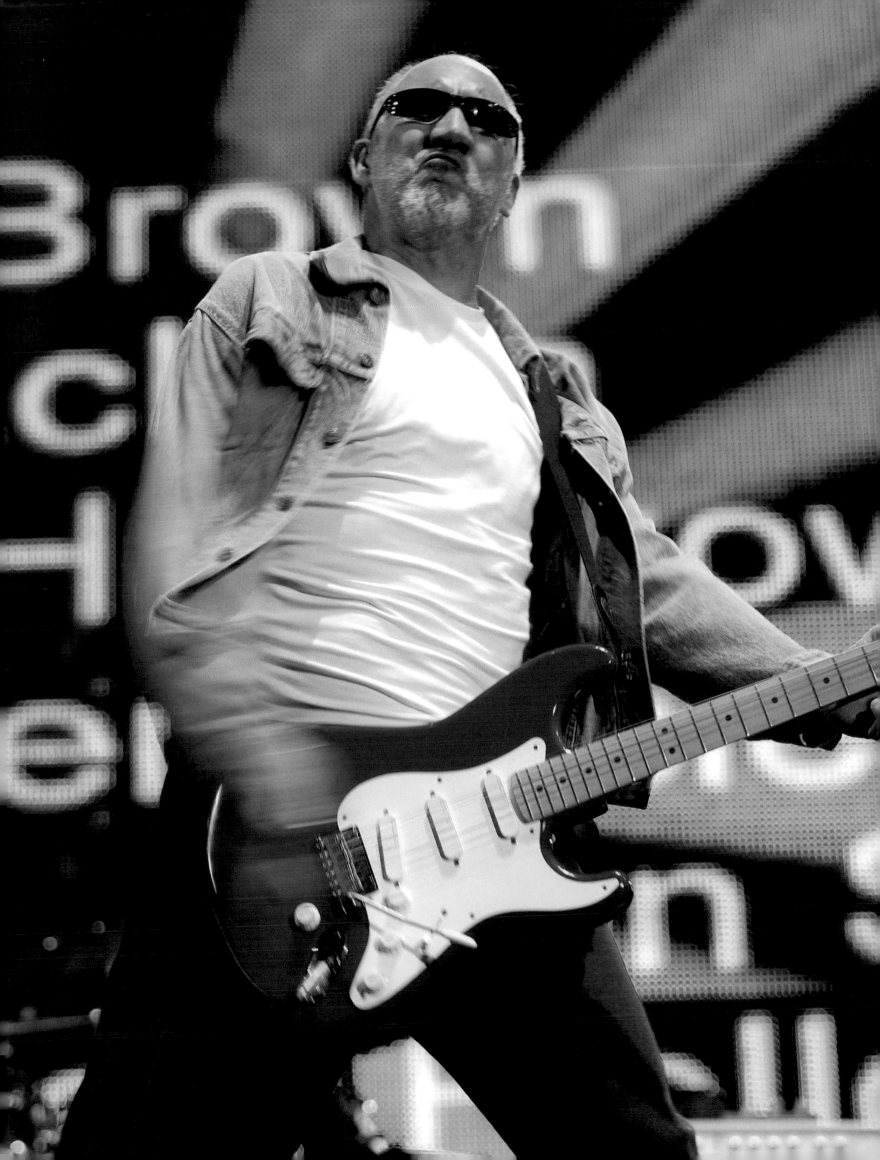

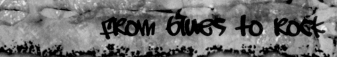

SYD BARRETT

FLOYD'S DESTRUCTIVE GENIUS

Legendary 'lost' psychedelic genius Syd Barrett (1946–2006) was born Roger Keith Barrett in Cambridge. He learned to play guitar at the age of 14 and formed his first band in 1965. While attending art college in London, he joined the embryonic Pink Floyd.

Floyd began by playing blues and rhythm and blues covers, but soon developed the improvisational style that made them the premier band of London's underground scene. In January 1967, their debut single 'Arnold Layne' was a minor hit and was followed by the Top 10 success 'See Emily Play'. Barrett penned both, but neither was truly representative of the band in concert. Similarly, Barrett's short whimsical songs dominate *Piper At The Gates of Dawn* (1967), although 'Astronomy Dominé' and the freeform 'Interstellar Overdrive' were more representative of the band's live sound.

By the time of *Piper*'s release, Barrett's behaviour had become increasingly unpredictable. He was often unable to function onstage and, ultimately, too difficult to work with. His breakdown was caused by a combination of deep unease with the trappings of fame and an excessive intake of LSD. Barrett's old Cambridge friend David Gilmour was drafted at first to cover for him, replacing him altogether early in 1968. Barrett was an innovative guitarist who was influenced by the improvisatory technique of Keith Rowe of underground band AMM.

Although no virtuoso, Barrett achieved unique effects by playing through a Binson echo unit and employing a Zippo lighter or plastic ruler as bottlenecks. This experimental approach heralded new ways of playing rock guitar. His favoured instrument was a Telecaster Esquire decorated with mirrors.

Barrett's solo career was short, consisting of *The Madcap Laughs* and *Barrett* (both 1970), and *Opel* (1988), a collection of outtakes and unreleased material. After some ill-fated live outings as a member of Stars in 1972 and an abortive return to the studio in 1974, Barrett gave up music and retreated to Cambridge, where he spent his time painting and gardening. His reclusiveness fuelled the legend, and successive generations of musicians from David Bowie to the Damned to Kasabian have cited his influence. Barrett died in July 2006 of pancreatic cancer.

ROBBY KRIEGER

OPENING DOORS

Eclectic guitarist Robby Krieger (b. 1946) was born in Los Angeles. Krieger started to play the blues on piano and began to learn guitar at the age of 17 on a flamenco model. 'I switched around from folk, to flamenco to blues to rock'n'roll,' he recalled. The Paul Butterfield Blues Band was an important influence. 'If it hadn't been for Butterfield going electric, I probably wouldn't have gone rock'n'roll.'

For Krieger, rock'n'roll offered almost as much musical freedom as jazz but with greater earning potential. While playing in the Psychedelic Rangers with drummer John Densmore, they hooked up with keyboardist Ray Manzarek and singer Jim Morrison (pictured left) to form the Doors. The band was unusual in having no bassist; in concert Manzarek played keyboard bass with his left hand while session musicians were used in the studio. Their debut album *The Doors* (1967) was an instant sensation. 'Light My Fire' became a massive Summer of Love hit in America and featured Krieger's guitar sparring with Manzarek's swirling organ in the jazzy middle section. His discordant solo on 'When the Music's Over' from *Strange Days* (1967) anticipated Robert Fripp's style, while his vibrato on the introduction to 'Riders on the Storm' from *LA Woman* (1971) evoked gentle rainfall. He generally favoured a Gibson SG, although he has also used a Les Paul Sunburst and a Fender Stratocaster.

After Morrison's death in 1971, the Doors made two more albums with Manzarek and Krieger sharing the vocal duties. They reunited in 1978 for *An American Prayer*, adding music to recently discovered tapes of Morrison reading his poetry. Krieger has also made several jazz-tinged solo albums. The Doors' enduring popularity and influence on successive generations of bands, starting with the Stranglers and Echo & the Bunnymen, inspired Krieger and Manzarek to assemble a new version of the band in 2002 with former Cult singer Ian Astbury but without Densmore, who subsequently took legal action to prevent the use of the Doors name. The move forced the outfit to tour as Riders On The Storm.

PETER GREEN

FLEETWOOD MAC'S FOUNDER

Blues-rock guitarist Peter Green (b. 1946) was born Peter Greenbaum in Bethnal Green, London. He began playing guitar at the age of 10. Among his early influences were Hank Marvin, Muddy Waters and B.B. King. After Green played bass in several semi-pro outfits, keyboardist Peter Bardens invited him to play lead in his band. Three months later, he joined John Mayall's Bluesbreakers, initially filling in for Eric Clapton for three gigs and becoming permanent when the guitarist left altogether. Replacing Clapton, of whom he was a great admirer, was a formidable task, but Green quickly established himself, developing an economical, sweetly melancholic style on his favoured Gibson Les Paul. His album with the Bluesbreakers *Hard Road* (1967) contains two Green compositions, including the instrumental 'The Supernatural'.

Originally billed as 'Peter Green's Fleetwood Mac', his next band utilized Bluesbreakers' rhythm section Mick Fleetwood (drums) and John McVie (bass), with Jeremy Spencer (slide guitar, vocals) and Green on lead and vocals. Debut album *Fleetwood Mac* (1968) was a mix of blues classics and original material. *Mr Wonderful* (1968) was straight-ahead blues, recorded live in the studio. Additional guitarist Danny Kirwan joined shortly before the 1968 No. 1 single 'Albatross', which showcased Green's stately, mournful blues playing.

Green struggled with fame and success, and his personality changed after a three-day LSD trip. He began appearing on stage in long robes, wearing crucifixes, and demanded that the band give all their money away to charity. After the chilling 'Green Manalishi', which seemed to address his mental struggles, he left Fleetwood Mac in May 1970. After an experimental jam session was released as a solo album, *The End Of The Game* (1970), Green disappeared, taking a succession of menial jobs, undergoing electroconvulsive therapy and spending time in mental institutions. He re-emerged as a recording artist in 1979 but suffered a relapse in 1984, living like a tramp for several years until rescued by his family. He made another comeback in the Nineties in the Peter Green Splinter Group, making nine albums up to 2003, but he has since stated that his medication affects his concentration and ability to play.

DUANE ALLMAN

SOUTHERN SLIDE STAR

Southern-rock guitarist Duane Allman (1946–71) was born in Nashville, Tennessee. Allman was inspired to take up guitar by his brother Gregg. At first they played country music, their initiation to the blues coming when the brothers saw B.B. King performing in Nashville. The pair began playing professionally in 1961, first in the Allman Joys and then the Hour Glass, who made two albums before splitting up in early 1968. Around this time Allman began playing electric slide, inspired by Jesse Ed Davis, and using an empty glass medicine bottle as a slide, a technique later adopted by Rory Gallagher and Lynyrd Skynyrd's Gary Rossington.

The Hour Glass recording led to Allman being offered session work on Wilson Pickett's *Hey Jude* (1968) album, which in turn led to him becoming a full-time session musician at Muscle Shoals Studio in Alabama, where he contributed to albums by Aretha Franklin, Percy Sledge

and Boz Scaggs. Frustration at the limitations of session playing led Allman to form the Allman Brothers Band in March 1969 with Gregg (organ, vocals), Dickey Betts (second lead), Berry Oakley (bass) and twin drummers Butch Trucks and Jai Johanny 'Jaimoe' Johanson. The band became one of America's most influential in the early Seventies, pioneering Southern rock and paving the way for Lynyrd Skynyrd and the Marshall Tucker Band. After gigging extensively, they made their recorded debut on the largely overlooked *The Allman Brothers Band* (1969), building momentum with *Idlewild South* (1970). Allman also played with Eric Clapton in Derek & the Dominos, memorably on the classic 'Layla'. He returned to the Allman Brothers Band as they recorded one of the seminal live albums, *At the Fillmore East* (1971), which captured their incendiary double-lead guitar attack at its peak. A few months after its release, Allman was killed in a motorcycle accident. The band elected to carry on without him.

Allman is remembered as one of the greatest guitarists of all time, admired not only for his slide technique but also for the improvisatory skills he displayed on his 1959 Gibson Darkburst Les Paul and 1968 Gibson Cherry SG.

DAVE DAVIES

THE KINKS' RIFFING LEGEND

Trailblazing Kinks lead guitarist Dave Davies (b. 1947) was born in Muswell Hill, London. The Davies were a close-knit, musical family and Dave acquired his first guitar, a Harmony Meteor, at the age of 11. He taught himself to play, citing blues pioneer Big Bill Broonzy as his earliest influence. Other inspirations were James Burton, Chuck Berry, Muddy Waters, Scotty Moore and jazz guitarist Tal Farlow.

The teenage Dave was a rebel, frequently truanting from the secondary school where the Kinks came together with elder brother Ray on rhythm guitar and vocals and Pete Quaife on bass (drummer Mick Avory was recruited later). The Kinks' third single 'You Really Got Me' proved their breakthrough. Davies played its famous two-chord riff on his Harmony

Meteor, creating the distortion effect by slashing his speaker with a razorblade. His work on the song is often credited as establishing the blueprint for heavy metal. A more reflective, melancholic vein soon crept into in the Kinks' work, which developed into a unique Englishness, perhaps a side effect of the Musicians' Union ban that prevented the band from visiting America from 1965 to 1969.

Davies's occasional solo career got underway with the single 'Death of a Clown', co-written with Ray, which subsequently appeared on *Something Else By The Kinks* (1967). Three other singles followed, but it was not until 1980 that he issued his first solo album *Dave Davies* (also known by its catalogue number *AF1-3603*). In the Seventies and Eighties, the Kinks became a major live attraction in America and with Ray playing less onstage, Dave adopted a dual purpose rhythm-lead style, primarily on a Gibson L5-S, using very few effects. Other instruments played in his lengthy career include a Gibson Flying V Futura, a Gibson Les Paul and a Fender Telecaster, plus an Ovation and a Martin for acoustic work.

Although a split was never formally announced, the Kinks last performed together in 1996, after which both brothers began work on solo projects. In 2004, Davies suffered a stroke, which has affected his ability to sing and play, although he has since recorded a solo album *Fractured Mindz* (2007) and in 2010 a DVD, *Mystical Journey*.

RY COODER

SESSION AND SOLO SUPREMO

Versatile American-roots guitarist Ry Cooder (b. 1947) was born in Los Angeles, California. As a child he mastered the fundamentals of guitar, and at the age of 17 played in a blues outfit with singer/songwriter Jackie DeShannon. In 1965, Cooder teamed up with blues legend Taj Mahal and future Spirit drummer Ed Cassidy in the Rising Sons. The project was short-lived, falling apart when the release of their album was vetoed by CBS.

Producer Terry Melcher later employed Cooder as a session player on many records, including some by Paul Revere & the Raiders. This led to his unique slide-guitar work gracing Captain Beefheart & the Magic Band's first album *Safe As Milk* (1967). Cooder turned down the Captain's offer to join the band permanently and continued his session career, working with Randy Newman, Van Dyke Parks and Little Feat. Cooder was a candidate to replace Brian Jones in the Rolling Stones, but clashes with Keith Richards precluded that, although he did contribute to the Stones' album *Let It Bleed* (1969) and played slide on 'Sister Morphine' from *Sticky Fingers* (1971).

His solo debut *Ry Cooder* (1971) featured covers of blues songs by Leadbelly, Blind Willie Johnson and Sleepy John Estes. Subsequent albums showcased his guitar work and explored diverse areas of American roots music. *Into The Purple Valley* (1971) embraced folk, while the ebullient *Paradise And Lunch* (1974) saw him hailed as a major figure. *Chicken Skin Music* (1976) and *Showtime* (1976) blended Tex-Mex and Hawaiian, and Cooder (pictured left with John Lee Hooker) turned his hand to *Dixieland On Jazz* (1978). *Bop Till You Drop* (1979), the first rock album to be recorded digitally, was more mainstream and yielded his biggest American hit, a cover of Elvis Presley's 'Little Sister'. Cooder has composed numerous soundtracks, notably for Wim Wenders' 1984 movie *Paris, Texas*. The title piece's haunting, atmospheric slide guitar, recorded on a Fifties Martin 000-18, was evocative of the American South. Cooder's main acoustic is a Thirties Gibson Roy Smeck model. His other guitars include a Fender Stratocaster (his foremost bottleneck guitar) and a Gibson ES-P. He has also played Japanese Guyatone models and a Ripley Stereo Guitar.

CARLOS SANTANA

SANTANA'S SEARING COLOSSUS

Multi-talented guitarist Carlos Santana (b. 1947) was born the son of a Mariachi musician in the Mexican town of Autlan de Navarro. The family moved to Tijuana when he was nine, and Carlos, who first played violin before changing to guitar, became interested in rock'n'roll and blues. At 13, he was earning money playing in cantinas and strip joints. When his family immigrated to San Francisco, he stayed behind to continue working as a musician but was persuaded to join them and soon became involved in the city's burgeoning music scene.

In 1966, the Santana Blues Band was formed. Despite the name, they operated as a collective, and Carlos was not regarded as the leader, a situation which persisted for several years, even

after the name was shortened to Santana in 1968. Embarking on a two-month tour of colleges and universities in California, the band developed their distinctive sound, incorporating the Afro-Cuban rhythms of Latin America, which complemented Santana's lyrical guitar style.

Carlos (pictured left with John Lee Hooker) quickly made a name for himself; his first appearance on record was as a guest on *The Live Adventures Of Mike Bloomfield And Al Kooper* (1968), which came about as a result of legendary promoter Bill Graham taking the band under his wing. Graham pulled off a remarkable coup in securing Santana a slot at the Woodstock Festival in August, 1969. By then, they had signed to CBS and recorded their debut album *Santana* (1969), a collection of free-form jams with which the band were largely dissatisfied. Woodstock proved a turning point for Santana; their rendition of the 11-minute instrumental 'Soul Sacrifice' was one of the highlights of the movie, making the band internationally famous. Santana were also on the bill at the Rolling Stones' disastrous free gig at Altamont later in the year. Their second album, *Abraxas* (1970), went to No. 1, and its mix of salsa, rock'n'roll, Latin and jazz was more successful for being compressed into structured songs. The album featured Santana's expressive guitar on two well-known pieces, Peter Green's 'Black Magic Woman' and 'Samba Pa Ti'.

The recruitment of teenage prodigy Neal Schon gave the band a harder-edged dual guitar sound for *Santana* (1971), also known as *Santana III* to avoid confusion with the first album. *Caravanserai* (1972) veered into jazz-rock fusion territory, and Santana's commercial fortunes started to decline. Next came *Amigos* (1976). By returning to the Latin feel and adding a dose of funk, Santana arrived at a formula that served him for many years.

Santana made an acclaimed appearance during the American leg of Live Aid in 1985. The year 1988 saw a reunion tour with various former members of the Santana band. During the Nineties, however, his career was at a low point, and he was without a record contract, but he pulled off a remarkable comeback by signing to Arista Records and assembling an all-star cast for *Supernatural* (1999), which won nine Grammy Awards. It was followed by *Shaman* (2003) and *All That I Am* (2005), which mined the same vein, mixing hip hop and pop with Santana's familiar lyrical Latin guitar.

In 2008, Santana worked with Marcelo Vieira on the album *Marcelo Vieira's Acoustic Sounds*. Santana performed at the 2009 American Idol finale show. In 2009, he appeared at the Athens Olympic Stadium in Athens with his 10-member all-star band as part of his 'Supernatural Santana – A Trip through the Hits.' Santana is featured as a playable character in the video game Guitar Hero 5.

Carlos Santana is famous for his searing lead lines and, largely thanks to the Woodstock movie, his gurning facial expressions as he wrings every drop of emotion from his instrument. He tends not to use many effects pedals other than wah-wah and delay. He was associated with Gibson guitars for a long time, endorsing them in advertisements during the Seventies. At Woodstock, he played a red Gibson SG Special, and on *Supernatural* he used a Gibson Les Paul. Carlos now favours Paul Reed Smith guitars, and the company have produced a signature series in his honour, including the Santana SE and Santana III, the necks and fretboards of which are made of Brazilian rosewood to help create his trademark smooth tone. For classical guitar, Santana favours an Alvarez Yairi.

RORY GALLAGHER
KEEPING THE FAITH

Highly respected blues guitarist Rory Gallagher (1948–95) was born in Ballyshannon, Ireland, and grew up in Cork. After learning his trade as a teenager playing in Irish show bands, Gallagher formed the power trio Taste in 1966. The band released two studio and two live albums. Shortly after their appearance at the 1970 Isle of Wight Festival, Taste split acrimoniously. Gallagher, already established as a virtuoso, went solo.

The Seventies were prolific years for Gallagher with 10 albums to his name. *Live In Europe* (1972) captured his high-octane live show, and a second live album *Irish Tour* (1974) sold in excess of two million copies worldwide. His later output was more sporadic, but he remained a hugely popular live attraction and toured constantly.

His formative influences were Lonnie Donegan, Chuck Berry, Muddy Waters, Leadbelly and Woody Guthrie. In turn, he influenced many other guitarists, including Johnny Marr, Slash, Glen Tipton, the Edge and Brian May. Gallagher was closely identified with his sunburst Fender Stratocaster, believed to have been the first in Ireland, which he bought in 1961, impressed with its appearance and swayed by Buddy Holly's use of the same model. He modified the guitar several times and after extensive use it was extremely battered and had virtually lost its sunburst finish. The Strat was invaluable to Gallagher for its bright tone and because he could achieve a wah-wah effect by manipulating its tone control rather than using

a pedal. Soloing on the Stratocaster, Gallagher creates an exquisite flurry of notes on 'Daughter of the Everglades' from *Blueprint* (1973). His other guitars included a Fender Esquire and Telecaster, Danelectro Silvertone, Gretsch Corvette and National Resophonic. A Martin D-35 was his favoured acoustic. Gallagher's bottleneck technique was widely admired by his peers and was showcased on the title track of *Calling Card* (1976).

Having been in poor health for several years, Gallagher died in June of 1995 of complications following a liver transplant. He is remembered as a talented singer and songwriter as well as an uncompromising musician who, although he dabbled in country, hard rock and folk, remained a bluesman at heart.

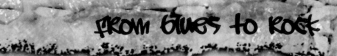

MICK TAYLOR

BLUESBREAKING STONE

Blues-rock guitarist Mick Taylor (b. 1949) was born in Hatfield, Hertfordshire. A guitarist from the age of nine, he was in his teens when he formed a group with some school friends that subsequently evolved into the Gods. Taylor made two singles with the band. When Eric Clapton failed to turn up for a Bluesbreakers' gig in Welwyn Garden City, the 16-year-old Taylor stood in for Clapton for the second half of the set. When Peter Green left the Bluesbreakers in 1967, Mayall signed Taylor as his replacement.

He became known for a style that is based on the blues with overtones of Latin and jazz. His reputation as a slide guitarist was second to none. These attributes made him ideally

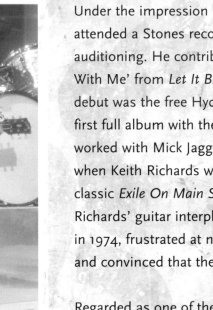

qualified to replace Brian Jones in the Rolling Stones. Under the impression he was doing session work, Taylor attended a Stones recording, soon realizing that he was auditioning. He contributed to 'Country Honk' and 'Live With Me' from *Let It Bleed* (1969) and was hired. His live debut was the free Hyde Park concert in 1969. On Taylor's first full album with the Stones, *Sticky Fingers* (1971), he worked with Mick Jagger on 'Moonlight Mile' and 'Sway' when Keith Richards was absent from the studio. The classic *Exile On Main Street* (1972) featured Taylor and Richards' guitar interplay at its peak. He left the Stones in 1974, frustrated at not receiving songwriting credits and convinced that the band was about to collapse.

Regarded as one of the finest guitarists in the world, Taylor was expected to pursue a high-profile solo career but instead joined Jack Bruce's band. His first solo work was the largely overlooked blues and jazz-tinged album *Mick Taylor* (1978). He spent much of the Eighties battling heroin addiction, a legacy from his time in the Stones, and he guested for Bob Dylan and Mark Knopfler. Taylor is usually associated with the Gibson Les Paul. He used a Gibson ES-355 for the recording of *Sticky Fingers* and *Exile On Main Street*, a Gibson SG on tour, and, on occasion, a Fender Stratocaster and Telecaster.

BONNIE RAITT

COUNTRY BLUES CLASS

Blue-eyed soul and country guitarist and singer-songwriter Bonnie Raitt (b. 1949) was born in Burbank, California, the daughter of Broadway vocalist John Raitt and pianist-singer Marge Goddard. At the age of eight, she was given a Stella guitar as a Christmas present, which her parents insisted she play at family gatherings. Bonnie became a devotee of blues and folk music at 14 upon hearing an album recorded at the Newport Blues Festival.

She began studying at Harvard in 1967 and started to play clubs and coffeehouses in the Boston area supporting blues legends like Muddy Waters, Son House and John Lee Hooker. Leaving college for a full-time career in music, she was opening for Mississippi Fred McDowell in New York in 1970 when word began to spread of her talents, which led to a recording contract with Warner. Her debut album, *Bonnie Raitt* (1971), mixed covers of blues standards with Bonnie's own material. Subsequent albums matched its critical acclaim but sold in modest quantities until she achieved a breakthrough with 'Runaway' from *Sweet Forgiveness* (1977). Her momentum stalled, however, and she was dropped by Warner in 1983.

Without a record contract for much of the Eighties, Bonnie was struggling with alcohol and drugs but kept touring and remained politically active, singing on the anti-apartheid song 'Sun City' and appearing at Amnesty International benefits. After signing to Capitol in 1989, Bonnie finally achieved commercial success with three chart-topping albums: *Nick Of Time* (1989), *Luck Of The Draw* (1991), and *Longing In Their Hearts* (1994), which earned her an armful of Grammy awards. Raitt was inducted into the Rock And Roll Hall of Fame in 2000. Since then she has mixed recording and performing with political activism. *Silver Lining* was released in 2002; *Souls Alike* in 2005.

Since 1969, Bonnie has used her Fender Stratocaster at every gig, backed up by her signature-model Stratocasters, to avoid constant retuning. She also has a Gibson ES-175 and a Guild F-50. Bonnie prefers to adapt her playing style to suit each song.

BILLY GIBBONS

ZZ TOP'S TALENT

Billy F. Gibbons (b. 1949), also known as the Reverend Willie G, led his Texas boogie band, ZZ Top, to international superstardom in the early days of MTV, combining a unique image with driving Southern rock and a series of eye-catching videos. At the music's core was Gibbons' tasteful blend of rhythmic crunch and fiery soloing, created on his 1959 Gibson Les Paul, named Miss Pearly Gates.

Gibbons grew up in Houston, Texas. In the 1960s he formed the psychedelic group the Moving Sidewalks, which recorded *Flash* (1968), and opened for the Jimi Hendrix Experience during the Texas leg of Hendrix's first American tour. He formed ZZ Top in 1969 with bassist-vocalist Dusty Hill (pictured below) and drummer Frank Beard. They released *ZZ Top's First Album* on London Records in 1971. The follow-ups *Rio Grande Mud* (1972) and *Tres Hombres* (1973) with its driving paean to a Texas bordello 'La Grange', combined with extensive touring, cemented the band's reputation as a hard-rocking power trio.

It was in the 1980s, however, that ZZ Top really exploded. The band changed record labels, and Gibbons and Hill, during a hiatus from recording, each grew chest-length beards, unbeknownst to each other. The band also updated its sound, incorporating synthesizers into their music. The results were their three biggest albums, *Eliminator* (1983), *Afterburner* (1985), and *Recycler* (1990). A series of videos for the hit singles 'Legs', 'Gimme All Your Lovin'', and 'Sharp Dressed Man', among others, became staples of the young music video channel MTV.

Although ZZ Top lost some of their early fans with its more radio-friendly sound and missteps like the effects-laden remixed box set *Six Pack* (1987), the band's unique blend of boogie and funny, sometimes raunchy, lyrics, anchored by Gibbons' blues-based virtuosity, continued to draw fans. In 2004, ZZ Top was inducted into the Rock And Roll Hall Of Fame.

In recent years Gibbons has made appearances with other bands and acted on television shows. ZZ Top played at the 2007 Orange Bowl game in Miami. The *Eliminator Collector's Edition* CD/DVD celebrating the 25th anniversary of the album was released in 2008. Gibbons continues to perform and guest on the albums of various artists.

PAUL KOSSOFF

FREE FOR ALL

Blues and hard-rock guitarist Paul Kossoff (1950–76), son of British actor David Kossoff, was born in Hampstead, London. He studied classical guitar as a child but had given it up by his early teens. Inspired by John Mayall's Bluesbreakers, featuring Eric Clapton, he resumed playing and teamed up with drummer Simon Kirke in the rhythm and blues band Black Cat Bones in 1966.

The band often supported Fleetwood Mac, and a friendship arose between Peter Green and Kossoff, based on their shared enthusiasm for the blues. Kossoff saw singer Paul Rodgers singing in Brown Sugar, which led to the formation of Free at the height of the British blues boom in 1968. Bassist Andy Fraser, another former Bluesbreaker, was recruited at the suggestion of pioneering blues musician Alexis Korner, who also came up with the band's name. All four members of Free were in their teens at the time.

Korner helped broker a deal with Island Records, and Free's debut *Tons Of Sobs* (1969) was recorded on a minimal budget. The album showcased the band's blues rock at its most raw, driven by Kossoff's guitar. 'Goin' Down Slow', one of only two non-originals on the album, featured his long, complex solo. *Free* (1969) was more polished, with Fraser's rhythmic bass coming to the fore and providing a springboard for Kossoff's lead. Before *Fire And Water*

(1970), Kossoff was disillusioned by the band's lack of commercial success until the classic single 'All Right Now' rectified that. Kossoff's aggressive riff, played on his trademark Gibson Les Paul, remains his best-known work. Free temporarily split after the failure of *Highway* (1971) but reconvened for *Free At Last* (1972). But Kossoff's drug problems spiralled out of control, and he had minimal input to the final Free album *Heartbreaker* (1973).

The guitarist was able to complete a solo album *Back Street Crawler* (1973) and subsequently assembled a band of the same name, which made two albums with him. Still struggling with drug addiction, he almost died in rehab in 1975, and on a flight from Los Angeles to New York in March 1976 Kossoff suffered a fatal, drug-induced heart attack.

SONNY LANDRETH

LOUISIANA LEGEND

A blues guitarist best known for his slide-guitar work, Sonny Landreth (b. 1951) was born in Canton, Mississippi. The family relocated to Lafayette, Louisiana, where Sonny was immersed in the area's swamp-pop and Zydeco music. Beginning as a trumpeter, he was already a virtuoso guitarist in his teens. His earliest role model was Scotty Moore, and he was later influenced by the Ventures and Chet Atkins.

Landreth's first professional appearance was with Zydeco accordionist Clifton Chenier, in whose Red Hot Louisiana Band Landreth was the only white. He recorded two albums for the Louisiana independent Blues Unlimited label, *Blues Attack* (1981) and *Way Down* (1985), the second of which came to the attention of record companies in Nashville. This in turn led to Landreth recording and touring with John Hiatt. His reputation led to his being offered more session work, notably with John Mayall, who recorded Landreth's song 'Congo Square'.

Ultimately, he also worked with guitar legend Leslie West, Kenny Loggins, Dolly Parton, Junior Wells, Beausoleil, Bonnie Raitt, Allen Toussaint, Mark Knopfler and soul singer Jimmy Buffett. He resumed his solo recording career with *Outward Bound* (1992). His music is rooted in Louisiana, and evokes the sounds, smells and sights of the state. As he says: 'Playing this music is as natural for me as going to the crawfish festival. It's something I think I was born to do.' Landreth's latest album, *From the Reach*, was released in 2008.

Landreth is held in high esteem by his peers. His unique style of playing slide guitar has left many guitarists puzzling over how he achieves the powerful and sweet sound from his trademark National guitar. Landreth's strings are positioned high off the frets, allowing him to play notes, chords and chord fragments behind the slide, which is placed on his little finger. His right-hand technique is highly distinctive, involving slapping, tapping and picking the strings with his fingers. He also employs numerous different tunings, so many that he has developed an automatic tuner that is mounted on the guitar.

GARY MOORE

SKID ROW TO SOLO

Blues and hard-rock guitarist Gary Moore (b. 1952) was born in Belfast, Northern Ireland. He began playing the acoustic guitar at the age of eight, acquiring his first electric model at 14. Moore learned to play right-handed, despite being naturally left-handed. In 1969 he joined Skid Row, an Irish blues-rock group that featured Phil Lynott on vocals. When the latter was sacked, Moore took over as singer of the slimmed-down power trio.

Skid Row supported Fleetwood Mac, then featuring Peter Green, who was a massive influence on the young guitarist. With Green's help, the band signed a contract with CBS, releasing two albums that were very influential on Irish rock before Moore left in 1971. His debut album *Grinding Stone* (1973) was credited to the Gary Moore Band, but his initial solo career was short-lived, as he was reunited with Phil Lynott, replacing Eric Bell as Thin Lizzy's lead guitarist for a short spell. Moore returned to the band briefly in both 1976 and 1978. In between, he was a member of Colosseum II, the second version of the British jazz-fusion band that featured a heavier sound than its original incarnation largely because of Moore's guitar work.

With a little help from Lynott on vocals, Moore's solo career resumed in 1979, when his distinctive bluesy, wailing guitar graced the singles chart on 'Parisienne Walkways'. The pair

charted again with the heavier 'Out In The Fields' in 1985. The Eighties saw him concentrating on rock, but he returned to his first love on *Still Got The Blues* (1990). After some puzzling experiments with dance beats, he went back to basics once more on *Back To The Blues* (2001). More recently. he has released *Close As You Get* (2007) and *Bad For You Baby* (2008).

Of the many guitars that he has used in his lengthy career, Moore is probably most attached to the Gibson Les Paul that he bought from his mentor Peter Green when the latter quit the music business. His fondness for Gibson guitars was recognized by the company when he became one of the first artists to have a signature model. Moore has also played the Fender Stratocaster and guitars by Charvel, Paul Reed Smith and Ibanez.

NEAL SCHON

JOURNEY'S SOUL

Rock and jazz guitarist Neal Schon (b. 1951) was born in Oklahoma, son of a jazz saxophonist and composer. A precocious talent, he learned guitar at the age of 10 and joined Santana at 15, turning down an invitation to join Eric Clapton in Derek & the Dominos. Schon made two albums with the band, *Santana III* (1971), on which he was credited as co-producer, and *Caravanserai* (1972), a departure into jazz fusion. In 1972, he played with Azteca, a Latin jazz-rock fusion ensemble that on stage consisted of up to 25 members.

In 1973, Schon formed Journey with former Santana band member Greg Rolie on keyboards and vocals. The band was originally intended to serve as a back-up outfit for musicians in the San Francisco area, but this notion was quickly abandoned and Journey made their first live appearance at the city's Winterland Ballroom. Signed to Columbia Records, the debut album *Journey* (1975), the follow-up *Look Into The Future* (1976) and *Next* (1977) were all firmly in the jazz-rock mould, featuring long tracks and lengthy instrumental workouts. The albums sold poorly, prompting a change in direction on *Infinity* (1978) to a pomp-rock sound similar to Boston and Foreigner.

This marked the start of a run of success for Journey that would bring them to a whole new audience, peaking with their best-selling work *Escape* (1981). Schon also recorded two albums with keyboardist Jan Hammer in 1981 and 1982 and has issued sporadic solo recordings since. After Journey split, he joined forces with former Baby's singer John Waite in Bad English in 1988. Journey reunited in 1995 and released *Trial By Fire* in 1996. Schon announced a new Journey album for 2010.

Schon was inspired by bluesman B.B. King and jazz-fusionist Al Di Meola. His first guitar was an acoustic Stella, followed by a Gibson ES-355, and a Les Paul Goldtop. He currently uses Gibson guitars, and the company produced a limited-edition signature-model Les Paul. In the Eighties, he inaugurated his own brand, the Schon, manufactured by Jackson Guitars and later Larrivee. Schon suffers from tinnitus after many years of playing live.

hard rock and metal

Jazz has its saxophonists. Blues has its harmonica players. Pop has its synthesizers and dancers. But take the guitar hero out of hard rock and heavy metal, and you've gutted the genre. Nowhere has the guitar had a greater impact than on the sound and style of heavy music, and no other genre of music has produced as many guitar heroes. From Tony Iommi's dark, spine-chilling tritones heralding the birth of heavy metal in 1970 to John 5's twisted, high-tech fretboard fury inspiring this century's guitar hero-in-waiting, the power of guitar has rarely seen such champions as the 25 iconic players chronicled here.

RITCHIE BLACKMORE

RULER OF THE RIFF

His contemporaries Eric Clapton, Jimmy Page and Jeff Beck might receive more time in the spotlight, but guitarist Ritchie Blackmore (b. 1945) has been similarly influential and innovative during his 40-plus-year career.

Born in Weston-Super-Mare, England, in April 1945, Blackmore was given his first guitar at the age of 11 and began taking classical lessons, an education that would later reveal itself in both his neoclassical rock leanings and his Renaissance work in Blackmore's Night. His early influences include rockers Hank Marvin and Cliff Gallup as well as country legend Chet Atkins. By the mid-Sixties, Blackmore began working as a session guitarist with legendary producer Joe Meek, appearing on tracks such as Heinz's Top 10 hit 'Just Like Eddie' (1963).

In 1968, Blackmore joined forces with keyboardist Jon Lord and formed Deep Purple. Later that same year, the band released its first album, *Shades Of Deep Purple*. The disc included a cover of Joe South's 'Hush', which reached No. 4 on the charts and put Blackmore's group on the map. After a few more albums and a line-up change, Deep Purple released *Machine Head* (1972), which would become not only the band's high-water mark but also one of the most influential hard-rock and heavy metal albums of all time. The album was to be recorded at a casino in Montreux, Switzerland, but the night before recording, during a Frank Zappa & the Mothers Of Invention show, an audience member fired a flare gun inside the casino, igniting a fire that would burn the place to the ground. This turn of events proved to be a fortuitous one for Deep Purple, as it became the inspiration for their signature hit, 'Smoke On The Water' (1973), which contains arguably the greatest – and most widely recognized – guitar riff ever written. In fact, so powerful were the inverted power chords Blackmore used to create that riff that he revisited them to create the riffs to the later Deep Purple hits 'Woman From Tokyo' (1973) and 'Knockin' At Your Back Door' (1984), as well as Rainbow's 'Man On The Silver Mountain' (1975).

'Smoke On The Water' may have the riff that made Blackmore's guitar work immortal, but his solo in 'Highway Star', another standout track on *Machine Head*, is even more significant to his legacy. With his fiery double-picked lines, Blackmore ushered in the neo-classical shred style of guitar playing. It's no secret that future shred-god Yngwie Malmsteen borrowed nearly as much from Blackmore as he did from Bach – from the scalloped fretboard of his Fender Stratocaster paired with several Marshall stacks to his employment of exotic scales in a hard-rock format.

Following *Machine Head*, Deep Purple's reign began to dissolve. Further line-up changes would bring undesirable alterations to Blackmore's hard-rock blueprint. Unhappy with the direction of the band's emerging sound, the guitarist hooked up with Elf singer Ronnie James Dio and formed Rainbow in 1975. Their first album together, *Ritchie Blackmore's Rainbow* (1975), produced the iconic rock hit 'Man On The Silver Mountain', the signature guitar riff of which could be second cousin to that of 'Smoke On The Water'. In later years, Blackmore

would shift Rainbow's focus to a more commercial tack, resulting in yet more line-up changes (including vocal turns from Graham Bonnet and Joe Lynn Turner), but nonetheless producing such AOR hits as 'Since You've Been Gone', 'Stone Cold' and 'Street Of Dreams'.

In 1984, Blackmore rejoined Deep Purple, and released *Perfect Strangers*, the band's best and most successful album since the same line-up released *Machine Head* 12 years earlier. The record produced major rock radio hits in both its title track and the rock anthem 'Knockin' At Your Back Door'. For Blackmore, the timing couldn't have been better, for just as metal guitarists like Eddie Van Halen, Yngwie Malmsteen and George Lynch were taking technical guitar chops to a whole new level, *Perfect Strangers* served as a not-so-subtle reminder that the old-school Deep Purple guitarist still had plenty of fuel left in his tank.

In 1997 Blackmore flipped off the switch on his Marshalls and formed Blackmore's Night, a primarily acoustic stew of Renaissance, folk, world and new-age music featuring lyricist and vocalist Candice Night. Over the past decade, the band of minstrels has released five studio albums and several live recordings, including the 2007 CD/DVD *Paris Moon*.

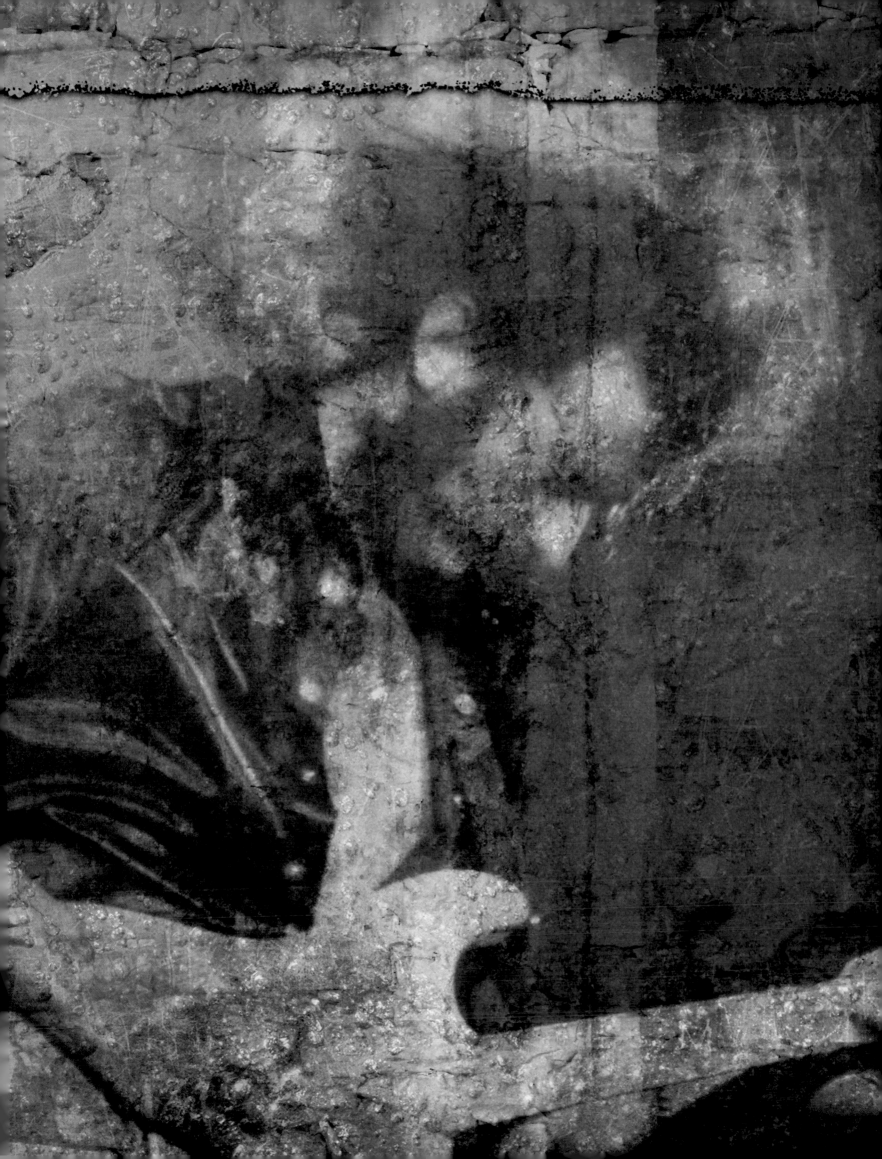

LESLIE WEST

MOUNTAIN MAESTRO

A pioneering hard-rock guitarist with a tone as big as his waistline, Leslie West (b. 1945) is one of the most underrated guitar heroes in rock history. Best known as the leader of the hard-rock trio Mountain, which was named by VH1 as one of the Top 100 Hard Rock Bands of All Time, West's monster guitar sound was made immortal on the group's timeless hit 'Mississippi Queen'.

Born in New York City, West first made a name for himself in the mid-Sixties with the Vagrants, an East-Coast powerhouse band that had a minor hit with a cover of Otis Redding's 'Respect', in 1967. After leaving the Vagrants, West teamed up with bassist Felix Pappalardi, who also produced the Vagrants and Cream. Soon after, they recruited drummer Corky Laing to complete the band they decided to call Mountain, a name reportedly derived from West's rather rotund figure, and released their self-titled debut album in 1969. The group debuted at the Fillmore later that year and went on to play at the Woodstock festival. Although Mountain's existence was relatively brief, the band racked up three gold albums and a handful of hit singles, including 'Never In My Life', 'Theme From An Imaginary Western' and, of course, 'Mississippi Queen'.

It's rare that a single song can launch an enduring legacy, but that's exactly what the giant riff and fat intro solo to 'Mississippi Queen' did for West. He possessed a rare gift of a signature guitar sound that would influence a new generation of rock guitar icons, including Michael Schenker, Richie Sambora, and even tone-god Eddie Van Halen. Key to his monster tone, aside from his special touch, was the Gibson Les Paul Jr, which he paired to Sunn amplifiers. Though West these days favours his Dean Soltero signature-model guitar along with Marshall amplifiers to churn out fat blues lines for Blues Bureau International (*Got Blooze*, 2005; *Blue Me*, 2006), his greatest legacy is that magical guitar tone of 1970 that set the standard for hard rock and heavy metal to come.

GLENN TIPTON

JUDAS PRIEST TO ROCK GOD

Clad head-to-toe in studded black leather and featuring a thundering rhythm section, a dynamic twin-guitar assault and one of the purest rock vocalists in music history, it simply doesn't get any more 'metal' than Judas Priest. And the man behind many of the band's greatest riffs and solos is guitarist Glenn Tipton (b. 1947).

Born in Blackheath, England, Tipton was a latecomer to the guitar, first picking it up at the age of 21. By the early Seventies, he was making a name for himself on the Birmingham club circuit in the Flying Hat Band, an early metal outfit in the vein of Black Sabbath. In 1974 guitarist K.K. Downing asked Tipton to join his own burgeoning metal band, Judas Priest. The partnership, with Tipton's classically influenced style contrasting with Downing's more straight-ahead, heavy blues-rock approach, proved a winning formula. Priest became one of the most influential heavy metal acts of the Seventies, and the two guitarists spearheaded the twin-guitar harmony approach that ruled the new wave of British heavy metal.

In those formative years Tipton maintained a primarily blues-influenced approach to his metal noodlings, occasionally adding neo-classical phrasing. An early example of his affinity for more complex harmony is heard in his solo in 'Beyond The Realms Of Death', from *Stained Class* (1978). Sonically, Tipton favoured a Fender Stratocaster, later switching to a modified Strat, swapping its standard single-coil pickup for a fatter-sounding humbucking pickup. As Priest's sound began to modernize, with the mainstream success of *British Steel* (1980), *Point Of Entry* (1981) and *Screaming For Vengeance* (1982), so did Tipton's sound and approach. During the Screaming For Vengeance tour, he switched to the metal-approved Gibson SG, before getting an endorsement deal with Hamer Guitars, which crafted Tipton's signature-model Phantom GT, a guitar he still uses today.

After a lull through the Nineties, which saw singer Rob Halford replaced by Tim 'Ripper' Owens, Judas Priest reunited with Halford and revived their career. In 2009, they released *A Touch of Evil: Live*, featuring previously unreleased live tracks. 'Dissident Aggressor' won the 2010 Grammy Award for Best Metal Performance.

TONY IOMMI

BLACK SABBATH'S IRON MAN

Frank Anthony Iommi (b. 1948) was born in Birmingham, England. Like so many other teenage boys in Sixties Britain, he was inspired to pick up the guitar upon hearing Hank Marvin & the Shadows. In 1967, after playing in various local acts, Iommi hooked up with three former school mates – Bill Ward (drums), Terry 'Geezer' Butler (bass) and John 'Ozzy' Osbourne (vocals, pictured below) – to form the blues-rock outfit Earth. But just as Iommi was set to begin a full-time music career, he suffered a horrific accident on the last day of his job at a sheet-metal factory, where a machine sliced the tips off his right hand's index and ring fingers. Crafting artificial fingertips from melted plastic bottle-caps covered with leather, the disciplined young guitarist persevered.

Earth later changed their name to Black Sabbath, and with it a new, darker and heavier musical direction emerged. When the band entered the studio in 1970 to record their self-titled debut, Iommi, like his idol Marvin, was a dedicated Fender Stratocaster player. While recording the first track, one of his pickups blew, so he picked up a Gibson SG he had as a backup, and the iconic sight and sound of Iommi paired to an SG was born. When Sabbath released their landmark *Paranoid* in 1971, it was clear that heavy metal was here to stay, and the band's next three albums, *Master Of Reality* (1971), *Vol. 4* (1972) and *Sabbath Bloody Sabbath* (1973), cemented their position as the most influential heavy metal band of all time. With such leaden yet glorious riffs as 'Black Sabbath', 'Paranoid', 'War Pigs', 'N.I.B'. and 'Iron Man' Iommi secured his place as the father of heavy metal guitar.

Although Osbourne left the band to pursue a solo career in 1979, Iommi kept the Sabbath locomotor chugging with a rotating stable of singers. In late 1998, the original Black Sabbath line-up released *Reunion*, a live album that earned the band a second chance at the spotlight. They headlined summer festivals several times in the Noughties, inspiring a new generation of metal fans and musicians to carry the heavy metal torch.

In 2007 Iommi teamed with Geezer Butler, Ronnie James Dio and Vinny Appice to form Heaven and Hell. They toured the US and UK in 2007 and released their first studio album, *The Devil You Know*, in 2009.

TED NUGENT

MOTOR CITY MADMAN

Theodore 'Ted' Nugent (b. 1948), the Motor City Madman, first gained fame as the lead guitarist of the Amboy Dukes. With the Dukes and later as a solo artist, Nugent's intense playing formed the backbone of songs like 'Journey To The Center Of The Mind', 'Stranglehold', 'Free For All', 'Cat Scratch Fever', 'Motor City Madhouse', 'Paralyzed', and 'Wango Tango'.

Born in Detroit, MI, Nugent picked up the guitar in his teens, inspired by British blues-rockers like the Rolling Stones and the Yardbirds. Nugent, a lifelong conservative with a taste for hunting and distaste for drugs and drinking, didn't fit the image championed by the Dukes' psychedelic material. The band issued three albums before Nugent, as the sole original member, rechristened the band Ted Nugent & the Amboy Dukes, and began conducting guitar duels on stage.

By the mid-1970s Nugent was a solo artist with a backing band and stage show that wowed the metal crowd. With *Cat Scratch Fever* (1975) Nugent rose to the top of the charts and became one of the biggest concert draws in rock. His live set, 1978's *Double Live Gonzo!*, cemented his success, but over the course of *Weekend Warriors* (1978), *State Of Shock* (1979) and *Scream Dream* (1980), desertions by band members and bad business decisions drove Nugent into bankruptcy.

Nugent released a series of albums that failed to catch fire in the Eighties. He tried his hand at acting and became known as much for his right-wing views as for his music. At the end of the decade he joined rock supergroup Damn Yankees, which scored a hit with 'High Enough' from their self-titled 1990 album. The band dissolved after one more release and Nugent became a solo act again, turning out the well-received *Spirit Of The Wild* (1995). The 1990s also saw re-releases of his best work: 1993's three-disc box set *Out Of Control*, *Live At Hammersmith '79* (1999), and his first three albums, remastered, in 1999. He has continued to tour, and his third live collection, *Full Bluntal Nugity*, was released in 2001.

A well known conservative and survivalist, Nugent played the US national anthem using alternate picking and whammy bar at the Alamo in Texas for a Tax Day Tea Party in 2009.

JOE PERRY

GUITAR WIELDING TOXIC TWIN

One half of the infamous 'Toxic Twins', along with vocalist Steven Tyler, Aerosmith's Joe Perry (b. 1950) projects a swagger and ultra-cool stage presence that few guitarists can match. Fewer still possess his capacity for muscular, gritty soloing and hook-laden riffing. For over 30 years now, Perry and his stinging guitar tone, generated most often via his signature Gibson Les Paul through Marshall amps, have inspired countless aspiring guitarists to cut out the fluff and rock with soul.

Anthony Joseph 'Joe' Perry was born in Lawrence, Massachusetts, in September 1950, and by the age of six was turned onto the rock'n'roll sounds of Little Richard and Bill Haley & his Comets. Later, inspired by the music of the Beatles and Rolling Stones, the teenaged Perry picked up the guitar and soon discovered the playing of such British blues-rock guitar greats as Jeff Beck, Jimmy Page and Peter Green. In 1969, while playing in the Jam Band (with Aerosmith bassist Tom Hamilton), Perry met singer Steven Tyler (pictured below), and the two decided to join forces, calling themselves Aerosmith.

Combining the gritty rock of the Stones with the heavy riffing of Led Zeppelin and the boogie of American blues, Aerosmith would become the top American hard-rock band of the Seventies. Their albums *Toys In The Attic* (1975) and *Rocks* (1976) are generally recognized as two of the most important hard-rock albums of the seventies, producing such timeless hits as 'Walk This Way', 'Sweet Emotion' and 'Back In The Saddle'. Tragically, the Toxic Twins' heavy drug and alcohol abuse would lead to the demise of Aerosmith in 1979.

In 1980, working as the Joe Perry Project, the guitarist released *Let The Music Do The Talking*, a vastly underrated album of incendiary guitar work. After two more Project albums, Perry rejoined the original Aerosmith line-up in 1984 for a reunion tour. A surprising collaboration with rap group Run-DMC on the classic hit 'Walk This Way' put the Toxic Twins back on the mainstream map. They sobered up and went on to huge success with *Permanent Vacation* (1987), *Pump* (1989) and *Get A Grip* (1993). Perry continued to work on solo projects as well, even receiving a Grammy nomination for the song 'Mercy', from his 2005 release *Joe Perry*. In late 2009 Perry released a new Joe Perry Project album *Have Guitar, Will Travel*.

MALCOLM YOUNG

POWER BEHIND THE THRONE

Hailed as one of hard rock's greatest rhythm guitarists, Malcolm Young (b. 1953) was born in Glasgow, Scotland. When he was 10, the family immigrated to Sydney, Australia where Malcolm and younger brother Angus were taught to play guitar by elder sibling George, a member of the Easybeats. Malcolm founded AC/DC with Angus in 1973. The recruitment of vocalist Bon Scott the following year provided the catalyst for the band's unstoppable rise from their early Australian-only albums to international stardom with *Highway To Hell* (1979). AC/DC survived Scott's death from acute alcohol poisoning in 1980, bouncing back to even greater success (and excess) with new frontman Brian Johnson.

Although less visible than the band's charismatic singers and ostentatious lead guitarist Angus, Malcolm Young is the power behind the throne of AC/DC, he is chief decision-maker and co-songwriter. Providing the foundation for his younger brother's guitar heroics, Malcolm nails down the rhythm on his 1963 Gretsch Jet Firebird, although for the tours in support of *Back In Black* (1980) and *For Those About To Rock (We Salute You)* (1981), he played a Gretsch White Falcon. His long association with Gretsch guitars was recognized by the introduction of the Malcolm Young signature model, based on the Firebird.

His style is simple, direct and brutal; he plugs straight into the amps and shuns the use of effects. AC/DC standards like 'Highway To Hell' and 'Problem Child' are built on his insistent three-chord riffs, creating a powered-up version of Chuck Berry's rock'n'roll blueprint. AC/DC's guitar sound influenced the New Wave of British Heavy Metal which arose in the late Seventies; bands like Saxon and Iron Maiden have acknowledged their debt to the expatriate Scots, whilst Malcolm Young's riffs have inspired speed metal, thrash and grunge.

The rock'n'roll lifestyle caught up with Malcolm when he was forced to miss the band's 1988 tour because of problems with alcohol. Lookalike cousin Stevie Young substituted until Malcolm resumed his rightful place as the unassuming general in AC/DC's engine room.

ALEX LIFESON

RUSH TO ROCK LEGEND

For over 30 years, guitarist Alex Lifeson (b. 1953) has quietly served as the cohesive key to success for progressive rockers Rush – arguably the most enduring and successful hard-rock band of all time. A guitarist always more interested in finding the right chord voicing or textural effect to make a chorus work than in shredding the frets off his axe du jour, it's no wonder every one of his power trio's 18 studio albums have achieved gold sales.

Born Alex Zivojinovich in Fernie, Canada, in August 1953, Lifeson grew up in Toronto and received his first guitar at the age of 13. He drew inspiration from the usual crowd of guitar heroes, like Jimi Hendrix and Eric Clapton, and in the autumn of 1968 he formed his first substantive band, teaming with drummer John Rutsey and bassist Geddy Lee and calling themselves Rush. After several years on the Toronto covers circuit, the trio signed a deal with Mercury Records and released their self-titled debut in 1974. Soon after, Rutsey left the group, opening the door for virtuoso drummer and gifted lyricist Neil Peart. After two more albums in 1975, *Fly By Night* and *Caress Of Steel*, the trio broke through in 1976 with *2112*, an album of epic, complex tunes that carried the band to the top of the progressive-rock mountain.

The band's next three albums – *A Farewell To Kings* (1977), *Hemispheres* (1978), and *Permanent Waves* (1980) – burnished the trio's reputation as superior instrumentalists, while songs like

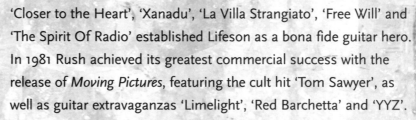

'Closer to the Heart', 'Xanadu', 'La Villa Strangiato', 'Free Will' and 'The Spirit Of Radio' established Lifeson as a bona fide guitar hero. In 1981 Rush achieved its greatest commercial success with the release of *Moving Pictures*, featuring the cult hit 'Tom Sawyer', as well as guitar extravaganzas 'Limelight', 'Red Barchetta' and 'YYZ'.

During the Eighties Rush experimented heavily with synthesizers, crafting a more futuristic sound to go with Peart's often sci-fi and Cold-War lyrical themes. But by 1993's *Counterparts* the band had largely gone back to guitar- and riff-driven songwriting; their 2007 release, *Snakes And Arrows*, contained no keyboards whatsoever. In an interview with *Guitar One* magazine in 2007, when asked if keyboards would ever again be used in Rush, Lifeson replied, 'Yes – over my dead body'. Spoken like a true guitar hero.

GEORGE LYNCH

TOP OF THE MOB

With his wide range of standard and unorthodox techniques, George Lynch (b. 1954) became a guitarist's guitarist as he cruised through the various incarnations of his bands Dokken and Lynch Mob. Born in Spokane, Washington, and raised in California, Lynch became lead guitarist of Dokken in 1980 after auditioning for Ozzy Osbourne in 1979 and losing out to Randy Rhoads.

Dokken had a string of platinum albums such as *Under Lock and Key* and *Back For The Attack*, which feature Lynch's inventive lead guitar work. The instrumental track 'Mr Scary' on the latter album contributed to his popularity among guitar players. The band earned a Grammy nomination for Best Rock Instrumental in 1989. Dokken disbanded in 1989 and Lynch formed Lynch Mob, a distinct stylistic departure. In 1993, he released his first solo album, *Sacred Groove*. Dokken reunited in 1994 and released *Dysfunctional*, but the album was unsuccessful. Dokken released an unplugged concert from a 1994 show titled *One Live Night*, but three years later the band again split up and Lynch reassembled Lynch Mob.

In 1999, Lynch Mob adopted a new sound with *Smoke This*, and in the intervening years, Lynch continued to release albums and tour with various assemblages of bandmates from the two groups. In 2003, Lynch formed the George Lynch Group. *Furious George* (2005) featured covers of classic rock tunes from ZZ Top, Jimi Hendrix and Led Zeppelin, among others. Lynch Mob released *Smoke and Mirrors* in 2009.

Lynch has been an endorser of ESP guitars since 1986. His famed Skull and Bones guitar, named 'Mom', is actually a J Frog guitar with a neck by ESP. Several George Lynch signature guitars have been produced by ESP. Common Lynch techniques include using open-string chords, root-5 power chords, tritone accents and right-hand picking techniques to create unique tones. He uses unusual scales, and employs string bends and the whammy bar to slide into pitches. Jimi Hendrix, Jeff Beck and Michael Schenker, along with Eddie Van Halen and Yngwie Malmsteen, are cited as his influences.

ULI JON ROTH

SCORPIONS TO SKY GUITAR

Born in Düsseldorf, Germany, Ulrich 'Uli' Jon Roth (b. 1954) began his lifelong musical journey on the trumpet, before switching to the classical guitar at the age of 13. This training, combined with his passion for classical music, would help Roth become one of the main protagonists of the neo-classical shred guitar style, later brought to the forefront by Swedish guitarist Yngwie Malmsteen.

From 1973 until 1978 Roth was the primary songwriter and lead guitarist for legendary German rock group the Scorpions, having replaced guitarist Michael Schenker, who left to form UFO in 1973. Roth recorded five albums with the band, the final one being 1978's *Taken By Force*, which featured the Roth-penned 'Sails Of Charon'. This track, which Roth says was musically inspired by a Tchaikovsky violin concerto, is significant in that it represents arguably the first example of neo-classical shred guitar, and it would also come to be Roth's best-known song in the US.

Soon after *Taken By Force* was released, Roth left the Scorpions, dissatisfied with the commercial turn the band's sound was taking. He next formed Electric Sun, which lasted from 1978 until 1985. It was during this time, too, that Roth focused more on the neo-classical aspects of his guitar playing. To execute his classically based compositional ideas, he replaced his long-beloved Fender Strat with a newly commissioned six-octave 32-fret guitar. The result, the Sky Guitar, made its debut on Electric Sun's final album, *Beyond The Astral Skies* (1984) and has been Roth's weapon of choice for over 20 years now.

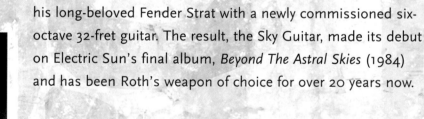

Starting in 1985 Roth spent much of his time working in the classical music spectrum, writing four symphonies and two concertos, and playing with symphony orchestras throughout Europe. In 1991 he served as music director for the television special *A Different Side of Jimi Hendrix*. In 1998 he joined Michael Schenker and Joe Satriani on the European leg of the G3 tour. In 2000 he released the two-CD set *Transcendental Sky Guitar*, and in 2004 the concerto *Metamorphosis Of Vivaldi's Four Seasons*, a twenty-first-century incarnation of the spirit of Vivaldi's music. Roth's *Under a Dark Sky* was released in 2008.

MICHAEL SCHENKER

UFO GUITAR LEGEND

Though he has been cited by countless rock guitarists as a major influence, and despite the fact that he co-founded legendary metal band the Scorpions, guitarist Michael Schenker (b. 1955) remains one of the most underrated and underappreciated guitarists of all time.

Born in Sarstedt, Germany, Schenker was first turned on to the guitar when his older brother Rudolf brought home a Gibson Flying V. Inspired by the heavy tone of Mountain's Leslie West and the nimble fretwork of Hank Marvin, Michael taught himself to play and would then join Rudolf in forming the Scorpions, recording their first album, *Lonesome Crow* (1972), when he was just 17. But even at this young age, it was clear that Michael possessed considerable talent.

During the ensuing tour, British space-metal group UFO witnessed Schenker's formidable guitar chops at a sound check and asked him to join the band as lead guitarist. With Rudolf's blessing, Michael took the gig, and it was with UFO that Schenker's reputation as a guitarist would begin to be formed. His first album with UFO, *Phenomenon* (1974), contained such future hard-rock classics as 'Doctor Doctor' and 'Rock Bottom'. The album also contained an instrumental track titled 'Lipstick Traces', which Schenker played entirely with his *feet*! It was also around this time that he would begin playing his famous black and white Gibson Flying V, an instrument with which Michael would become synonymous.

After several more successful albums, Schenker's alcohol abuse led to his exit from UFO in 1979. He rejoined the Scorpions later that year, staying just long enough to record *Lovedrive*, before leaving again. He next set out on his own, starting the first of many incarnations of the Michael Schenker Group (MSG). Craving commercial success, however, he steered away from his hard-rock roots, and in the mid- to late Eighties came to the cusp with singer Robin McCauley supplying the 'M' in MSG. Since then, Schenker has focused mostly on solo albums, including three releases in 2001 alone (*MS 2000: Dreams And Expressions, Odd Trio* and *Be Aware Of Scorpions*). The MSG album *In the Midst of Beauty* was released in 2008. Most recently, Schenker has received an endorsement deal with Dean Guitars, which makes the black and white Michael Schenker Signature V guitar.

ANGUS YOUNG

ON A HIGHWAY TO HERO

AC/DC guitarist Angus Young (b. 1955) – all five feet two inches of him – is nonetheless larger than life. Rising up from working-class Scottish roots to become the heart and soul of one of the greatest rock'n'roll bands of all time, Young, with his schoolboy outfit and Gibson SG in hand, has become the definitive rock-guitar icon.

Born in Glasgow, Scotland, in March 1955, Young moved to Australia with his family in the Sixties. Inspired by their big brother George (guitarist in the Easybeats) as well as by Chuck Berry, Muddy Waters and the Rolling Stones, the brothers Young teamed up to form AC/DC in 1973. After a couple of years, the brothers hooked up with singer Bon Scott and subsequently signed a deal with Atlantic Records, releasing their debut, *High Voltage*, in 1975.

Contrary to the glam-rock and disco sounds that were popular in the mid-Seventies, AC/DC pounded out no-nonsense three-chord rock with a good-time message, thus setting the band apart from the crowd. Although there were countless rock guitarists playing power chords and minor pentatonic licks on Gibson SGs through Marshall amps, *nobody* sounded like Angus Young. His singular tone and vibrato, in addition to his wild stage antics not only made Young a rising guitar hero but also turned AC/DC into a must-see live act.

After several more highly successful albums, including 1979's *Highway To Hell*, tragedy struck AC/DC, when singer Scott died of acute alcohol poisoning after a night of heavy partying. Downhearted, the band nearly called it quits, until they met British singer Brian Johnson. The fit was perfect, and AC/DC rebounded with one of the top five albums in rock history, *Back In Black* (1980). Songs like the title track, 'Hells Bells', and 'You Shook Me All Night Long' helped enshrine AC/DC as the world's greatest rock'n'roll band.

Thirty years and millions of albums later, AC/DC remain an iconic hard-rock band, and guitarist Young, who has never strayed from his SG-Marshall sound or from his schoolboy uniform and high-voltage stage act, remains a bona fide hard-rock guitar hero.

JAKE E. LEE

OZZY TO BADLANDS TO LEGEND

Jakey Lou Williams (b. 1957) was born in Norfolk, Virginia. His father was a member of the US Navy, which meant frequent relocation. Finally, however, the Williams family settled down in San Diego, California, where Jake began taking classical piano lessons, and, upon hearing his older sister's Jimi Hendrix, Led Zeppelin and Black Sabbath records, soon turned to the guitar.

During high school, Jake formed a band called Teaser, with whom he would dominate the San Diego club scene. He next joined Stephen Pearcy's band Mickey Rat, which moved to Los Angeles and changed its name to Ratt. After developing a huge following on the LA scene, Lee decided to leave the band. After a few gigs with Rough Cutt and abbreviated writing sessions with the great metal singer Ronnie James Dio, singer Ozzy Osbourne (pictured right) asked him to audition for the lead guitarist spot made available by the tragic death of Randy Rhoads. Brimming with confidence, Lee gave it a shot and was chosen from 500 other guitarists to stand at Ozzy's side on stage and in the studio for the next four years.

Lee's first record with Ozzy was 1983's *Bark At The Moon*. Knowing his worthiness to fit Rhoads' sizeable shoes would be questioned, Lee's playing shone bright on the record, particularly on the title track. *The Ultimate Sin* (1986) followed and, anchored by the MTV video hit 'Shot In The Dark', peaked at No. 1 on the album charts. Despite the album's success, Osbourne was in the midst of a drug and alcohol funk, and in the midst of one of his frequent rages, he fired Lee.

After taking some time off Lee hooked up with ex-Black Sabbath singer Ray Gillen in 1989 to form the blues-metal outfit Badlands. Their self-titled debut received critical acclaim but weak public support. Their follow-up, *Voodoo Highway* (1991), represented an even deeper journey into the blues and again earned critical raves. Since Badlands, Lee has been invited to play on several compilation and tribute albums, including tributes to Rush, Jeff Beck and Van Halen. He also released a solo album called *A Fine Pink Mist* in 1996, and more recently recorded an album of blues covers from the Sixties and Seventies, called *Retraced* (2005).

ADRIAN SMITH
IRON MAIDEN TO ICON

With the exception of Judas Priest, no metal band has been more influential than Iron Maiden. And it is no coincidence that Maiden first took flight when guitarist Adrian Smith (b. 1957) joined the band one month into recording their second album, *Killers*, in 1981.

Adrian Frederik 'H' Smith was born in Hackney, East London, in February 1957. At school, he was drawn to the rock-guitar sounds of Jimi Hendrix and Ritchie Blackmore, and so set about learning how to play. While at school, he became friends with Dave Murray and the two would eventually form a band called Urchin, though Murray would soon leave to form Iron Maiden. While Maiden rose to become one of England's most popular metal bands, Urchin fell apart, and so Smith welcomed the invitation to once again play alongside Murray in 1981. Starting with *Killers*, and continuing with *Number Of The Beast* (1982), *Piece Of Mind* (1983), *Powerslave* (1984), *Somewhere In Time* (1986), and *Seventh Son Of A Seventh Son* (1988), Smith's deceptively 'lazy' and melodic soloing approach would play perfect straight man to Murray's often fiery, scalar lines, and their harmony parts would set a metal-guitar standard adhered to even today.

Smith played a variety of guitars during this era, including an Ibanez Destroyer, Gibson Les Pauls and SGs, various Dean models, custom Jacksons, Lado models and, of course, his preferred Fender Stratocasters. His amplification was – and continues to be – Marshall.

Equally important to Maiden's sound and success during this era was Smith's songwriting sensibilities. He wrote or co-wrote such classic FM radio hits as 'Flight Of Icarus', '2 Minutes To Midnight', 'Wasted Years' and 'Can I Play With Madness', and helped steer the band into ever more progressive waters. This direction, however, collided with bassist Steve Harris's musical vision, which was to return to a more straightforward metal sound. Thus, Smith left Iron Maiden to pursue solo ambitions. Recording under the acronym A.S.A.P. (Adrian Smith And Project), he released *Silver And Gold*, in 1989, and later formed the alternative rock-influenced Psycho Motel, releasing *State Of Mind* (1996) and *Welcome To The World* (1997). Smith then rejoined Maiden in 1999 for the Ed Hunter tour and continues to record and tour with them now.

CHRIS POLAND

MASTER OF MEGADETH

In the early Eighties, as the new wave of British heavy metal was taking the US by storm, an American music revolution called 'thrash metal' was brewing, combining the heavy sounds of metal with the unabashed aggression and speed of punk. At the centre of this sonic storm was a young quartet called Megadeth, which featured the lightning-fast yet fluid lead licks of guitarist Chris Poland (b. 1957).

Though best known for his work in Megadeth, Poland was drawn to the complex musical style of jazz fusion as a young man, playing in a jazz-rock band called Welkin while still at high school. Upon graduation, he moved to LA where he played in a jazz-fusion outfit called the New Yorkers from 1977–82. Their complex songs and improvisations, informed by such fusion luminaries as Mahavishnu Orchestra and Weather Report, proved fertile for Poland, who would later use these fusion roots to set himself apart from the myriad metal clones lining the Sunset Strip in the Eighties.

Poland joined Megadeth in 1984, recording the band's debut, *Killing Is My Business...And Business Is Good* (1985), and their breakthrough follow-up, *Peace Sells...But Who's Buying*

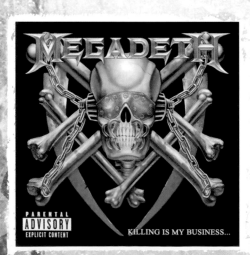

(1986), which finds the multifaceted guitarist's commanding chops on full display in both the title track and 'Wake Up Dead'. Suffering from substance abuse issues, Poland was fired from the band. Poland eventually kicked his habits and returned to the music scene, first as a bass player with punk band the Circle Jerks and then with his first solo album, a jazz-metal opus titled *Return To Metalopolis* (1990). He subsequently formed the progressive fusion outfit Damn The Machine, and later, Mumbo's Brain. Poland would once again play with Megadeth, recording several solos on the band's 2004 release, *The System Has Failed*.

Poland's greatest labour of love recently has been OHM, a progressive metal-fusion project that spotlights his recognizable style. In 2009, Poland formed OHMPHREY, a side-project with Robby Pagliari of OHM, and Jake Cinninger, Kris Myers and Joel Cummins of progressive rock band Umphrey's McGee. OHMPHREY released an eponymous debut album in 2009.

DAVE MURRAY

IRON MAIDEN TO ICON 2

More than any other hard-rock or heavy metal duo, Iron Maiden guitarists Adrian Smith and Dave Murray (b. 1956) set the standard for twin-guitar harmony lines and riffs. Indeed, their killer riffs and epic songs have helped to make Iron Maiden, arguably, the most influential metal band of all time.

Murray was born in Edmonton, England. Inspired by the early rock sounds of Jimi Hendrix, Free and Deep Purple, he got his first guitar at the age of 15 and started a band called Stone Free, which also happened to contain future Maiden guitarist Adrian Smith. In 1976, he met bassist Steve Harris, who asked him to join his fledgling metal band, Iron Maiden. Murray accepted the gig, but left almost immediately after, citing irreconcilable differences with singer Dennis Wilcock. Murray then rejoined Smith, this time in a metal band called Urchin. Together, they recorded one single, but when informed that Wilcock had left the band, Murray bolted back to Maiden.

In 1980, Iron Maiden released their eponymous debut, followed in 1981 by *Killers*. To this day, metal guitarists cite these two records as among the most influential metal albums of all time. But in terms of worldwide superstardom, it would be the arrival of singer Bruce Dickinson and Maiden's subsequent amazing string of albums from 1982 to 1984, including *Number Of The Beast* (1982), *Piece Of Mind* (1983) and *Powerslave* (1984), that would put the band on top of the world.

During this time of exploding publicity and recognition, Murray began to garner ever-increasing coverage in guitar magazines and metal-based fanzines, his 1957 black Fender Strat ubiquitously present. Murray's legato-fuelled lines proved technically proficient yet unpretentious, presenting aspiring guitarists a 'more metal' yet robust alternative to the emerging neo-classical stylings of Randy Rhoads and Yngwie Malmsteen.

Though subsequent album sales gradually faded (2010's *The Final Frontier* is the band's latest), Iron Maiden's appeal as a live act has never waned. From their 1984 World Slavery Tour, which saw them play 322 gigs in 20 countries over a 14-month period, to headlining festivals like Reading, Monsters Of Rock and Rock In Rio, Iron Maiden has by unofficial count entertained more fans than any band in music history. That is their, and Murray's, greatest legacy.

RICHIE SAMBORA

A GUITAR HERO AMONG US

Though guitar playing in the decade of the Eighties was often thought of as a 'guitar Olympics' of sorts, Bon Jovi guitarist Richie Sambora (b. 1959) typically eschewed fretboard flights of fancy in favour of melodic, tastefully arranged solos designed to serve the band's infectious hit songs. While this approach has kept him on the outside of the guitar-hero clubhouse, his impact on the greater musical community is rarely matched.

Richard Stephen Sambora was born in Perth Amboy, New Jersey, in July 1959. He began playing guitar in his early teens, inspired by Jimi Hendrix, Eric Clapton, Jeff Beck and the Beatles. In 1978, he made his recording debut with his band Shark Frenzy, but the mix tapes were damaged in a flood and thus never saw the light of day. (Shark Frenzy member Bruce Foster eventually remastered the tapes, and the album was released on Sanctuary Records in 2004.) In 1983, fellow New Jerseyan Jon Bongiovi (pictured below) hired Sambora to replace guitarist Dave Sabo in his newly signed band Bon Jovi. The rest, as they say, is history. Over the past 25 years, Bon Jovi has released 10 studio albums that have collectively sold over 120 million copies, and the band has played over 2,500 shows in over 50 countries. Additionally, Sambora has released two critically acclaimed solo albums – *Stranger In This Town* (1991) and *Undiscovered Soul* (1998). Suffice it to say, few guitarists have spent as much time onstage as Sambora has in his remarkable career.

Through the years, Sambora – an avid guitar collector – has played just about every guitar possible. In the early years of Bon Jovi, he favoured custom Gibson Les Pauls, often equipped with floating tremolo systems. He then went through a period of 'super-Strats', from such manufacturers as Charvel, Jackson and Kramer, which made his first signature model guitar, in 1987. He was also one of the top endorsers of Ovation acoustic guitars, as featured in the video for 'Wanted Dead Or Alive' (1986).

Since then, the guitarist has continued to mix it up, using various vintage Fenders and Gibsons, as well as the 'Sambora' guitar, made by his long-time associate and luthier Chris Hofschneider. In 2008 Sambora announced his new ESP endorsement deal, and in 2009 the ever-popular Bon Jovi released *The Circle*.

VITO BRATTA

WHITE LION'S LEGEND

When Eighties hair-metal band White Lion released the video for their breakthrough hit 'Wait', in 1987, guitar fans saw arguably the second coming of Eddie Van Halen. Guitarist Vito Bratta (b. 1961) brought forth tasty rhythm guitar parts, masterly single-note technique, and above all a two-hand tapping technique that, while in the style of Van Halen, found a new direction and thus provided Bratta his own identity.

Born in Staten Island, New York, Bratta took up the guitar at the age of 12. Five years later, he heard Van Halen, and it changed his world forever. Prior to joining White Lion, Bratta played in a New York band called Dreamer, where he earned the respectful nickname 'Vito Van Halen', for his own amazing tapping technique.

In 1983 Bratta teamed up with Danish singer Mike Tramp (pictured right) and formed White Lion, releasing their debut album, *Fight To Survive* (1984) on Grand Slamm Records. After several personnel changes in their rhythm section, the band signed a major-label deal with Atlantic Records in 1987 and released *Pride*. The single 'Wait' exploded on MTV, and White Lion was quickly thrust into the spotlight. But their biggest success would come more than a year after the album's release, when the tender acoustic ballad 'When The Children Cry' would take the band to the top of the hair-metal genre. For Bratta, the exposure brought well-deserved recognition for his instrumental prowess. He also received critical acclaim as a guitarist whose playing had substance and direction in an era of 'guitar wars' repetitiveness. He further set himself apart via his preference for a Steinberger guitar, when his contemporaries were all solidly camped primarily in the Charvel, B.C. Rich and Kramer camps.

The band's follow-up album, *Big Game* (1989), while a commercial success, didn't measure up to the expectations set by *Pride*. They released one more album, *Mane Attraction* (1991), before caving in to the onrushing winds of grunge music in 1992. In 1995 Bratta decided to take a break from the instrument he had played every day since the age of 12, finally picking it up again in 1997, only to experience a wrist injury that would prevent him from playing again for several years.

KIRK HAMMETT
METALLICA'S MASTER OF GUITAR

When singer-guitarist Dave Mustaine was dismissed from the original Metallica line-up, it opened the door for a young Bay Area-based guitarist named Kirk Hammett (b. 1962) to come in and lead the thrash-metal charge. What Hammett and his mates in Metallica would accomplish from that point no one could have predicted.

Born in San Francisco, California, Hammett benefited from his older brother's extensive hard-rock record collection, which included albums by Jimi Hendrix, Led Zeppelin and UFO. Inspired, Hammett picked up a Montgomery Ward catalogue guitar at the age of 15. He soon upgraded to a 1978 Fender Stratocaster, and then a 1974 Gibson Flying V, matching it to a Marshall amp. With his powerful new rig, the guitarist soon hooked up with vocalist Paul Baloff and formed Exodus. The pioneering thrash band would later support Metallica twice, in late 1982 and early 1983.

In the spring of 1983, after giving guitarist Mustaine the boot, Metallica called Hammett and invited him to audition in New York. He hopped a flight, nailed the gig and before long was in the studio recording the band's debut, *Kill 'Em All* (1983). After the ensuing tour, Hammett began taking lessons from virtuoso Joe Satriani. His hard work paid off, and Hammett began to make a name for himself in the guitar community via his incendiary scalar lines in solos such as 'Fade To Black' from

1984's *Ride The Lightning*. Two years later, in 1986, the band released what many believe to be their magnum opus, *Master Of Puppets*.

In 1987, Hammett began an association with ESP guitars, becoming their biggest endorser. With his signature guitar in hand, Hammett laid down some of his scariest lines to date on Metallica's 1988 release, *...And Justice For All*. But it was the band's 1991 self-titled release, the 'Black Album', that enshrined them as the reigning kings of metal. Ironically, while the band had achieved mass commercial success, Hammett's bluesier, wah-drenched soloing approach on this and later releases saw his stock among some in the guitar community drop. But as evident in his 2007 endorsement deal with Randall amplifiers and ESP's limited-run 20th anniversary Kirk Hammett model guitar, the Metallica guitarist maintains his relevancy. In 2009, Metallica was inducted into the Rock And Roll Hall Of Fame.

MARTY FRIEDMAN

SHREDDING SUPERSTAR

Many guitarists of the 'shred' variety unfortunately stick to scalar lines and diatonic arpeggios in straight major or minor keys. Marty Friedman (b. 1962) is not one of them. Indeed, Friedman's tendency toward Eastern, Middle Eastern and other ethnic sounds has distinguished him as one of the most musically gifted super-pickers the guitar world has ever seen.

Martin Adam Friedman grew up in the Baltimore area. He began playing guitar at the age of 15, shortly before his family moved to Hawaii. While there, he played in several local bands and began seeking out Asian and Middle Eastern music to incorporate their exotic sounds into his own. His constant practising and unquenchable thirst for musical knowledge paid off in 1982, when he hooked up with Shrapnel Records. Five years later, working with fellow shredder Jason Becker, the duo recorded *Speed Metal Symphony* under the moniker Cacophony. It was a hit in the shred community, and Friedman's solo debut, *Dragon's Kiss*, followed a year later, in 1988.

The exposure, combined with Friedman's virtuosity, led to his joining thrash giants Megadeth in 1990. Their first album together, *Rust In Peace* (1990), is generally recognized as one of the most technically accomplished thrash albums in history. Friedman's fretboard explorations on such tracks as 'Holy Wars...The Punishment Due' and 'Tornado Of Souls' ably demonstrate how effective shred

stylings can be when phrased appropriately. His second album with Megadeth, *Countdown To Extinction* (1992), further demonstrated the chemistry that had seemingly eluded singer/leader Dave Mustaine for most of his career, thanks largely to Friedman's fretwork.

Around this time, Friedman began to seek outlets for his non-metal, exotic compositions. He formed a partnership with new-age musician Kitaro and released the Asian-themed instrumental record *Scenes* (1992). In the coming years, he released two other solo-guitar albums in the same vein, before recording his final album with Megadeth, *Risk*, in 1999. Since then he has moved to Japan, where he regularly appears with various Japanese artists and continues to record exotic-rock instrumental guitar albums, including *Loudspeaker* (2007). In 2008, his eighth solo album, *Future Addict*, was released in Japan, featuring reworked versions of some of his past work.

TOM MORELLO

A MUSICIAN WITH A MESSAGE

Driven by a fierce intelligence, a relentless pursuit of social justice and a wide-ranging taste in sounds and songs, Tom Morello (b. 1964) was the driving force behind the bands Rage Against the Machine and Audioslave. Morello has won Grammys and performed around the world inspiring and uniting people with music. Known for innovative guitar solos and varied, effects-laden tones, he has been ranked number 26 on *Rolling Stone*'s list of the 100 Greatest Guitarists of All Time.

Morello was born to a Kenyan father and Irish-Italian mother. His mother exposed him to politics and the classics from an early age, and Morello became the first person from his Illinois town to enroll at Harvard after graduating with honors from high school. After college, he moved to Los Angeles. Morello had studied guitar throughout high school, initially influenced by Kiss, Iron Maiden and Alice Cooper, later by the Clash, the Sex Pistols and Devo. In LA he formed a band with vocalist Zack de la Rocha, drummer Brad Wilk and childhood friend Tim Commerford on bass. After frequenting the LA club circuit, Rage Against the Machine signed to Epic Records in 1992. That same year, the band released their self-titled debut, and eventually three more studio albums.

In 2000, de la Rocha quit the band, and Morello, Wilk and Commerford formed Audioslave with ex-Soundgarden singer Chris Cornell, releasing three albums and a DVD of the band's unprecedented free concert in Cuba. In 2007, Rage Against the Machine reunited at the Coachella Music Festival. Though they have played for big events, RATM do not play together regularly.

In recent years, Morello has performed and recorded folk music under the alias The Nightwatchman and has toured in support of activist causes, joining likeminded musicians, including Bruce Springsteen, for a slew of projects and performances. He has contributed to albums by artists including Primus, Johnny Cash, the Crystal Method. Morello has appeared in movies, such as *Iron Man* (2008) in which he played a terrorist, as well as contributing to soundtracks.

SLASH
APPETITE FOR BRILLIANCE

The man beneath the top hat, Saul 'Slash' Hudson (b. 1965) was born in the Hampstead area of London. When he was 11, his family moved to Los Angeles, California, where at the age of 14 he heard Aerosmith's *Rocks* for the first time and found his life's calling.

Practising guitar for hours on end, learning the licks of his heroes Joe Perry, Eric Clapton and Angus Young, among others, Slash set about forming his own band to play the famed Sunset Strip. Teaming up with friend and drummer Steven Adler, Slash formed the blues-rock act Road Crew. Soon, the two friends hooked up with singer Axl Rose, guitarist Izzy Stradlin and bassist Duff McKagan to form a new band called Guns N' Roses.

In 1987, GN'R released its debut, *Appetite For Destruction*, an album that would go on to become one of the biggest rock'n'roll albums in history. The album would catapult the band (and its excesses) into the realms of Aerosmith and the Rolling Stones. But on an individual level, it would install Slash as the era's premier guitar anti-hero, a role model for aspiring guitarists uninterested in the fretboard flash of players like Steve Vai or Yngwie Malmsteen.

Slash's meteoric ascension would impact the guitar-gear world as well. With his low-slung Les Paul harking back to the sights and sounds of Led Zeppelin's Jimmy Page and Seventies-era Joe Perry, the once grand but then-stalled Gibson brand was suddenly resurrected to its prior position of esteem.

Following the demise of GN'R, Slash released two albums with Slash's Snakepit and recorded sessions with dozens of top-name artists ranging from Michael Jackson to Alice Cooper to the Yardbirds. Then, in 2003, he reunited with former Gunners McKagan and Matt Sorum and recruited guitarist Dave Kushner and singer Scott Weiland to form Velvet Revolver. The band's two releases, *Contraband* (2004) and *Libertad* (2007), have helped to return Slash to the world's biggest stages and positioned him as one of the enduring guitar heroes of his generation.

DIMEBAG DARRELL

CUT OFF IN HIS PRIME

Despite a life cut tragically short by violence, Darrell Lance Abbott (1966–2004), known as 'Dimebag Darrell,' achieved stardom not only as a founding member of the bands Pantera and Damageplan, but also in death as an icon who succumbed on stage and carried his passions to the grave.

Darrell Abbott took up guitar when he was 12. He was a devoted fan of Black Sabbath and KISS. (He later had an autograph on his chest by KISS guitarist Ace Frehley tattooed in place.) Abbott formed Pantera in 1981 with his brother, drummer Vinnie Paul. Influenced by metal acts from Iron Maiden to Slayer, Pantera became a force in the subgenre 'groove' metal. Pantera scored with *Cowboys from Hell* in 1990 and cemented their reputation with *Vulgar Display of Power* in 1992, as the band adopted a heavier vocal and guitar sound. However, by 2003, frictions with vocalist Phil Anselmo caused the group to split.

A year later, Dimebag and Vinnie formed Damageplan with guitarist Pat Lachman and Bob Zilla on bass, and released the hit album *New Found Power*. Throughout the runs of Pantera and Damageplan, Dimebag performed as a guest on multiple projects, including cuts for Nickelback, country singer David Allen Coe and the Dallas Stars hockey team. He was called 'the sixth member of Anthrax', because of his many guest appearances on the band's albums.

In 2004, Abbott was performing with Damageplan at a club in Columbus, Ohio. Nathan Gale, a paranoid schizophrenic, approached the stage and shot Abbott five times, killing him instantly, along with three others, and wounding seven more. Gale was shot and killed by police officer James Niggemeyer. Dimebag was buried in a KISS Kasket with Eddie Van Halen's Charvel Hybrid VH2 – a black and yellow Frankenstrat guitar, known as 'Bumblebee', that was on the cover of *Van Halen II*.

Dimebag wrote a column for *Guitar World*, and three of his solos, 'Walk,' 'Cemetery Gates' and 'Floods,' are ranked among the magazine's top 100 of all-time.

NUNO BETTENCOURT

EXTREME GUITAR STAR

As a guitarist and songwriter Nuno Bettencourt (b. 1966) draws from many styles and influences. Born in the Portuguese archipelago of the Azores, Bettencourt grew up in Boston, Massachusetts. As a teenager, he began playing drums, bass and keyboards, but ultimately chose guitar as his primary instrument, drawing heavy influence from Eddie Van Halen as well as the Beatles, Led Zeppelin and Queen.

Bettencourt joined Extreme in 1985, and the band released its self-titled debut album in 1989. In 1991, the band released *Pornograffitti*, which included the acoustic hits 'More Than Words' and 'Hole Hearted'. But it was the extraordinary technical prowess Bettencourt displayed on such tunes as 'Get The Funk Out' and 'He-Man Woman Hater' – from speed picking to string skipping to tapped arpeggios – that solidified him as one of the era's top guitarists. It was also during this time that Washburn guitars unveiled the Nuno Bettencourt N4 signature-model guitar, a model that endures today.

After Extreme disbanded in 1996, Bettencourt released his solo debut, *Schizophonic* (1997), on which he played all instruments. He next assembled a new group, Mourning Widows, which incorporated a variety of alternative-rock styles. The band released its self-titled debut

CD in 1998, and followed up with *Furnished Souls For Rent*, which was released in Japan in 2000. In 2002, Bettencourt formed the recording entity Population 1 and released the self-titled and self-produced 2002 album, *Population 1*. *Sessions From Room 4* followed in 2004, and in 2005 the band changed its name to the DramaGods and released *Love*. In 2007, Bettencourt teamed up with singer Perry Farrell in Satellite Party, releasing *Ultra Payloaded* that same year, but Bettencourt departed soon after its release.

In addition, Bettencourt can be heard and seen on the Universal/Japan CD and DVD release of *Guitar Wars* (2004). He also has written, recorded and toured with several artists including Tantric, BBMak, Toni Braxton and Wyclef Jean and Rhianna, among numerous others.

PAUL GILBERT

RACER X'S MR BIG

Too often, the music created by so-called 'shred' guitarists comes across as too cerebral and serious to elicit enjoyment from any but the most die-hard shred fan. Fortunately for the rest of instrumental guitar fans, Paul Gilbert (b. 1966) prefers to dish out his hungry man portions of notes with humour and irreverence matched only by his technical ferocity.

Gilbert first picked up the guitar at the age of five, but did not fully understand music until he was nine. In 1982, he sent a tape of his band Missing Lynx to Shrapnel Records' head Mike Varney, who upon hearing it put Gilbert into his Spotlight column in *Guitar Player* magazine (Yngwie Malmsteen also appeared in that issue's column!). In 1984, Gilbert moved to Hollywood, California, to attend the Guitar Institute of Technology, where he met the future members of Racer X. The band recorded their debut album, *Street Lethal*, in 1985, with such tracks as 'Y.R.O'. helping Gilbert quickly become one of the most talked-about guitarists on the scene. By the time they released their second album, *Second Heat* (1987), which featured the downright terrifying guitar instrumental 'Scarified', the band was selling out all the big clubs on the LA scene and Gilbert was being recognized as one of the most technically proficient guitarists of the Eighties.

Whereas Racer X was essentially one giant adrenaline rush, Gilbert's next band, Mr. Big, offered him the opportunity to stretch his songwriting wings, and the band's 1989 self-titled debut reached No. 46 on the *Billboard* Top 200 album chart. But it was 1991's *Lean Into It*, featuring the No. 1 acoustic ballad 'To Be With You' as well as 'Just Take My Heart' and 'Green-Tinted Sixties Mind' that brought Gilbert more widespread acclaim.

In 1997, Gilbert left Mr. Big to pursue a solo career. He has since released 10 studio albums, including the all-instrumental *Get Out Of My Yard* (2006). His signature-model Ibanez PGM guitars continue to be top sellers, and his instructional videos, particularly *Intense Rock I* and *Intense Rock II* are generally considered in the guitar-playing community to be among the best ever produced. In 2009, Gilbert reunited with the original Mr. Big band members Eric Martin, Billy Sheehan, and Pat Torpey for a reunion world tour.

ZAKK WYLDE
THE LAST TRUE HERO

Though he maintains a gruff, beer-drinking, hell-raising public persona, guitarist Zakk Wylde (b. 1967) is one of the most talented, dedicated and hard-working guitarists of the past 20 years and, as some in the guitar community have speculated, the last true guitar hero.

Wylde was born Jeffrey Phillip Wiedlandt in Bayonne, New Jersey. He started playing guitar at the age of 15, drawing influence from such guitar legends as Jimmy Page, Eddie Van Halen and Randy Rhoads. He soon started a band called Stone Henge, playing *Animal House*-style house parties in central New Jersey. A few years later, while playing a gig in Sayreville, New

Jersey, a photographer offered to get his press kit into the hands of Ozzy Osbourne, who was looking for a new guitarist. A short while later, Wylde was making his debut with the Prince of Darkness at Wormwood Scrubs prison, in London, England.

Wylde's first album with Ozzy was *No Rest For The Wicked* (1988), featuring the rock hits 'Miracle Man' and 'Crazy Babies'. From the start, Wylde's minor pentatonic-based lines, aggressive vibrato and screaming pinch harmonics proved a perfect fit for the Osbourne sound. Their next studio record, *No More Tears* (1991), which produced the rock hits 'No More Tears' and 'Mama I'm Coming Home', solidified Wylde's reputation as a guitarist here to stay. Indeed, since that time, Wylde has recorded three more studio records with the madman, including 2007's *Black Rain*.

In addition to his Ozzy gig, Wylde has worked on several side projects, like *Pride And Glory* (1994) and a solo album titled *Book Of Shadows* (1996). But Wylde's most prolific work has been with his own Black Label Society, formed in 1999. In a period of just eight years, BLS has released seven studio records along with several live albums and DVDs. Additionally, Wylde has several signature-model Gibson Les Paul Customs – the most famous being his black and antique-white bulls-eye design – and a signature-model Marshall head.

ALEX SKOLNICK

TESTAMENT TO REMEMBER

Alex Skolnick (b. 1968) is best known as a metal guitarist with thrash pioneers Testament. But metal is just one facet of the talented guitarist's abilities. Skolnick was born in Berkeley, California. At the age of nine, he discovered Kiss and subsequently decided to learn guitar. He was later inspired by the highly technical work of Eddie Van Halen and Randy Rhoads. At the age of 16, he joined a band called Legacy. Two years later, the band changed their name to Testament and entered the studio to record their first album, *The Legacy*, which was released in 1987. Skolnick would go on to record five more albums with Testament before disbanding in 1992.

During that era, Skolnick earned well-deserved praise in the guitar community, regularly appearing at the top of readers' polls in guitar magazines as Best Thrash Guitarist or Most Underrated Guitarist. It was also during this time that Skolnick saw one of jazz legend Miles Davis's guitar-driven bands on television, sparking an intense passion for jazz music. He began to study the jazz language intently, eventually moving to New York City to attend New School University, where he earned a degree in jazz performance in 2001.

While attending New School he founded the Alex Skolnick Trio. Their first recording, *Goodbye To Romance: Standards For A New Generation* (2002), featured jazz arrangements of classic metal songs. Subsequent releases *Transformation* (2004) and *Last Day In Paradise* (2007) featured similar arrangements of metal tunes, accompanied by original bebop compositions.

In recent years, Skolnick has toured as a member of the Trans-Siberian Orchestra, a classical-rock odyssey that performs technically demanding arrangements of Christmas songs to sold-out arenas. He is also featured in Jekyll & Hyde In Concert, the touring version of the hit Broadway show *Jekyll & Hyde*, and has begun working with composer Jim Steinman on the Dream Engine project, performing new songs and classics. In 2005, Skolnick reunited with Testament for a highly successful series of sold-out concerts in Europe and Japan. *The Formation of Damnation* was released in 2008. It was the first studio album of all new material for Testament in nine years and the first to feature Skolnick on guitar since 1992's *The Ritual*.

JASON BECKER

A TRUE HERO

Jason Becker (b. 1969) is an American neo-classical metal guitarist and composer whose steady rise to the top of the guitar world was cut short by illness. Becker was born and raised in Richmond, California. In high school, he performed Yngwie Malmsteen's 'Black Star' with his band at a talent show. At 16, he formed Cacophony with his friend Marty Friedman. Produced by Mike Varney, the duo released *Speed Metal Symphony* in 1987 and *Go Off!* in 1988, touring the US and Japan in support. By 1989, Becker was a solo act, having recorded *Perpetual Burn* on his own in 1988.

At the peak of his abilities, Becker was known as a shredder with exceptional technique who demonstrated his mastery at clinics. He studied the works of violinist Niccolò Paganini, arranging the composer's *Fifth Caprice*, and performing it in an instructional guitar video. Becker's compositions feature high-speed scalar and arpeggio passages.

At 20, Becker replaced Steve Vai in David Lee Roth's band. While recording *A Little Ain't Enough* in 1989 and preparing for a tour, Becker began to feel limpness in his left leg. He was diagnosed with Amyotrophic Lateral Sclerosis (Lou Gehrig's Disease) and given a grim prognosis. Becker finished the album, but quickly lost the ability to perform on stage. As

the disease progressed, Becker turned to composing, using a keyboard after he was unable to use both hands, and controlling a computer system – eventually with his eyes – as his mental acuity remained unaffected by the disease.

In 1996, Becker released *Perspective*, an instrumental album composed by him (with the exception of Bob Dylan's song 'Meet Me In The Morning'). The writing of the music had begun before ALS completely crippled his abilities. Later Becker released *Raspberry Jams* (1999) and *Blackberry Jams* (2003), collections of demos and alternate versions of songs that were later reworked and released on his albums. Two tribute albums, *Warmth in the Wilderness* (I and II), featuring guitarists Steve Vai, Paul Gilbert, Marty Friedman and others, have been released, with profits aiding Becker with his medical expenses.

JOHN 5

THE MODERN-DAY HERO

Guitar One magazine declared him a 'modern-day master of the Telecaster'. In the 2007 *Guitar World* readers poll, his instrumental guitar tour de terror *The Devil Knows My Name* was named Best Shred Album of 2007. Also in 2007, he graced the covers of *Guitar Player* and *Guitarist* magazines. And in 2008, he was featured on the cover of *Guitar Edge* magazine, which proclaimed him one of the 'new guitar heroes'. Finally, it seems, guitarist John 5 (b. 1971) is shedding the cloak of 'underrated' for some hard-earned and long-overdue time in the spotlight.

John 5 was born John Lowery in July 1971 in Grosse Point, Michigan. He started playing guitar at the age of seven, inspired by the US country television show 'Hee Haw'. When he turned 18, John moved to California to pursue a career as a professional session guitarist. There he met producer Bob Marlette and began working on a number of TV shows, commercials and film soundtracks.

After touring with Lita Ford and k.d. lang, and working on short-lived projects with drummer Randy Castillo and singer Rob Halford, John landed a gig with David Lee Roth's DLR Band.

Shortly thereafter, shock-rocker Marilyn Manson invited John for lunch and hired him on the spot, dubbing him with his current 'John 5' moniker. John 5 would play with Manson until April 2004, at which time – at the urging of the legendary Les Paul – he set out to record his first solo album, *Vertigo* (2004).

With *Vertigo* and his subsequent release *Songs For Sanity* (2005), John 5 revealed to his primarily metal fan base a multifaceted approach to guitar that includes heavy bluegrass and country influences. That unusual musical pedigree created an underground buzz in the guitar community. Since then, a permanent gig with metal superstar Rob Zombie has garnered John 5 even greater mass appeal. In 2007, John released an album of instrumental guitar music called *The Devil Knows My Name*. Featuring guest appearances from the likes of Joe Satriani and Eric Johnson, it contains all the no-holds-barred shred essentials, but its injections of country and bluegrass phrasing, mixed with industrial and futuristic sounds, breaks the old mould and sets the twenty-first-century standard for instrumental guitar music. John 5 works on projects with various artists, including Rob Zombie, with whom he tours.

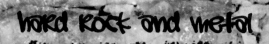

MARK TREMONTI

A STORY OF SUCCESS

Mark Tremonti (b. 1974) rose to fame as the lead guitarist of Creed, enjoying enormous success at the turn of the 21st century with metal-influenced songs that crossed over to the pop charts. Tremonti's tasteful power has garnered him many fans. His instructional DVD, *The Sound and the Story*, adds tips from several guitarists, including Michael Angelo Batio, Rusty Cooley, Troy Stetina, Bill Peck and Myles Kennedy.

Tremonti was born and grew up near Detroit, Michigan. He got his first guitar at age 11 for about $25. Tremonti learned guitar by ear and with the help of books and videos. At 16, Mark and his family moved to Florida, where he met future Creed singer Scott Stapp in high school. Although the two were not friends at the time, Tremonti encountered Stapp again at Florida State University. They formed Creed with guitarist Brian Brasher, bassist Scott Phillips and drummer Brian Marshall.

Creed's debut album, *My Own Prison*, was released independently in 1997. After Wind-Up Records picked up the group and re-released the album it became a surprise success, spinning off several hit singles, including 'My Own Prison.' When Creed's second album, *Human Clay*, was released in 1999, 'Higher' and 'With Arms Wide Open' also hit No. 1. Overall, the band had seven consecutive hits on rock radio and sold over 30 million records worldwide in seven years. Internal squabbles led to Creed's splitting and Tremonti's forming Alter Bridge in 2004. The band released two studio albums: *One Day Remains* (2004) and *Blackbird* (2007). A third album was recorded for release in 2010. After ten years apart, Creed reunited in 2009 with a tour and the album *Full Circle*.

Tremonti has contributed to many artists' records over the years, including Sevendust's *Hope & Sorrow*, and Fozzy's *All That Remains*. He also played on the cover of Deep Purple's 'Burn,' from Michael Angelo Batio's *Hands Without Shadows*. Mark Tremonti plays several of his signature-model Paul Reed Smith guitars with Fender and Bogner amps and Mesa/Boogie heads and cabinets. He also uses a Taylor 614CE acoustic.

soft rock and pop

Some guitar heroes blaze trails with fiery histrionics and outrageous behaviour
while others simply revolutionize music with good taste and a unique sound.
There can be no doubt that the 12-string shimmer of Roger McGuinn, the inspiring
textures of the Edge and the history making lead lines of George Harrison made
these legendary icons burn as brightly as their hard-rock counterparts. They passed
the torch to a new generation that would pour fuel on to the rock'n'roll fire, even
as direct descendants like Trey Anastasio and Lenny Kravitz continued to create
new and tasty licks in both high- and low-intensity musical settings.

JAMES BURTON

CHICKEN PICKIN' MASTER

Louisiana native James Burton (b. 1939) is one of several guitarists weaned on country music who parlayed his unique talent into session and tour work with rock musicians while maintaining his ties to the country community.

Burton first achieved local fame as a backup musician on the popular 'Louisiana Hayride' radio show, which spotlighted a young Elvis (pictured below) and rivalled the 'Grand Ole Opry' as a radio institution in Fifties America. In Louisiana Burton got his first significant exposure with his guitar solo on the 1957 Dale Hawkins hit 'Suzie Q'. Soon Burton was in California, and his talents were deemed perfect for the sound of the emerging teen idol Ricky Nelson, whose family television show, 'The Adventures Of Ozzie And Harriet', was another American pop culture icon. Burton spent six years recording and touring with Ricky, even appearing on the TV show himself while establishing Nelson as a pop presence with distinctive guitar riffs on hits like 'Hello Mary Lou', 'Lonesome Town' and 'Teenage Idol'.

Burton's 'chicken pickin'' mastery on dobro and guitar landed him studio gigs with artists as diverse as Joni Mitchell, the Monkees and Merle Haggard, as part of the legendary LA studio band known as the Wrecking Crew. Burton soon began an eight-year stint with Elvis's TCB

band, which lasted until the singer's death in 1977. Almost immediately thereafter Burton began a 16-year relationship with John Denver, again recording and touring wth the singer up to his untimely death in 1997. Burton is unrivalled in his melding of country and rock guitar idioms and in his association with pop superstars (Nelson, Presley and Denver) whose lives ended tragically.

Burton was also part of the acclaimed Cinemax special, 'Roy Orbison And Friends, A Black And White Night'. Beginning with *King Of America* (1987), Burton also recorded and toured with Elvis Costello for about a decade. Burton was elected to the Rock And Roll Hall Of Fame in 2001. He was elected to the Musicians Hall Of Fame in November 2007 as a member of the Wrecking Crew.

ROGER McGUINN

SIGNATURE SOUNDS

James Joseph McGuinn (b. 1942) was raised in Chicago and became a fan of folk music as a teenager. He asked for and received a guitar from his parents after hearing Elvis's 'Heartbreak Hotel'. In 1957 McGuinn entered Chicago's Old Town School of Folk Music, where he studied five-string banjo and guitar.

McGuinn's skills and solo performances attracted the attention of recording artists in the burgeoning folk-music craze, and by 1964 he had been a member of the Limeliters, the Chad Mitchell Trio and Bobby Darin's band. As a session musician for Darin's New York publishing company, he recorded with Hoyt Axton, Judy Collins and a young duo named Tom & Jerry, soon to become Simon & Garfunkel. Relocating to Los Angeles in 1964 was the move that would initiate the making of McGuinn's legend.

In LA McGuinn met singer-guitarist David Crosby and singer-songwriter Gene Clark, with whom McGuinn released a failed single as the Beefeaters before adding bassist Chris Hillman and drummer Michael Clarke to form the Byrds. The goal was to bring elements of the British Invasion sound to the folk-influenced modern songs of Bob Dylan and the band's writers. The first single, Dylan's 'Mr. Tambourine Man', featured McGuinn's new, revolutionary guitar sound: a Rickenbacker 12-string heavily compressed in the studio to create a jingly sustain that would influence guitarists for decades. McGuinn later would adapt the sound for the spacey ambience of the Byrd's psychedelic hit 'Eight Miles High' (1966).

Along the way Chicago's Jim McGuinn was renamed Roger by the founder of the Subud spiritual group. The original Byrds would enjoy enormous success, but would soon split, reform and spawn solo careers. McGuinn would continue to tour, release solo albums and eventually become an Internet pioneer artist covering classic songs on his Folk Den website. In November of 2005 McGuinn released a four-CD box set containing 100 of his favourite songs from the Folk Den. But he will forever be remembered as the guitarist who melded folk, country, rock and psychedelia into a signature guitar sound.

GEORGE HARRISON

BEATLEMANIA

Pigeonholed as the 'quiet one', misunderstood as an adopter of Eastern religion and music, and overshadowed (sometimes maligned) by his prolific, trailblazing bandmates Lennon and McCartney, George Harrison (1943–2001) might have become a footnote in musical history. But as a member of the Beatles Harrison made the words 'lead guitar' a household term and steadily developed as a songwriter and player to the point of equal artistic footing with his mates, as evidenced by his contributions to the band's penultimate album *Abbey Road* (1969) and the abundant creativity of his early solo career. He demonstrated amply that there was life (and love and peace) after the Beatles.

Influenced by the British skiffle star Lonnie Donegan, American rockabilly guitarist Carl Perkins and Nashville stalwart Chet Atkins, Harrison was already developing a unique style when, at the invitation of schoolmate Paul McCartney, he joined John Lennon's Quarrymen and became part of rock history. Harrison would endure the mayhem of Beatlemania and find solace in the music and faith he encountered in India. As a songwriter he would grow slowly from the telling solitude of 'Don't Bother Me' to the universality of 'Something' and 'Here Comes The Sun'. As a guitarist he would often defer to the wishes of McCartney and producer George Martin on solos (and to the talents of Eric Clapton on 'While My Guitar Gently Weeps'). But his carefully crafted solos and phenomenal exposure with the band inspired millions to take up guitar, while making the Gretsch Country Gentleman and Rickenbacker 360 12-string two of the world's most recognized instruments.

Embracing Indian music (along with the Hare Krishna faith), Harrison exposed the western world to the sitar and brought exotic sounds to the Beatles' records as they shifted their focus from live performing to studio work. As a solo artist Harrison was the first ex-Beatle to score a major hit with his three-disc 'All Things Must Pass'. He adopted a signature slide-guitar sound and branched out with historic work as a humanitarian (*The Concert For Bangladesh*), filmmaker (Handmade Films) and bandmate (the Travelling Wilburys). When he died of brain cancer in 2001 he left a legacy of guitar music and influence that justified his 2004 entry as a solo artist into the Rock And Roll Hall Of Fame.

CLARENCE WHITE

INNOVATOR OF COUNTRY ROCK

In his short life California guitarist-mandolinist Clarence White (1944–73) conceived innovations that would inspire country and rock guitarists from both a stylistic and technical perspective long after his death. He brought bluegrass picking to the forefront of rock, turning acoustic guitar into a solo instrument. He developed a device for electric guitar that let traditional guitarists sound like pedal steel players. As a member of the Byrds (pictured below) from 1968 to 1973 he brought a new level of musicianship to a band that, with the exception of Roger McGuinn, didn't even play on their first hit single.

Born into a family of musicians, White played with his brothers in the Country Boys, which became the Kentucky Colonels. His skills led to session work on many mid-Sixties pop and rock albums as well as live gigs alongside Gene Parsons, Gib Gilbeau and former Byrd Gene Clark. White joined Parsons and Gilbeau in the band Nashville West and was invited to record with the Byrds as the band was leaving behind their British Invasion bent for a tighter focus on the marriage of country and rock. White's innovative string bending and solos on the group's seminal *Sweetheart Of The Rodeo* (1968) album enlivened tracks like 'The Christian Life' and 'One Hundred Years From Now'. In 1968 he joined the band and toured with them until their final split in 1973. He had continued studio work during his tenure, alternating with Ry Cooder as guitarist on Randy Newman's *12 Songs* (1970) and collaborating with Jackson Browne on his albums.

With fellow Byrd Gene Parsons White developed a device, the B-Bender, that would allow guitarists to bend strings independently of their fretting hands, giving six-string guitarists the

mournful sound of a pedal steel with less work. The sound is perhaps most familiar from Bernie Leadon's solo on the Eagle's 'Peaceful Easy Feeling' (1972), but has been used on records by artists as diverse as Led Zeppelin and Donna Summer. White, however, wouldn't live to see his invention gain its following. He was killed by a drunk driver while loading gear into his car after a performance with the Kentucky Colonels in 1973.

STEPHEN STILLS

CROSBY, STAR AND NASH

Stephen Stills (b. 1945) turned acoustic guitar into a fiery blues instrument as a solo artist and performer. That alone might have made him a rock icon, but of course Stills was also busy producing, composing and singing with the most popular rock vocal group of all time, creating hit singles on his own, teaming with individual members of his band and forming new groups for successful albums, and enjoying a 40-year career in the rock spotlight.

An oft-travelled military child, Stills gravitated to California in 1965 after stints with New York-based groups the Au Go Go Singers, which included a young singer named Richie Furay, and the Company, a folk-rock group that toured Canada, where Stills met Squires guitarist Neil Young. In California Stills recruited the relocated Furay and Young to form Buffalo Springfield and make his first international splash as the composer, singer and guitarist of the socially conscious 'For What It's Worth' (1967). But the Springfield dissolved after two years.

A jam session at the home of Joni Mitchell united Stills and former Byrd David Crosby with Hollies singer Graham Nash. As Crosby, Stills & Nash (pictured left), the trio made a landmark appearance at Woodstock in 1969, and their eponymous debut album from the same year, featuring 'Marakesh Express' and 'Suite: Judy Blue Eyes', became an international smash. The band added Neil Young for the second album *Déjà Vu* (1970), and have continued to perform together in various combinations into the twenty-first century.

Along the way Stills branched off with projects like the *Manassas* albums with another former Byrd, Chris Hillman. *Manassas* allowed Stills to show his songwriting mastery in hard rock and Latin genres as well as acoustic and country rock. Stills' first two solo albums spawned the hits 'Love the One You're With' and 'Change Partners' (both 1970). As a guitarist Stills was notorious for wild experimentation, and CSNY's sound is identifiable for the rich acoustic guitars utilizing D5 (D-A-D-D-A-D) and Drop D tunings as well as the iconic 'Suite: Judy Blue Eyes' with its E-E-E-E-B-E tuning. Stills' solos on songs like the CSNY hit 'Woodstock' (1970) and the bluesy solo turn 'Black Queen' (1970) show the fire in the playing of this soft-rock superstar.

TERRY KATH

CHICAGO'S PARAGON

Terry Kath (1946–78) was the guitarist and a founding member of the jazz-rock ensemble Chicago Transit Authority (soon shortened to Chicago), which, like their contemporaries Blood, Sweat & Tears, brought a jazzy, horn-based sound to hard rock with their early albums, before settling into a superstardom built around anthemic pop ballads. Early on, however, it was the virtuoso playing and guttural blues singing of Kath that helped define the band's unique sound.

Kath grew up in Chicago, playing bass and guitar in local bands in the early and mid-Sixties. Towards the end of the decade he joined his pal, saxophonist Walter Parazaider, and two other horn players in a big band of serious songwriter/instrumentalists, including keyboardist Robert Lamm and bassist Peter Cetera. The Chicago Transit Authority's first (eponymous) album from 1969 was a smash, driven by Kath's self-styled masterpiece 'Introduction', his rhythmic acoustic strumming on 'Beginnings', his inspired wailing on the cover of 'I'm A Man' and his Hendrix-like adventurousness on 'Free Form Guitar'. (Kath knew and admired Hendrix, who famously told Parazaider, 'Your guitar player is better than me'.) The follow-up *Chicago II* (1970) was an even bigger smash, with Kath blazing a fiery solo on the hit '25 or 6 to 4' and perhaps initiating the group's appeal as a ballad band with his vocals on the popular make-out classic 'Colour My World'.

Kath most often played a Gibson SG or a Fender Strat and used multiple effects boxes, including a wah-wah pedal that he used to great effect, along with his vocals, on the *Chicago*

III (1971) social commentary 'Dialogue'. Kath was a major part of the first seven Chicago albums, but was known to be unhappy in 1978 and working on a solo album. He would not live to see its release, however. At a party in January 1978, Kath, a gun aficionado, was pointing a handgun to his head and pulling the trigger, reassuring friends, 'Don't worry, it's not loaded'. But Kath was mistaken, and he died from a self-inflicted head wound a week shy of his thirty-second birthday.

MICK RONSON

BOWIE'S BACKING

In the 25 years before cancer ended his life at the age of 46 Mick Ronson (1946–93) became a guitar icon through his seminal work as part of David Bowie's Spiders From Mars band, work that would lead to production and performance assignments with artists such as Ian Hunter, Lou Reed and Morrissey, as well as American roots rockers such as Bob Dylan and John Mellencamp.

Ronson played in local bands throughout the mid-Sixties in his native Hull and endured a failed stint trying to establish himself in London before returning to Hull and joining the Rats. In 1970 former Rat John Cambridge came back to Hull to recruit Ronson as guitarist in David Bowie's backup band. The band, originally called the Hype, at points included producer Tony Visconti and keyboardist Rick Wakeman. Ronson's flair for arranging and playing grounded Bowie (pictured below) as he developed his outsized persona on the early albums *Space Oddity* (1969), *The Man Who Sold The World* (1970), *Hunky Dory* (1971) and *The Rise And Fall Of Ziggy Stardust And The Spiders From Mars* (1972).

Ronson's playing and arranging brought him the producer's hat in 1972 for Lou Reed's *Transformer* with Bowie, as well as the unlikely leap to work on American country-rock group Pure Prairie League's *Bustin' Out* (1972), on which Ronson contributed string-ensemble arrangements along with guitar and vocals. Ronson played on Bowie's *Aladdin Sane* and *Pin Ups* (both 1973) but

left Bowie after the 'Farewell Concert' in 1973. In the ensuing years Ronson released three solo albums. The first, *Slaughter On 10th Avenue* (1974), featured Ronson's best-known solo piece, 'Only After Dark'.

After a brief stint with Mott The Hoople, Ronson worked steadily with former Hoople singer Ian Hunter. Ronson also was part of Dylan's Rolling Thunder Revue and worked on records by Elton John, T-Bone Burnett and Roger McGuinn. His last high-profile live performance was his appearance at The Freddie Mercury Tribute Concert in 1992.

For his work with Bowie, Ronson favoured a stripped-paint Gibson Les Paul and Marshall amp. Thereafter he often used a Fender Telecaster. Ronson died of liver cancer in April 1993.

RICK NIELSEN

NO CHEAP TRICKS HERE

As lead guitarist and primary songwriter of the rock band Cheap Trick, Rick Nielsen (b. 1946) fired the band's melting pot of pop melodies and punk energy. Nielsen also became a highly coveted session player in the 1970s. With his legendary guitar collection (numbering over 250) and a unique stage wardrobe featuring bowties and baseball caps, Nielsen's style made him one of the true rock iconoclasts.

Richard Nielsen was born in December 1946 in Rockford, Illinois. He took up guitar in the wake of the British Invasion, and had a short-lived record deal in the late Sixties with his band Fuse. Later, Nielsen and bassist Tom Petersson started Cheap Trick with drummer Bun E. Carlos and vocalist Randy 'Xeno' Hogan. In 1974, Hogan left the band and was replaced by Robin Zander.

Epic signed the group in 1976, and released its self-titled album in February 1977. Neither the debut nor their next two albums, *In Color* (1977) and *Heaven Tonight* (1978), were well received at the time, although *Heaven Tonight*, with its teen anthem 'Surrender', is now considered by many to be the group's best album. But Cheap Trick's real strength was their live show, and on tour in Japan in 1978 they recorded the breakthrough live album *At Budokan*. By the spring of 1979 it was No. 4 on the US Top 40 album charts, fuelled by the single 'I Want You To Want Me' (originally on *In Color*), which was written by Nielsen.

Cheap Trick would endure many ups and downs, but Nielsen's reputation would continue to build. He performed on Alice Cooper's *From The Inside* (1978), Hall & Oates' *Along The Red Ledge* (1978) and, along with Carlos, the sessions for John Lennon's *Double Fantasy* (1980) album. His work has turned up frequently on American TV shows such as 'That 70's Show'. Nielsen wrote, and performed with Cheap Trick, the theme for the comedy news show 'The Colbert Report'.

Nielsen's unique guitars, including a five-necked monster, have been stars of the band's shows. Nielsen has collaborated with guitar manufacturer Hamer on several 'themed' guitars, including the Rockford and Doctor models.

JOE WALSH

THE OUTRAGEOUS EAGLE

Joe Walsh (b. 1947) was born in Kansas and spent his childhood in Ohio and his high-school years in New Jersey before returning to Ohio to attend college at Kent State. He played bass in various bands before adopting guitar for a stint in the local group the Measles from 1965 to 1969. That led to a spot with Cleveland-based trio the James Gang, with whom Walsh appeared on the band's debut *Yer Album* (1969). The follow-up *James Gang Rides Again* produced the rock-radio staple 'Funk #49' (1970).

Walsh found the James Gang confining and relocated to Colorado, forming the group Barnstorm and hitting big with the solo follow-up *The Smoker You Drink, The Player You Get* (1973) and its smash hit 'Rocky Mountain Way'. In the wake of expanding solo success Walsh adopted an even bigger profile in 1976 as the new guitarist in the Eagles, replacing Bernie Leadon and helping change the band's sound from mellow West-Coast country to the harder rock of *Hotel California* (1976).

Walsh continued to impact the Eagles until their breakup in 1980, all the while releasing his own solo material, including *But Seriously Folks* (1978), which included his brilliant comic statement on the rock life, 'Life's Been Good'. In the Eighties Walsh maintained a lower profile, dealing with alcohol addiction, and returned to touring with Ringo Starr in 1989. With the Eagles' reunion in 1994, Walsh returned to the road and the studio for the band's live *Hell Freezes Over* set and 2007 studio album *Long Road Out Of Eden*.

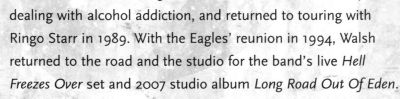

Walsh's rhythm-guitar playing defines classic funk-rock and his fluid lead lines on tracks like 'Life In The Fast Lane' and 'Hotel California' are textbook meldings of rock and soul. Combined with an outrageous personality that has made him a staple on American comedy radio and TV shows, his considerable talents helped Walsh forge one of the best-known and most endearing personalities in rock. But his comic freewheeling personality belies his skills as one of the most tasteful, precise and accomplished guitarists in rock.

PETER FRAMPTON

LEGEND COMES ALIVE

Peter Frampton (b. 1950) rode a slow-developing wave of popularity that transported him from British teen idol to international pop megastar, only to see the wave crash in a show-business wipeout of legendary proportions. In the ensuing 30 years, Frampton has managed to mix a fair amount of successes with disappointments while navigating much calmer musical seas.

Frampton got his first guitar at the age of eight and took classical lessons. But by the age of 10, he was playing rock'n'roll and by his mid-teens was in the Preachers, who were produced and managed by Bill Wyman. By 1966 he was lead singer and guitarist in the Herd, with whom he scored a handful of British hits. In early 1969, at 18, he co-founded Humble Pie. In two years Frampton recorded five albums with Humble Pie, leaving to concentrate on a solo career just as the band's *Rockin' The Fillmore* (1971) ascended the American charts.

Guesting on George Harrison's *All Things Must Pass* (1970), Frampton encountered an effects device, the talk box, for the first time. He released four solo albums between 1972 and 1975, and his buzz began to build through non-stop touring. His show, as recorded at San Francisco's Winterland in 1975, was released in February 1976 as *Frampton Comes Alive!*. Within months, Peter Frampton was the biggest pop-rock star in the world.

The album became the biggest-selling live LP of all time. But Frampton was pressured to record a follow-up quickly. The result, *I'm In You* (1977), was deemed a disappointment in the wake of *FCA!*. Then, the film *Sergeant Pepper's Lonely Hearts Club Band* (1978), in which Frampton starred, flopped. The crash was complete when Frampton suffered a near-fatal car accident in the Bahamas and an ensuing bout with drug dependency. Frampton was never able to regain the popularity that attended *Frampton Comes Alive!*, though he would continue to record and tour, sometimes in support of pals like David Bowie and Ringo Starr. Frampton, however, never lost his dedication to guitar. In 2006 he released an all-instrumental work, *Fingerprints*. In 2007 it won the Grammy for Best Pop Instrumental Album. A new album entitled *Thank You Mr Churchill* was released in 2010.

DAVEY JOHNSTONE

VERSATILITY AND COMMAND

Davey Johnstone (b. 1951) rocketed to fame with the Rocket Man himself, Elton John (pictured below), as the former Reg Dwight exploded on the music scene in the early Seventies, rising from thoughtful love balladeer to raucous glam rocker/showman to international pop-music institution and legend. Except for a short period from the late Seventies to early Eighties, Johnstone always occupied the nucleus of John's band, along with drummer Nigel Olsson and bassist Dee Murray (pictured below), who died in 1992.

Johnstone was a busy studio acoustic guitarist when he was asked to join the British folk group Magna Carta. Johnstone was part of the band for three albums, during the recording of which he played a wide variety of instruments including guitar, mandolin, sitar and dulcimer. Magna Carta producer Gus Dudgeon asked Johnstone to play on a self-titled 1970 solo album by a new artist, Bernie Taupin. Taupin's collaborator, John, then invited Johnstone to play on his 1971 album *Madman Across The Water*. Johnstone found a sonic niche for himself on the prolific John's piano-based arrangements, ranging from *Madman*'s moody atmospherics to the spacey effects of *Honky Chateau*'s 'Rocket Man', to his signature crunch on 'Saturday Night's Alright For Fighting' (*Goodbye Yellow Brick Road*).

Johnstone did work with other acts occasionally, including future wife Kiki Dee, Joan Armatrading, Leo Sayer, Alice Cooper, the Who, Meat Loaf, Stevie Nicks, Yvonne Elliman, Bob Seger, Rod Stewart, George Jones, Belinda Carlisle and Vonda Shepherd. The who's who list is a testament to Johnstone's versatility and command of genre. Johnstone also released a solo album, 1973's *Smiling Face*, and has created the *Warpipes* project with other John alumni and a well-received album of acoustic instrumentation, 1998's *Crop Circles*, with ex-John and Hellecasters guitarist John Jorgenson. In 1996, Johnstone released a video of instructional guitar called *Davey Johnstone: Starlicks Master Sessions*, on which he plays a wide variety of Elton John classics, joined by Billy Trudel on vocals and Bob Birch on bass. In 2009, Johnstone played his 2,000th show as a member of the Elton John band.

TiM FARRiSS

MASTER OF THE UNDERSTATED

Tim Farriss (b. 1957) was born in Perth, Western Australia, and found fame with his brothers Andrew and Jon as a member of the band INXS, originally known as the Farriss Brothers Band. The oldest of the Farriss children, Tim was classically trained on the guitar for four years, starting at the age of eight. He attended high school in Sydney, where he met Kirk Pengilly (pictured below), the future guitarist and saxophonist of INXS. Eventually adding lead singer Michael Hutchence (pictured below), the band released its debut album, *INXS*, in 1980. The album featured 'Just Keep Walking', their first Australian hit single. Its follow-up, 1981's *Underneath The Colours* (produced by Richard Clapton), became a hit album in Australia.

The band followed with *Shabooh Shoobah* (1982), which featured the single 'The One Thing', their first Top 30 hit in the United States. With *The Swing* in 1984, the band built its international reputation, as 'Original Sin' became their first No. 1 single and an international hit. 'Original Sin' didn't fare as well in the UK, and INXS had only marginal success on the charts until 1986 with the release of *Listen Like Thieves*, on which the band displayed its Rolling Stones and Chic influences. In the US the second single, 'What You Need', became a Top 5 Billboard hit, bringing INXS their first breakout US success.

Farriss became known as a versatile guitarist who could move smoothly from the funk-influenced style of INXS's early works and the crunchy grooves of their hard-rock material; a master of the

understated, tasty riff more than the flamboyant solo. Farriss suffered from bone disease and injuries throughout his life, but always recovered to lend his defining guitar work to the band throughout their 25-year history.

An avid sportsman, Farriss made a fishing video in 1989 called 'Fish In Space', a playful reference to Michael Hutchence's film *Dogs In Space*. In 1996 Farriss released a sample CD, *Deep Inside*, which featured over 1,000 samples of various instruments. INXS gained new attention in 2007 with a reality based TV show 'Rock Star: INXS', in which they chose a new lead singer.

STEVE LUKATHER

TOTO TO THRILLING LICKS

Although his band of high-school buddies achieved international fame under the name Toto, Steve Lukather (b. 1957), session guitarist extraordinaire, has had to struggle under the same suspicion under which his bandmates have toiled: that the whole may add up to less than the sum of its parts. For Toto, despite achieving wide fame with singles like 'Rosanna' and 'Africa' in the early Eighties, was first and foremost a band of extraordinarily talented and seasoned studio players who emerged in the Los Angeles recording scene of the Seventies.

Lukather, a native of LA, first played drums and keyboards but switched to guitar when he discovered the Beatles as a boy. In high school he met drummer Jeff Porcaro and keyboardist Steve Porcaro, as well as keyboardist/singer David Paich, son of veteran film and TV arranger/ conductor Marty Paich. All were becoming active in the burgeoning LA studio scene, and the Porcaro brothers were crucial to Lukather's obtaining session work and burnishing his reputation as a multi-style studio guitarist. By the time he was asked to join the Porcaros, Paich, bassist David Hungate and singer Bobby Kimball in Toto, Lukather had already recorded and toured with Boz Skaggs. In the coming years he would play on hundreds of hit records, including releases by Leo Sayer, Boz Scaggs, Alice Cooper, Barbra Streisand, the Pointer Sisters, Cher and Cheap Trick – in the Seventies alone.

Toto garnered a lot of buzz with their debut album and exploded two years later with *Toto IV* (1982), but after that the band settled into a long run with a mostly international cult following. With a breakout performance on Michael Jackson's *Thriller* (1982), he became a superstar guitarist and took on a larger role with Toto, co-writing most of the group's songs and taking over lead vocals, along with his constant stream of studio gigs. He launched a solo career in the late Eighties and won a Grammy for his collaboration with Larry Carlton, *No Substitutions* (2001). Toto continued to tour internationally, but the band couldn't regain its early popularity in the US, In 2008, Lukather left Toto, and the band dissolved. He continues to work on solo projects and perform on other artists' recordings. Lukather plays his own MusicMan signature model 'Luke', which incorporates his signature EMG pickup system.

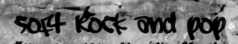

STEVE STEVENS

BILLY IDOL TO GUITAR IDOL

Brooklyn's Steve Stevens (b. 1959) grew up as a fan of progressive rock and honed his chops by studying guitar at Manhattan's LaGuardia High School of Performing Arts. He worked the Long Island and Manhattan club scenes with bands and eventually was hired for session work, including tracks for ex-Kiss drummer Peter Criss. But Steven's star really began to shine when he met former Generation X frontman Billy Idol (pictured below) in the early Eighties.

With Stevens' flamboyant shredding jumping out of his songs and videos, Idol's new solo works became smashes, as albums such as 1982's *Billy Idol* and 1983's *Rebel Yell* drove the new music channel MTV. Idol and Stevens collaborated on a third album, 1986's *Whiplash Smile*, another big hit, after which Stevens embarked on a solo career.

Stevens' work with Idol led to work with Michael Jackson (*Bad*), Ric Ocasek (*This Side Of Paradise*), Thompson Twins (*Here's To Future Days*) and Robert Palmer *Don't Explain*), and he won a Grammy for work with keyboardist Harold Faltermeyer on 'Top Gun Anthem' from the Tom Cruise film. From 1992 to 1994 Stevens worked with ex-Mötley Crüe singer Vince Neil on the album *Exposed*, which featured the cuts 'Sister Of Pain', 'Can't Have Your Cake' and 'You're Invited But Your Friend Can't Come'.

Stevens eventually got back to his prog-rock roots, working with bassist Tony Levin and drummer Terry Bozzio in the Bozzio Levin Stevens group, recording 1997's *Black Light Syndrome* and 2000's *Situation Dangerous*. Stevens reunited with Idol in 1999 for a series of tours across the USA and in Australia. They appeared in 2002 in an episode of 'VH1 Storytellers', which was subsequently released on CD and DVD. Stevens also appeared in the Billy Idol episode of VH1's 'Behind The Music'. Stevens, influenced by the great flamenco guitarist Paco deLucia, also recorded a solo release, *Flamenco A Go-Go*, which he recorded in his home studio. Stevens' renewed collaboration with Idol also resulted in Billy Idol's *Devil's Playground* (2005) with keyboardist Derek Sherinian. This was the first album to feature the trio since *Whiplash Smile*. Stevens recorded his latest album *Memory Crash* for Magna Carta Records in 2008.

THE EDGE
SEARCHING FOR SONIC MEANING

A master of texture and sonic architecture based on a minimalist style of playing, as opposed to contemporaries who sought impenetrable technique and unrestrained speed, Dave Evans (b. 1961) created a signature sound for a signature band, U2, just as surely as he created for himself a new identity – the Edge.

The Edge grew up in Dublin. He took piano and guitar lessons and often performed with his brother Dick while attending St. Andrew's National School. Later at Mount Temple Comprehensive School they answered an advertisement posted by drummer Larry Mullen, Jr., seeking musicians to form a band. At the initial practice in Mullen's kitchen the group featured Mullen on drums, Paul Hewson (Bono) on lead vocals, Dave and Dick Evans on guitar and Adam Clayton, a friend of the Evans brothers, on bass. Soon after, the group chose the name Feedback. Mostly they covered versions of songs they knew.

Along the way Dave Evans became the Edge. Exactly how this happened has taken on the mythic proportions of John Lennon's vision of a man on a flaming pie. At various times the moniker was said to have been inspired by the Evans nose, his overall angular features or his propensity to show off his fearlessness of high places by walking close to the edge of precarious perches. Whatever the source, it was not yet clear that U2 had an edge that would carry them to stratospheric heights.

Feedback became the Hype and then U2, a name they 'disliked least' among several possibilities, and became a four-piece with Dick Evans' departure. After winning a talent show in Limerick and landing manager Paul McGuiness, U2 released a pair of Ireland-only singles before signing with Island Records. The band's initial release *Boy* (1980), produced by Steve Lillywhite, won positive reviews, but the follow-up, *October* (1981), reflecting an immersion in spiritual themes, was a misfire. Then in 1984 the band released *War*, which contained

'Sunday Bloody Sunday' and 'New Year's Day'. Soon, U2 were gaining international attention for their striking sound, passionate lyrics and charismatic frontman, Bono.

U2 were looking for a new sound, however, and the Edge's interest in the unconventional work of Brian Eno and his engineer Daniel Lanois led to the pair's involvement with the band's biggest album to date. *The Unforgettable Fire* (1984) spawned the hit 'Pride (In the Name of Love)' and, helped by MTV, solidified U2's following in the US. The band's riveting performance at Live Aid in 1985 further expanded their worldwide audience. On tour in 1986 U2 developed songs for an album that would confront America's place, for better or worse, in the world. *The Joshua Tree* (1987) became the fastest-selling album in British chart history, and was No. 1 for nine weeks in the United States, winning the band their first two Grammy Awards. The ensuing tour spawned the film and album *Rattle And Hum* (1988), which wowed fans and divided critics. The band decamped to ponder another new direction at the end of the Eighties.

Throughout the Nineties and into the twenty-first century, U2 continued a phenomenal pattern of releasing albums (*Achtung Baby*, *Zooropa*, *Pop*) that were accompanied by critical praise and followed by tours that grew ever more elaborate in an attempt to comment on the superficiality of modern life, art and media. After each cycle the band would attempt to reinvent itself or its sound. It is in part this obsession with freshness, along with a commitment to social justice and the core talents of the band, that established U2 as one of the greatest bands in rock history, as they soldiered on with *All That You Can't Leave Behind* (2000) and *How To Dismantle An Atomic Bomb* (2004). The band released *No Line on the Horizon* in 2008 and launched the U2 360° Tour in 2009, continuing into to 2010.

Crucial to this achievement has been the Edge's search for sonic meaning as he crafted a guitar sound with delays, reverbs and a minimalist approach to playing that complemented the passion, pain and joy embedded in U2's music. Just as he salvaged the sessions for *Achtung Baby* when he came up with the chord progression for the song 'One', throughout U2's career it has been his dedication to artistic growth that has pushed the band to new sonic destinations.

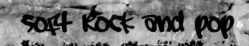

LENNY KRAVITZ

RETRO ROCKER AND TRENDSETTER

Producer-performer Lenny Kravitz (b. 1964) has explored multiple genres during his 25-year career as a music star, but has often been thought of as married to retro styles. Born in New York, Kravitz was raised in Los Angeles. His parents, a television producer and actress, were well connected in show business. Kravitz decided to pursue rock'n'roll while in high school. Heavily influenced by Prince, Kravitz at first patterned his style and approach directly after Prince and became known as Romeo Blue.

In the late Eighties, Kravitz moved back to New York and began looking to classic rockers for inspiration. Kravitz inked a recording and issued his debut release, *Let Love Rule* (1989). The title track became a hit single and video, and Kravitz gained a reputation as a trendsetter. He began to compose for other artists, writing Madonna's 'Justify My Love'.

Kravitz's work in the Nineties included: *Mama Said* (1992), which included the funk rocker 'Always On The Run' (a collaboration with Guns N' Roses guitarist Slash) and the soul ballad 'It Ain't Over 'Til It's Over'; 1993's *Are You Gonna Go My Way*, which made Kravitz an arena headliner and media star; and 1998's *5*, which included the biggest hit of his career, 'Fly Away', and the hit remake of the Guess Who's 'American Woman'.

In the twenty-first century, Kravitz continued to record and branched out with a design company. He recorded a funky version of John Lennon's 'Cold Turkey' for Amnesty International's 2007 benefit compilation *Instant Karma*. Kravitz was returned in 2008 with *It Is Time For A Love Revolution*. Kravitz released *Negrophilia* in 2010, and was scheduled to open for U2 on several 2010 tour dates. Kravitz's first guitar was a Fender Jazzmaster. 'I'd always wanted a Les Paul', he said in 2002. 'And then my dad got me the Jazzmaster, which was cool, but I always wanted a Les Paul. And so I traded it in when I had some money, a couple years later, and got my first Les Paul'. He has also used a Les Paul Goldtop with a Park amplifier, a Flying V that he designed and had built at Gibson, and a Les Paul Custom SG with three pickups, as well as an Epiphone Sorrento.

TREY ANASTASIO

STAR OF THE JAM SCENE

Princeton, New Jersey, native Trey Anastasio (b. 1964) became the star of the jam-band resurgence through his prolific work both with his band Phish and a multitude of side projects. Phish's touring and recording life spanned from 1983–2000, experienced a hiatus from 2000–03 and finally disolved in 2004. Inheriting the mantle and rabid following of the Grateful Dead and its departed guitar hero Jerry Garcia while attracting new fans to Phish's more complex, improvisatory works, Anastasio displayed a deep knowledge of rock, blues, jazz and country guitar styles.

As a boy Anastasio attended Princeton Day School, where he met future songwriting partner Tom Marshall. As a teenager, he helped his mother Dina write songs for children's records. At the University of Vermont, he teamed up with bassist Mike Gordon, drummer Jon Fishman and guitarist Jeff Holdsworth (later replaced by keyboardist Page McConnell) to form Phish. Anastasio was suspended for a year after breaking into the school's science building and stealing body parts for a prank. Transferring to Goddard College, he studied composition while he and the band developed Phish's early material.

Phish developed its loyal following by combining progressive rock-influenced compositions with a genial, inventive stage show that encouraged trading taped copies of performances and included

crowd-pleasing departures such as covers of Beatles and Queen tunes and a much-discussed detour into bluegrass. Constant touring helped the band's sound develop into highly focused works like *Rift* (1993) and on to more improvisational works such as *The Story Of The Ghost* (1997) and *The Siket Disc* (1998), both developed from hours of recordings of the band jamming. Anastasio has always played hollow-body electrics built by his friend and former audio technician Paul Languedoc. Since the dissolution of Phish, he has appeared onstage with many artists, including Phil Lesh & Friends, reaffirming Anastasio's allegiance to the legacy of the Grateful Dead and co-founder and guitarist Jerry Garcia. Anastasio ran afoul of the law as a result of drug use in 2007, and was sidelined for part of 2008. But the ever-expanding community of Phish fans that he helped create thrives online. Phish reunited in 2009 with shows in the US, and the band toured throughout 2009.

alternative and indie

Although its roots lie in late Seventies punk, indie and alternative rock have broadened to embrace such a diversity of guitar styles as to render labels irrelevant, particularly when many indie and alternative acts have crossed over into the mainstream and sold millions of records. The unifying factor between the guitarists in this category is perhaps a certain mindset, an attitude likely to regard the term 'guitar hero' with suspicion. For the majority of the musicians here, the guitar is a tool that serves the song; the effect achieved by the music, not the technical skill of the player, is of paramount importance.

TOM VERLAINE

EXPERIMENTER EXTRAORDINAIRE

A crucial figure in New York's late Seventies new-wave scene, Tom Verlaine (b. 1949) was born Thomas Miller in New Jersey. At an early age, he learned piano before switching to saxophone, inspired by John Coltrane. He took up guitar in his teens and began forging his own style, searching for new ways of expressing himself on the instrument.

At boarding school, Verlaine met kindred spirit Richard Hell, and in 1973 they formed the short-lived Neon Boys. The band became Television a few months later when Verlaine found second guitarist Richard Lloyd. Due to friction with Verlaine, Hell left to found the Heartbreakers. In 1975, Television began playing legendary New York venues Max's Kansas City and CBGB's, where the city's new-wave movement began to ferment. Verlaine briefly dated punk poetess Patti Smith. The band released their first single, 'Little Johnny Jewel', a tribute to Iggy Pop, independently in 1975. For the recording, Verlaine plugged his guitar straight into the mixing desk.

Television's debut album *Marquee Moon* (1977) was hailed as a masterpiece. After a disappointing follow-up, *Adventure* (1978), the band split up amidst musical and personal differences. Television's sound was characterized by dual interlocking guitars heard to stunning effect on the epic 'Marquee Moon'. The nominal roles of rhythm (Lloyd) and lead (Verlaine) were largely equivalent, with the backing as vital as the solo instrument. Influences came from twin-guitar bands Love, Quicksilver Messenger Service, Buffalo Springfield and the Rolling Stones.

Verlaine launched a solo career with *Tom Verlaine* (1979), which continued in a similar vein. Later albums showcased his sparkling guitar work, highlighted by a fine solo on 'Ancient Egypt' from *The Wonder* (1990) and the all-instrumental *Warm And Cool* (1992). Television reformed for a third, eponymous album in 1992 and have performed together occasionally since.

Verlaine has consistently sought unconventional guitar sounds. He favours Fender guitars and his use of the company's Jazzmaster and Jaguar models in Television's early days inspired Thurston Moore, Kevin Shields and John Frusciante to do likewise.

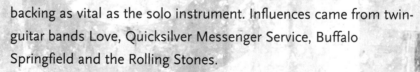

BERNARD SUMNER
RIDING THE NEW WAVE

New-wave guitarist Bernard Sumner (b. 1956) was born in Salford, Manchester. Seeing the Sex Pistols in Manchester in June 1976 inspired Sumner and Peter Hook to acquire their first instruments, guitar and bass respectively. Originally called Warsaw, later Joy Division, they recruited drummer Stephen Morris and singer Ian Curtis for their band, making some self-produced records before joining local independent label Factory. In-house producer Martin Hannett transformed Joy Division from an ordinary punk outfit into one of the most influential groups of all time.

The debut album *Unknown Pleasures* (1979) was edgy and atmospheric, Sumner's understated guitar adding texture and leaving space rather than seeking to dominate; 'She's Lost Control' is one example among many. Hailed as a classic by the critics, the album made an immediate impact on emerging bands like Echo & the Bunnymen, the Cure and U2. More recently, Joy Division's influence can be heard on Editors and Interpol.

Closer (1980) refined Joy Division's sound into a more stately affair, with Sumner's synthesizer lending extra gravitas. Shortly before its release, Curtis committed suicide. The others continued as New Order, adding Gillian Gilbert on keyboards, which gave the band a more electronic edge. Their debut album *Movement* (1981) saw Sumner emerge as lead singer and lyricist. New Order gradually freed themselves from the shadow of their previous incarnation to embrace the influence of the New York dance scene. *Power, Corruption And Lies* (1982) first showcased the pioneering crossover between dance, electronic music and rock which was to be their enduring

trademark and which proved almost as influential as the music of Joy Division. Their seventh album *Get Ready* (2001) returned the band to guitar-based rock. In between albums, Sumner worked with Johnny Marr as Electronic. Sumner's emphasis was primarily on rhythm, often leaving the bass or synthesizer to provide melody, as on 'Regret' from *Republic* (1993). He favoured a Gibson SG Standard (without vibrola) and also used a Shergold Masquerader and a Vox Phantom. Sumner served as musical director and arranger for both Joy Division and New Order. Sumner is currently the lead vocalist of the band Bad Lieutenant, which formed in 2007.

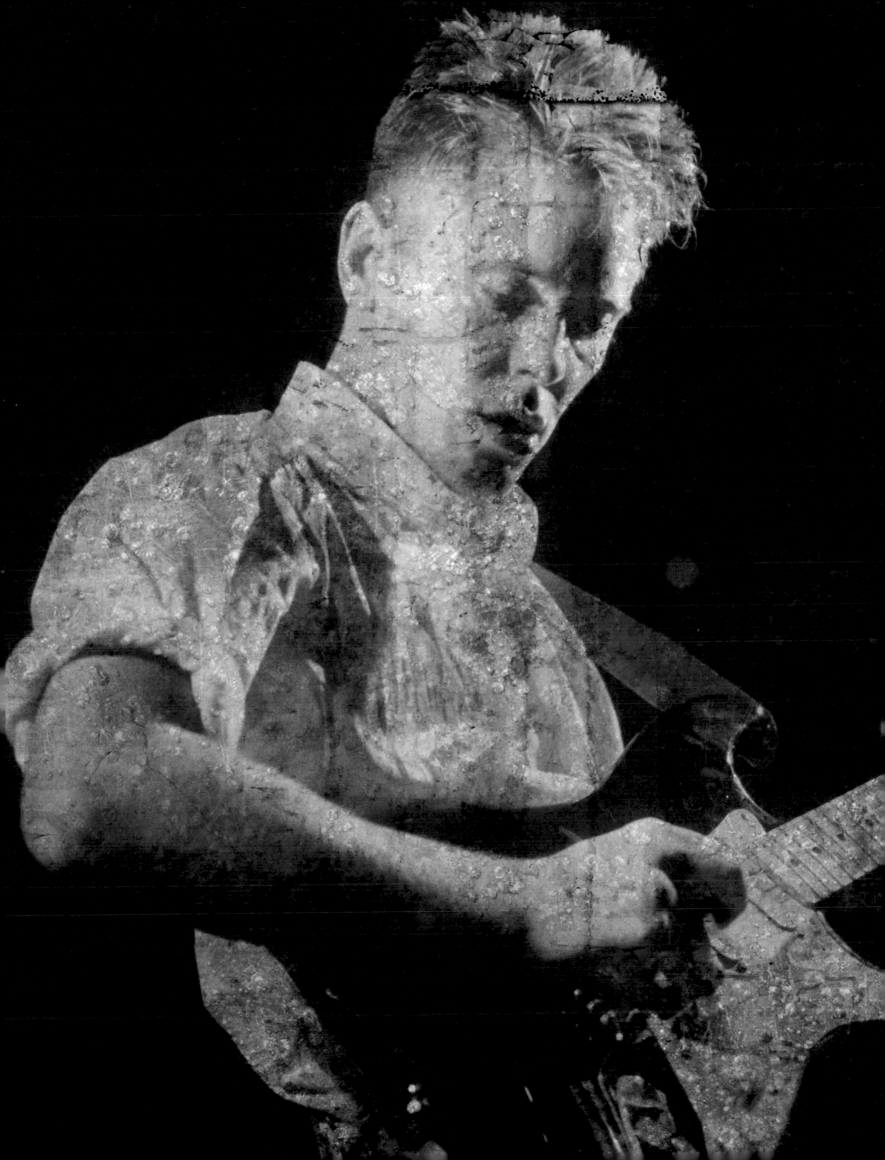

PETER BUCK
AVOIDING ROCK CLICHES

Alternative-rock guitarist Peter Buck (b. 1956) was born in Berkeley, California. After dropping out of college, he moved to Athens, Georgia, where he met singer Michael Stipe (pictured below) while working in a record shop. The pair discovered that they had similar tastes in music: punk rock, Patti Smith and Television. Together with Mike Mills (bass) and Bill Berry (drums), they formed R.E.M.. After achieving some popularity locally they recorded a single, 'Radio Free Europe', independently. The record was followed by an EP, 'Chronic Town', on the larger indie label IRS.

Debut album *Murmur* (1983) established R.E.M.'s alternative credentials, with the band deliberately avoiding what they saw as rock clichés. Buck's clear, bright guitar deftly added texture without seeking to dominate the production. His early, arpeggiated style was influenced by the Byrds' Roger McGuinn and was notable again on *Reckoning* (1984).

Buck remains most commonly associated with Rickenbacker guitars, particularly the black 'Jetglo' 360 model. 'Feeling Gravity's Pull' from the *Fables Of The Reconstruction* (1985) album featured an ominous chromatic guitar figure from Buck amidst its folk-rock vibe. *Life's Rich Pageant* (1986) was a more direct rock record, while *Document* (1987) was the band's most conventional album so far with Buck contributing bursts of angry guitar and taking a rare solo on 'Strange'.

R.E.M. became one of the first American alternative bands to cross over into the mainstream, and their major-label debut *Green* (1988) saw them balance experimentation and commercial appeal. *Out Of Time* (1991) was guitar-light but included 'Country Feedback', an innovative combination of the guitar styles of its title. The effect was heard again on 'Sweetness Follows' from *Automatic For The People* (1992). *Monster* (1994) was a leap into harder rock territory, powered by grunge-influenced guitars and glam-rock riffs. R.E.M. has continued as a three-piece since Bill Berry left in 1997. In 2006, Buck toured with Robyn Hitchcock and the Venus 3 as lead guitarist to support the band's first release, *Olé! Tarantula*. In 2008, Buck joined McCaughey and Steve Wynn in the band the Baseball Project.

alternative and indie

PAUL WELLER

THE MODFATHER

The enduring and iconic guitarist and songwriter Paul Weller (b. 1958) was born John William Weller in Woking, Surrey. He was a boyhood Beatles fanatic before discovering the Who and, through them, the mod movement. His father, who managed him for the majority of his career, bought his 12-year-old son an electric guitar for Christmas; at first neither realized that an amplifier was necessary too.

The Jam was formed at secondary school, and Weller played bass in early incarnations of the band. With Rick Buckler on drums and Bruce Foxton on bass, the Jam learned their trade by constant gigging. The band's arrival in London coincided with the burgeoning punk scene, and seeing the Sex Pistols live was a pivotal moment for Weller. While adopting punk's energy, the Jam remained distinct from the movement, not least because of the band's musical ability.

Weller's first role models on guitar were Pete Townshend and Dr. Feelgood's Wilko Johnson, whose dynamic rhythm-lead style impressed Weller. The Jam's best album *All Mod Cons* (1978) showcases Weller's maturing style and use of techniques ranging from power chords ('Billy Hunt'), to acoustic-electric work ('Fly') and backwards masking ('In The Crowd'). With the

Jam at the height of their popularity in 1982, Weller disbanded the outfit, citing frustration with the limitations of the three-piece format. His next project, the Style Council, a loose confederation of musicians based around Weller and keyboardist Mick Talbot, enabled him to explore more diverse musical areas, adding Latin and jazz to his repertoire. The Style Council folded in 1989, leaving Weller out of favour and without a recording contract. Influenced by the classic rock of Traffic, Free and Neil Young, Weller returned to basics by playing live and mounted an impressive comeback, beginning with his self-titled solo debut in 1992 and culminating in the million-selling *Stanley Road* (1995). Weller's influence was a rare point of unity between rivals Blur and Oasis. Weller's 2005 album *As Is Now* was a critical hit, and in 2006 he received the Lifetime Achievement Award at the BRIT Awards. His *Wake Up the Nation* was released in 2010.

THURSTON MOORE

SONIC YOUTH'S GROUNDBREAKER

Alternative experimental guitarist Thurston Moore (b. 1958) was born in Coral Gables, Florida. Inspired by New York's punk and new-wave scene, Moore moved to the city in 1977. While playing in a band called the Coachmen, he met Lee Ranaldo, an art student and member of Glenn Branca's avant-garde guitar orchestra. Moore assembled a band with bassist and future wife Kim Gordon, and along with Ranaldo they played on Branca's *Symphony No. 3* (1983).

The trio formed the core of Sonic Youth, which became part of New York's No Wave experimental scene. The band's early work was released on a variety of independent labels. *Bad Moon Rising* (1985) was their first album to be distributed widely in America, where it was largely ignored, and in the UK, where it received critical acclaim and encouraging sales. Switching to the influential independent label STT, Sonic Youth produced what is arguably their masterpiece *Daydream Nation* (1988) before moving to Geffen.

Sonic Youth are one of the most original guitar bands of all time due to the twin guitars of Moore and Ranaldo, which characterized their sound. In addition to Glenn Branca, they were influenced by Can, the Velvet Underground, the Patti Group and the Stooges as well as the speed and intensity of early Eighties hardcore punk bands Bad Brains, Minor Threat and Black Flag.

Moore relies on alternative tunings as part of his quest for new sounds. He and Ranaldo also make extensive use of prepared guitar – one that has had its timbre altered by placing objects, such as a drumstick, under the strings. In this way, cheap instruments like the Japanese Stratocasters, could produce amazing sounds. This experimentation resulted in their taking numerous instruments on tour, some of which have been specially prepared. Moore has used copious guitars, favouring Fender but also playing Gibson and Ibanez models. Sonic Youth were hailed as the godfathers of the American alternative scene, which went mainstream in the early Nineties, and were a major influence on Kurt Cobain and Nirvana. In 2007, Moore joined Original Silence for live-recorded *The First Original Silence*, followed by *The Second Original Silence* (2008).

BOB MOULD

GODFATHER OF GRUNGE

Alternative guitarist Bob Mould (b. 1960) was born in Malone, New York. Mould was 16 when, inspired by the Ramones, he took up guitar. While attending college in Minnesota in 1979 he founded Hüsker Dü, originally a hardcore punk/thrash band, with drummer Grant Hart and bassist Greg Norton.

The band's third album, *Zen Arcade* (1984), was a double album that broadened the noisy, guitar-driven style to embrace jazz, psychedelia, acoustic folk and pop. Hüsker Dü were instrumental in establishing alternative rock in America, making them one of the Eighties' most influential acts. Signing to major label Warner Brothers in 1986, they made *Candy Apple Grey* (1986) and another double set *Warehouse: Songs And Stories* (1987), which, although popular on college radio, failed to bring them to a wider audience. The band split in 1988 because of drug problems and the ongoing tensions between Mould and Hart, the group's other songwriter and vocalist.

Mould launched a solo career with *Workbook* (1989), which surprised many. His characteristic wall-of-guitars sound, which was to see him hailed as the godfather of grunge, was largely replaced by a more reflective, acoustic ambience. *Black Sheets Of Rain* (1991) returned him to familiar guitar-heavy terrain, which continued in Mould's new band Sugar, whose debut *Copper Blue* (1992) received widespread acclaim. Another power trio, Sugar were more accessible and melodic yet louder and angrier than Hüsker Dü, and Mould's guitars were very much to the fore. The mini-album *Beaster* (1993) was notable for the angst-ridden 'JC Auto' on which Mould's powerful playing achieved climactic momentum. For Sugar and his solo work, Mould

favoured an Eighties Fender Stratocaster. After *File Under: Easy Listening* (1994), he disbanded Sugar and resumed his solo career. He worked briefly as a pro-wrestling scriptwriter, before returning to music as performer and remixer. *DJ. Modulate* (2002) and *Body Of Song* (2005) added electronica to his rock template, while *Long Playing Grooves* (2002) was a full-on dance album released under the pseudonym LoudBomb. *District Line* was released in 2008, *Life and Times* the following year. A memoir was to be published in 2010.

KEVIN SHIELDS

MY BLOODY GENIUS

Alternative-rock guitarist Kevin Shields (b. 1963) was born in Queens, New York. When he was 10 the family relocated to Dublin, where he learned guitar as a teenager with Johnny Ramone as his role model. My Bloody Valentine came together in 1984. The band moved to Holland and then Berlin, where they recorded the mini-album *This Is Your Bloody Valentine* (1985). They reconvened in London the following year, going on to make three EPs, influenced by the Cramps and the Birthday Party. With Bilinda Butcher recruited as main vocalist, they made other recordings, but it was not until My Bloody Valentine signed to Creation Records in 1988 that they were allowed sufficient studio time to realize their vision.

After eight months of recording the band produced 'You Made Me Realise', an EP that brought them to wider attention and acclaim. The band followed up with *Isn't Anything* (1988). Influenced by the Jesus & Mary Chain, Dinosaur Jr. and the Cocteau Twins, the album defined My Bloody Valentine's idiosyncratic approach and established them as a major force in the British indie scene. Shields' onslaught of meticulously layered guitars was demonstrated on the single 'Feed Me With Your Kiss'. The band's wall of noise was complemented by a dreamy melodicism. Shields was a perfectionist in the studio, painstakingly assembling *Loveless* (1991), which consolidated their position as a leading indie band and inspired outfits like Ride, Chapterhouse, Slowdive and the short-lived shoe-gazing trend. It proved to be the last My Bloody Valentine album to date. Shields has continued to work as a producer and remixer.

Shields has customized the tremolo arms of his Fender Jaguar and Jazzmaster guitars to achieve his trademark sound. The process involves extending the tremolo arm, so that it sits high on the guitar for ease of operation and to allow for chord bending. This produces a warping effect, which initially caused some buyers of *Loveless* to return their vinyl copies. The thickness of his sound is achieved by using a reverse reverb effect. He plays at extremely high volume but does not make extensive use of effects pedals.

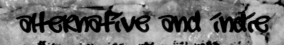

JOHNNY MARR

BONA FIDE BRITISH LEGEND

Indie guitar legend Johnny Marr (b. 1963) was born John Maher in Manchester, England to Irish Catholic parents. He grew up in a household where music was a constant fixture, and he recalled, 'I always had guitars, for as long as I could remember.' Guitar technique came easily to young Johnny, and he quickly mastered chord structures and progressions along with picking and fingering techniques.

As a teenager, he fell under the spell of Marc Bolan & T. Rex, which led him back to Howlin' Wolf. Marr went on to soak up an extensive range of influences, preferring American punk to its British counterpart, in particular Television, the Patti Smith Group and the Stooges' James Williamson. Intrigued by the guitar heroes of the Seventies like Keith Richards, Jimmy Page and Ritchie Blackmore, he was particularly taken with Irish bluesman Rory Gallagher. Inspiration came from English folk pickers Martin Carthy, Davey Graham and Bert Jansch. Also in the mix were Thin Lizzy, Neil Young, Nils Lofgren, Tom Petty, George Harrison and new wavers John McGeoch (Magazine, Siouxsie & the Banshees) and Pretenders guitarist James Honeyman-Scott.

Marr had been in various teenage bands before teaming up with singer and lyricist Steven Morrissey (pictured below) in 1982. They met when Marr called at Morrissey's house on the recommendation of a mutual acquaintance. The pair immediately struck up a songwriting partnership, and the Smiths were born. The band's ascent was rapid; in little more than a year they were on the charts with their second single, 'This Charming Man', ignited by Marr's exuberant, intricate riff played on a Fender Telecaster, not the 12-string Rickenbacker with which he mimed on 'Top Of The Pops' and in the video.

The Smiths became the most important and influential British indie group of the Eighties. Marr's music sometimes complemented and sometimes played counterpoint to Morrissey's frequently misunderstood lyrics.

Marr employed a diverse range of techniques to ensure that no two Smiths songs sounded the same. Highlights included the shimmering effect over the Bo Diddley shuffle on 'How Soon Is Now?'; the tumbling glam-rock intro to 'Panic'; the trebly, jangly opening of 'The Headmaster Ritual' from *Meat Is Murder* (1985), played on an Epiphone Cornet; the dynamic riffing of 'Bigmouth Strikes Again', and the wah-wah attack of 'The Queen Is Dead'. Marr aimed to be a modern guitar hero, serving the song rather than his ego. He took only two solos in the entire Smiths' canon, on the single 'Shoplifters Of The World Unite' and on 'Paint A Vulgar Picture' from *Strangeways, Here We Come* (1987).

Marr left the Smiths in 1987, frustrated with the direction of the group and exhausted by the demands of being the de facto manager. His first post-Smiths venture was controversial with the band's fans; 'The Right Stuff' was a collaboration with Bryan Ferry that adapted a Smiths' B-side, the bluesy instrumental 'Money Changes Everything'. He went on to work with many artists including Billy Bragg (pictured left, with whom he had guested in 1986), the Pet Shop Boys, Talking Heads, Kirsty MacColl, Beck and one of his heroes, Bert Jansch, on his album *Crimson Moon* (2000). He joined the The for *Mind Bomb* (1989) and *Dusk* (1992), with the latter in particular opening up new textures for the outfit's previously bleak sound.

In 1991 he formed the Mancunian supergroup Electronic with Bernard Sumner, an occasional pairing which produced three albums. In 2001, Marr put together his own band the Healers, handling lead vocals for the first time on *Boomslang* (2003). He became a member of US indie band Modest Mouse in 2006, appearing on the album *We Were Dead Before The Ship Even Sank* (2007), an American No. 1. In 2009 he began performing and recording with the Cribs, including the album *Ignore the Ignorant*.

Johnny Marr has acquired numerous guitars over the years. His 12-string Rickenbacker 330 once belonged to Pete Townshend and is one of three Rickenbackers, often used in the Smiths, which he owns. While in the The, he played a Fender Stratocaster and Telecaster. His other favourites are a 1959 Gibson ES-355, again frequently heard on Smiths records, and a 1959 Sunburst Les Paul. Marr was a role model for a younger generation of players. John Squire, Noel Gallagher and Bernard Butler have all given testament to his influence.

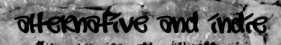

ADAM JONES

ALTERNATIVE ALL THE WAY

Alternative-metal guitarist Adam Jones (b. 1965) was born in Park Ridge, Illinois. He learned violin in elementary school, continuing with the instrument in high school before playing acoustic bass for three years in an orchestra and later teaching himself guitar by ear. Jones studied art and sculpture in Los Angeles before working in a Hollywood character shop sculpting models. His work appeared in several movies including *Ghostbusters 2* and *Predator 2*. He also worked on set design for various films.

In 1990, Jones formed Tool with Danny Carey (drums), Maynard James Keenan (vocals) and Paul D'Amour (bass), who was replaced in 1995 by Justin Chancellor. The band's recorded debut, the EP 'Opiate' (1992), was firmly in heavy-metal mode, but *Undertow* (1993), *Ænima* (1996), *Lateralus* (2001) and *10,000 Days* (2006) took the band in not so easily classifiable directions that have been described as art rock, alternative metal, progressive metal and psychedelic metal. The use of unpredictable time signatures, of which 'Schism' from *Lateralus* is a prime example, and their commitment to experimentation have resulted in Tool being hailed as standard bearers for the new prog rock. King Crimson, with whom the band has toured, were a major inspiration for Jones, along with Yes. Tool in turn have influenced alternative metal outfits System Of A Down, Breaking Benjamin and Deftones.

Jones employs multiple techniques: power chords, arpeggios, offbeat rhythms and minimalism. On Jambi', from *10,000 Days*, he played the solo on a talk box. Although wary of the overuse of effects, he has employed several, in particular the wah-wah, plus a flanger, digital delay and

volume pedal. He uses an electric hair remover in preference to an E-bow, claiming it produces a better sound. He favours Gibson Silverburst Les Paul Customs made between 1978 and 1985; he has also used a Gibson SG and is rumoured to have played a Fender Telecaster on *10,000 Days*. Jones utilizes his background in visual arts and film to create most of Tool's striking artwork and videos. On hiatus since 2008, Tool toured in 2009, headlining at Lollapalooza. They wrote songs for a new album throughout 2009 and 2010.

JOEY SANTIAGO

THE FORCE BEHIND THE PIXIES

Alternative-rock guitarist Joey Santiago (b. 1965) was born in Manila, Philippines, to a wealthy family, who emigrated to the United States when President Marcos declared martial law. The family eventually settled in Massachusetts. Joey first played guitar at the age of nine, becoming a fan of Seventies punk and David Bowie. At the University of Massachusetts, he met Black Francis (Charles Thompson) and they jammed together on guitar. On returning from a student exchange trip, Santiago dropped out of school and formed a band with Francis in January 1985. Bassist Kim Deal was recruited via a telling advertisement seeking someone into Peter, Paul & Mary and Hüsker Dü. Drummer David Lovering completed the line-up, which became the Pixies.

Securing a contract with British independent 4AD on the basis of their demo tapes, the Pixies debuted with the mini-album *Come On Pilgrim* (1987). The album utilized eight songs from the demos and established the band's powerful, guitar-driven sound. Santiago's innovative, angular

lead was evident on 'Holiday Song' and 'Vamos'. Their first full-length album *Surfer Rosa* (1988) was heavy and frenzied, while *Doolittle* (1989) was less raw and included some of their best-known songs, the poppy 'Here Comes Your Man' and ferocious opener 'Un Chien Andalou', which was distinguished by Santiago's chiming, churning guitar. He favoured the Gibson Les Paul but also used the company's ES-355. After two more albums the Pixies fell prey to internal tensions and disbanded in 1993.

Santiago maintained a good relationship with Francis, now known as Frank Black, and contributed lead guitar to several of his solo albums. He formed the Martinis with wife Linda Mallari, but the outfit only recorded one song in the Nineties and played live only occasionally; their debut album *Smitten* emerged in 2004. Santiago was influenced by jazz guitarists Joe Pass, Chet Atkins and Wes Montgomery as well as Jimi Hendrix and Iggy Pop. The Pixies were a force in late-Eighties and early Nineties alternative rock; Kurt Cobain was a great admirer. In 2006 Santiago began concentrating on film and commercial work, saying there would only be a new Pixies album 'if it happens in an organic manner'. He played a benefit concert in 2007 as part of the Martinis.

MIKE McCREADY

PEARL JAMMER

Alternative-rock guitarist Mike McCready (b. 1966) was born in Pensacola, Florida. His family moved to Seattle soon afterwards. He was 11 when he bought his first guitar and began to take lessons. In high school McCready formed a band that disintegrated after they were unsuccessful in obtaining a record contract in Los Angeles. Disillusioned, he did not pick up a guitar again for several months until inspired to resume playing by Stevie Ray Vaughan.

McCready was working with old friend and rhythm guitarist Stone Gossard when the pair were invited to participate in recording *Temple Of The Dog* (1991), a one-off project founded by Soundgarden singer Chris Cornell. McCready's four-minute-plus solo on 'Reach Down' remains one of his proudest achievements. Shortly after recording *Temple Of The Dog*, McCready and Gossard formed Pearl Jam with Eddie Vedder (lead vocals, guitar) and Jeff Ament (bass, pictured below). Their debut, *Ten* (1991), was lyrically dark, combining classic rock with an anthemic feel, informed by McCready's love of the blues in his prominent solos. *Ten* sold in excess of 15 million copies, establishing Pearl Jam as one of America's biggest rock acts.

Pearl Jam were associated with the Seattle grunge scene, which the band comfortably outlived, but were accused by their contemporaries of cashing in on the alternative rock boom. The band seemed uneasy with their own success and rebelled against music industry practices,

refusing to appear in music videos and boycotting the booking agency Ticketmaster. McCready fought his own battles against drug and alcohol addiction. He has participated in various side projects, including Mad Season, the Rockfords and UFO-tribute act Flight To Mars. Pearl Jam's eponymous eighth studio album was released in 2006, and its ninth studio album, *Backspacer*, in 2009.

Influenced by Neil Young, Jeff Beck, George Harrison, Jimmy Page, Joe Perry and Jimi Hendrix, Mike McCready has a reputation as a forceful blues guitarist. In live work, he hates to repeat himself, refusing to play the same solo twice and relishing improv. He is an energetic performer, sometimes soloing behind his head, Hendrix-style. He has used the Fender Stratocaster extensively along with the Gibson SG, Les Paul, Hummingbird acoustic and Flying V.

JEFF BUCKLEY

ECLECTIC BRILLIANCE

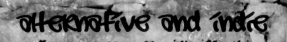

Alternative guitarist and singer Jeff Buckley (1966–97) was born in Anaheim, California. Jeff barely knew his father, singer-songwriter Tim Buckley, who died when he was eight. His mother, Mary Guibert, was a classically trained pianist and cellist, which meant that music was all around when Buckley was growing up. He started playing acoustic guitar at the age of six and received his first electric guitar at 13. His early influences were Led Zeppelin, Pink Floyd, Jimi Hendrix, the Who, and Kiss, later widening to embrace the progressive rock of Yes, Genesis and Rush, along with jazz-fusion guitarist Al Di Meola.

After graduating from high school, Buckley attended the Musicians Institute in Hollywood before working in a hotel and playing in a number of bands. He moved to New York City in 1990, where he continued his musical education, taking in Qawwali, the devotional music of Pakistan, Robert Johnson and hardcore punk. His first public appearance was at a tribute concert for his father in 1991, after which he joined future collaborator Gary Lucas in Gods And Monsters before opting to go solo. His performances at Manhattan's Sin-é club attracted intense record company attention and he signed with Columbia, who issued an EP of Buckley accompanying himself on a borrowed Fender Telecaster, 'Live at Sin-é', in 1993. Debut album *Grace* (1994) was remarkably confident, showcasing his songwriting ability and the amazing range of his voice. His eclectic guitar skills are evident on the closing tracks, where the hard-rock crunch of 'Eternal Life' is followed by the ethereal vibe of 'Dream Brother'. His favourite instrument was a Gibson Les Paul.

Buckley was writing songs and recording demos for the follow-up when he drowned in a tragic accident while swimming in a tributary of the Mississippi River in May 1997. Since then two albums have been issued: *Sketches For My Sweetheart The Drunk* (1998) featured unfinished studio material, and *Mystery White Boy* (2000) was a live compilation. *Grace* became a posthumous bestseller as Buckley's reputation mushroomed, with numerous artists covering his songs and Thom Yorke of Radiohead and Muse's Matthew Bellamy citing him as an influence.

KURT COBAIN
LEADING A GENERATION

Arguably the most important alternative guitarist of the Nineties, Kurt Cobain (1967–94) was born in Aberdeen, Washington. His parents divorced when he was seven, which had a traumatic effect on Cobain, tainting the remainder of his life. From an early age, he showed a keen interest in music, singing along to Beatles' songs on the radio. Given a guitar for his fourteenth birthday, he taught himself to play along to AC/DC and the Cars.

Cobain was influenced equally by hard rock, punk and pop, admiring Aerosmith, Black Sabbath, Led Zeppelin, Cheap Trick, Boston, Sex Pistols, Sonic Youth, the Pixies and, he claimed, the Bay City Rollers. He formed Nirvana with bassist and fellow punk-rock fan Krist Novoselic, and with drummer Chad Channing they formed part of the burgeoning Seattle scene, which would later be termed 'grunge'. The band recorded an album, *Bleach* (1989), for the local Sup Pop label.

Soon afterwards, Channing was fired and replaced by powerhouse Dave Grohl. In 1990, Nirvana signed to DGC Records and recorded the crossover smash *Nevermind* (1991) with producer Butch Vig. Trailed by the classic single 'Smells Like Teen Spirit' with its genre-defining quiet verse/loud chorus structure, *Nevermind* mixed abrasive guitar with pop melodies. Cobain felt that Vig had smoothed out the rough edges of the band's live sound and was determined that the follow-up would capture the real Nirvana; the booming, rumbling *In Utero* (1993) did just that. Best known for his raw, angry style, Cobain was adept at acoustic work as *Unplugged In New York* (1994) demonstrates. A notorious destroyer of guitars, Kurt favoured the Fender Mustang. He also used Stratocasters, Jaguars and occasionally a Telecaster, plus his beloved Sixties Mosrite Gospel.

The defiantly anti-establishment Cobain did not cope well with his newfound celebrity, and his life degenerated into a tabloid soap opera after his marriage to fellow rocker Courtney Love. Struggling with heroin addiction and stomach pains, which had plagued him since childhood, he tried to commit suicide in Rome while on tour in March 1994. A month later, he shot and killed himself at his home in Seattle.

NOEL GALLAGHER
BRITPOP'S TRAILBLAZER

Britpop guitarist Noel Gallagher (b. 1967) was born in Manchester, England. He began teaching himself guitar at the age of 13, later adopting Johnny Marr as his role model. His other inspirations were primarily British guitar bands: the Kinks, the Who, Slade, the Jam, and Stone Roses.

After unsuccessfully auditioning for the role of lead singer with Manchester indie group Inspiral Carpets, Gallagher became their roadie. Returning home in 1992 from an American tour, he discovered younger brother Liam singing in a band, Rain, with Paul 'Bonehead' Arthurs (guitar), Paul McGuigan (bass) and Tony McCarroll (drums). Noel allowed himself to be persuaded to join, on the condition that he take creative control. Renamed Oasis, their rise was swift, as the band graduated to stadium gigs within two years of the release of their debut single 'Supersonic' in 1994.

Oasis' first album *Definitely Maybe* (1994) was steeped in rock classicism, recalling the Sex Pistols with the bass buried beneath multiple layers of guitars. Further homage to his influences was evident in Gallagher's appropriation of T. Rex's 'Get It On' riff for 'Cigarettes And Alcohol'. New drummer Alan White joined for *(What's The Story) Morning Glory?* (1995), and his skills enabled Oasis to craft a more varied, Beatles-influenced collection. Noel's strident lead on the title track and adroit acoustic work on 'Wonderwall' stood out, but he is dismissive of his abilities: 'I'm more of a strummer than a lead guitarist.' Gallagher favours Epiphone Sheratons and has a signature blue 'Supernova' model. Carefully matching guitar to song, he also uses a Fender Stratocaster, Telecaster and Gibson Les Paul. Although naturally left-handed, he plays right-handed. Oasis spearheaded a revival in British guitar bands like Cast and Ocean Colour Scene and later Travis and Coldplay, who took their lead from the band's quieter side. The Gallagher brothers' pursuit of the rock'n'roll lifestyle resulted in an overproduced third album, *Be Here Now* (1997). Oasis subsequently recovered some of their early form. Further line-up changes fostered a more flexible musical approach while the Gallaghers' often combative relationship remained the core dynamic of the band. In 2009, however, the relationship between the two brothers reached breaking point, with Noel confirming on his blog that he had left Oasis to 'seek pastures new'.

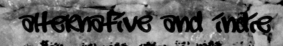

DAVE NAVARRO

MASTER OF ADDICTION

Alternative-rock guitarist Dave Navarro (b. 1967) was born in Santa Monica, California. After hearing Jimi Hendrix, Navarro began playing guitar at the age of seven and was in various bands in school. In 1986, he joined Jane's Addiction on the recommendation of drummer Stephen Perkins, a childhood friend. Inspired by the Velvet Underground, Joy Division, the Doors, PiL and Faith No More, the band quickly gained a following in Los Angeles and released their first album *Jane's Addiction* (1987) independently.

A live set with copious studio overdubs, the album was an unpredictable mix of folk, rock, funk and new wave punctuated by Navarro's unusual, angular guitar. Their second album for Warner Brothers, *Ritual De Lo Habitual* (1990), provided their breakthrough and is regarded as the band's masterpiece. It extends Jane's Addiction's musical palette to progressive rock with Eastern influences creeping in. Navarro's solo on 'Three Days' is one of his finest. After the trail-blazing Lollapalooza tour in 1991, which was organized by singer Perry Farrell and put alternative rock into large arenas for the first time, Jane's Addiction split up.

Navarro formed Deconstruction, whose sole album *Deconstruction* (1994) is now considered a cult classic, before joining the Red Hot Chili Peppers, making his live debut at the 1994 Woodstock Festival. After one album, *One Hot Minute* (1995), Navarro was dismissed in 1998

due to creative differences, as he was uneasy with the band's improvisational style. Navarro participated in a Jane's Addiction reunion tour in 1997, and the band reunited again in 2001 for an album and tour, disbanding in 2004. In between he worked with artists as diverse as Marilyn Manson and Christina Aguilera. Since the demise of Jane's Addiction, he was co-host of MTV's reality show 'Rock Star' and put together a new band, the Panic Channel. In recent years Navarro has worked on many projects with artists such as DJ Skribble and Billy Corgan, as well as the reformed Jane's Addiction. Navarro broadcasts an internet radio show called Dark Matter. From Jane's Addiction days, Navarro has played PRS guitars, notably his signature model. While a member of the Chili Peppers, he used Fender Stratocasters and has also played Telecasters and a Gibson Les Paul.

GRAHAM COXON
BRINGING GUITAR INTO FOCUS

Indie guitarist Graham Coxon (b. 1969) was born in West Berlin, the son of an army bandsman. His early years were characterized by the itinerant army life until the family settled in Colchester in the late Seventies. The young Coxon was a Beatles fan and possessed a talent for art. He began to learn saxophone and then at 12 obtained his first guitar, which he taught himself to play, inspired by the Jam and the Specials. At secondary school, he made the acquaintance of Damon Albarn.

In 1989, Coxon was studying for a degree in Fine Arts at Goldsmiths College, London, where he met bassist Alex James and which singer Albarn also attended. Together with drummer Dave Rowntree, they formed Seymour, renamed Blur on signing to indie label Food in 1990. Their first album *Leisure* (1990) was derivative of both the 'Madchester' and 'shoe-gazing' scenes. *Modern Life Is Rubbish* (1993) reacted against grunge and American culture by celebrating Englishness. The two-million-selling *Parklife* (1994) helped to popularize what was soon dubbed 'Britpop'. The theme continued on the oddly lacklustre *The Great Escape* (1995). Coxon's guitar added bite and aggression to Blur's early albums. Their fifth album *Blur* (1997) represented a radical change in direction, influenced by American indie-guitar bands, particularly Pavement. In this environment, Coxon's angular guitar work thrived. On *13* (1999) gospel and electronica were added to the blend.

Early in the sessions for Blur's seventh album, *Think Tank* (2003), Coxon's increasing distance from his bandmates led to his departure. Having already released four solo albums, his first post-Blur work and most successful solo venture was *Happiness In Magazines* (2004). Coxon plays most of the instruments on his albums and supplies the artwork for the covers. His differences with Blur have been resolved, but it remains unclear whether they will work together again. Coxon's seventh studio album, *The Spinning Top*, (2009) garnered critical raves. Coxon is an idiosyncratic guitarist much admired by his peers; Radiohead's Jonny Greenwood is an avowed fan. From early in his career, he has used the Fender Telecaster almost exclusively, although more recently he has started to diversify by playing a Gibson SG and Les Paul.

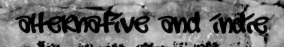

JOHN FRUSCIANTE

MELODIC MAESTRO

Alt-rock guitarist John Frusciante (b. 1970) was born into a musical family in Queens, New York. While living in Los Angeles after his parents' divorce, Frusciante became involved with the city's punk-rock scene and was particularly inspired by the Germs, teaching himself to play the songs on their first album before taking guitar lessons. He studied Jeff Beck, Jimmy Page and Jimi Hendrix; mastered the blues scale; and then became obsessed with Frank Zappa.

On seeing the Red Hot Chili Peppers at 15, he became a devotee, learning the guitar parts from their first three albums, as performed by the band's lead guitarist Hillel Slovak. When Slovak died from a heroin overdose in 1988, Frusciante successfully auditioned to replace his role model. His second album with the Chili Peppers *Blood Sugar Sex Magik* (1991) turned the band into stars, but Frusciante was unable to handle the newfound success and quit in May 1992. Struggling with depression, he became addicted to heroin, crack cocaine and alcohol for more than five years, once nearly dying from a blood infection, although he did manage to record and release two solo albums in that period. By 1998 he had been through rehab and cleaned up. He rejoined the Chili Peppers when his replacement Dave Navarro was fired. The band has since gone on to even greater worldwide success and acclaim. Frusciante's guitar is

particularly upfront on *Stadium Arcadium* (2005), which saw his playing receive belated recognition from critics and musicians. Following the Stadium Arcadium tour, the Red Hot Chili Peppers agreed to a hiatus of indefinite length. During this period Frusciante released his tenth solo album, *The Empyrean*, with contributions from Flea, Josh Klinghoffer and Johnny Marr.

Frusciante is an emotional and melodic guitarist who possesses great technical ability, and many of his live solos are improvised. He is a fan of guitarists with a melody driven style, such as Bernard Sumner, John McGeoch (Siouxsie & the Banshees) and XTC's Andy Partridge. He prefers pre-1970 guitars for their sonic qualities and selects the most appropriate instrument for the song. Since his return to the Chili Peppers he has used a 1962 Sunburst Fender Stratocaster.

BERNARD BUTLER

SUEDE'S CHAMELEON

Indie guitarist and producer Bernard Butler (b. 1970) was born in Tottenham, London. After learning violin as a child, he took up guitar at the age of 14, inspired by Johnny Marr, learning Smiths' guitar parts by watching the band play live. He was also influenced by Bernard Sumner and Aztec Camera's Roddy Frame. After replying to an advertisement in the 'Musicians Wanted' column of *Melody Maker*, he successfully auditioned for Suede in 1989.

Butler formed a songwriting partnership with singer Brett Anderson (pictured below), and the quality of their material saw Suede hailed by the music press as 'the best new band in Britain' before they had recorded anything. Suede spearheaded a shift from grunge towards a more British sound, which would culminate in the Britpop phenomenon of the mid-Nineties.

Since the early days of Suede, Butler has been associated primarily with his cherry red 1960 Gibson ES355 and also uses a black Gibson 330. His versatile approach was evident throughout the debut album, *Suede* (1993), mixing glam-rock aggression ('Metal Mickey') and subtle touches worthy of George Harrison ('She's Not Dead'). While recording the second album, *Dog Man Star* (1994), tensions between Butler and the others escalated and he left before its completion but after contributing some dynamic guitar, notably on 'We Are The Pigs' and 'New Generation'.

After brief encounters with the Verve and former All About Eve vocalist Julianne Reagan, he formed McAlmont & Butler with soul singer David McAlmont. Another acrimonious split followed after only two singles, but there was enough material in the can for an album *The Sound*

Of McAlmont And Butler (1996). The pair reunited in 2002. Meanwhile, Butler released two solo albums *People Move On* (1998) and *Friends And Lovers* (1999). Butler renewed his partnership with Brett Anderson shortly after the demise of Suede in 2003. Working as the Tears, they made *Here Come The Tears* (2005), which was inevitably reminiscent of Suede. The Tears have since announced a 'temporary' hiatus. Butler has become known as a producer-player in recent years, working with artists including the Veils, Duffy and Scott McFarnon.

JACK WHITE

REVIVING THE BLUES

Modern blues guitarist Jack White (b. 1975) was born John Gillis in Detroit, Michigan. He taught himself to play drums, starting at the age of five. On leaving school he played in various Detroit bands. In 1996, he married Meg White and, reversing normal practice, took her surname. The White Stripes were born when Meg, with no previous experience on the drum kit, started bashing along to his guitar, and he realized that her primitive beat was exactly the accompaniment he needed.

After two independent albums, the White Stripes breakthrough came on the release of *White Blood Cells* (2001) when DJ John Peel enthused about the band, and the excitement surrounding them in the UK transferred back to America. White was hailed as the most explosive rock performer in the world and credited with returning the blues to the forefront of modern rock. This was achieved with the setup of just guitar (occasionally piano) and drums. As White explained, 'All you need is two people. The music is from the guitar or piano and the rhythm is Meg's accompaniment. There is nothing else that needs to be there.' During downtime from the White Stripes in 2005, White formed the Raconteurs, a more conventional Sixties-influenced outfit. In 2009, he formed a new group called the Dead Weather with the Kills frontwoman Alison Mosshart.

In addition to blues masters Son House and Robert Johnson, White was equally inspired by Captain Beefheart, Dylan and obscure US garage bands the Sonics, the Monks and the Rats. The White Stripes' success initiated a new era of back-to-basics rock. White's most famous guitar is a red and white Airline, a cheap Sixties department-store model. For the White Stripes he also uses a Harmony Rocket, a Crestwood Astral and a Gretsch White Penguin. In the Raconteurs, he favours Gretsch guitars. To achieve the White Stripes' powerful live sound, he makes extensive use of effects, mainly a DigiTech Whammy to shift the pitch down and compensate for the absence of bass. When playing barre and power chords, he uses the little finger on his left hand partly because of an injury to his index finger sustained in a car accident in 2003.

MATTHEW BELLAMY

RULER OF THE RIFF

Twenty-first-century guitar hero Matthew Bellamy (b. 1978) was born in Cambridge, England. His father George was rhythm guitarist in the Tornadoes, who scored a massive transatlantic hit with the Joe Meek-produced 'Telstar'. Before learning guitar, Bellamy took piano lessons as a boy, equally inspired by Ray Charles and classical music. In the mid-Eighties, the family moved to Teignmouth, Devon, where Bellamy formed Muse with Chris Wolstenholme (bass) and Dominic Howard (drums).

The band served their apprenticeship through constant gigging while soaking up more influences, notably Jeff Buckley and Radiohead, to whom they would often be compared, much to Bellamy's irritation. After an independently released limited edition EP, Muse signed a major deal in 1998. Debut album *Showbiz* (1999) marked them as a band with the potential for crossover appeal to fans of indie, metal and prog rock. With the guitarist emerging as an energetic frontman, *Origin Of Symmetry* (2001) was a more expansive collection, featuring

Bellamy's untamed riffing and drawing on influences as diverse as Rage Against The Machine, Ned's Atomic Dustbin, Rachmaninov and Philip Glass. As remarkable as his guitar style was, Bellamy's soaring voice added emotion to the bombast. His riff from the single 'Plug In Baby' has been hailed as one of the greatest of all time.

Absolution (2003) developed the classical influences as Muse's popularity began to grow. Bellamy's lyrical themes of Armageddon, global conspiracy theories and corruption were explored further on *Black Holes And Revelations* (2006), with its political subtext expressed through a series of linked songs. Shortly after its release, Muse became the first group to play the rebuilt Wembley Stadium, confirming their status as one of the biggest bands in Britain. Muse released the live *HAARP* in 2008 and *The Resistance* in 2009. Bellamy uses guitars made by Manson of Exeter, principally a silver model that he helped design. Among its customized features is a built-in fuzz box, through which Bellamy achieves his unique sound and which also allows him to control feedback. He has also played a Fender Stratocaster, a Gibson SG, a Les Paul and a Yamaha Pacifica.

beyond Rock

Becoming a virtuoso requires heroic effort, but not all guitar heroes choose the life of the rock star. As befits rock's heritage in the marriage of country and rhythm and blues, many of music's greatest guitarists choose country or jazz as the genre for their life's work. Rock players are inspired by the great guitarists of bluegrass, classical, flamenco, fusion and other disciplines, and today many players of those styles, in turn, start out 'in the woodshed', learning Clapton, Page and Beck to help master the guitar skills that exist in the world beyond rock.

ANDRES SEGOVIA

A CLASSICAL LEGEND

Classical-guitar legend Andrés Segovia (1894–1987) was born in the city of Linares, Spain and reared in Granada. He received musical instruction at an early age and was tutored in piano and violin but warmed to neither. When he heard the guitar in the home of a friend, however, he was hooked. Disregarding the objections of his family and his teachers at the Granada Musical Institute, Segovia persisted in learning to play the guitar, teaching himself when he could not find satisfactory teachers.

Segovia was influenced by masters such as Francisco Tarrega, but developed his own style and technique. Segovia plucked the strings with a combination of his fingernails and fingertips, producing a sharper sound than many of his contemporaries. With this technique, he could create a wider range of tones. After the Second World War Segovia became among the first to endorse the use of nylon strings instead of gut strings, which improved stability in intonation.

Despite a lack of classical repertoire for guitar, Segovia dreamed of performing on the concert stage and continued to study and perfect his technique. As his talent developed, his reputation began to spread, and at the age of 15, in 1909, he made his public debut in Granada under the auspices of the Circulo Artistico, a local cultural organization. Numerous concerts followed, including ones in Madrid in 1912 and in Barcelona in 1916. In Madrid he had acquired from the craftsman Manuel Ramírez a guitar that he played for many years. In the mid-Thirties he began using an instrument made by Hermann Hauser of Munich.

By 1919 Segovia was ready for a full-fledged tour, and performed in that year in South America, where he gained an enthusiastic reception. Engagements kept him from returning to Europe until 1923. During this period Segovia was still considered something of a curiosity. At his London debut a sceptical *Times* critic became a devoted follower.

At his Paris debut in April 1924, a concert arranged by his countryman, cellist Pablo Casals, Segovia was a sensation, winning warm praise for turning the ugly duckling Spanish guitar into a beautiful swan. A successful Berlin debut later that year cemented his international reputation.

Still there was a limited repertoire for guitar, and so Segovia transcribed works written for other instruments. He relied primarily on Renaissance and Baroque pieces composed for lute or Spanish vihuela. In Germany he discovered the lute works of Sylvius Leopold Weiss, which were adaptable and effective. He also discovered a group of Bach's works that were well suited to the guitar. Segovia believed that many of Bach's solo pieces were originally written for lute and later transcribed by him for other instruments. Unconvinced critics nevertheless applauded Segovia's transcriptions. Demonstrating the suitability of Bach's music for the classical guitar was one of Segovia's greatest accomplishments.

Segovia's growing fame brought with it a rising interest in the instrument itself. The sound that Segovia produced and the intimacy of its presentation inspired thousands to take up guitar. During his career the guitar become one of the most popular and studied instruments in the world. Leading composers finally began to write for guitar. Over the years the instrument developed an extensive modern repertoire because of the efforts of other composers such as Turina, Torroba and Villa-Lobos. In a 1924 concert in Paris Segovia played a solo piece written for the guitar by Albert Roussel and entitled 'Segovia'.

The outbreak of the Spanish Civil War forced Segovia to leave Spain in 1936. After living for a time in Italy, he moved to Uruguay. He toured extensively in Central and South America. After an absence of five years Segovia returned to the United States in 1943 and had to rebuild his popularity. Over the next 20 years, through worldwide performances and with the help of the new medium of television, Segovia secured his place as the pre-eminent classical guitarist of the modern age. Segovia died in Madrid of a heart attack at the age of 94.

The boxed set *The Segovia Collection* (2002) is a widely praised 24-bit, 96-kHz remastering of the guitarist's 1952–69 mono and stereo performances for Decca by the Deutsche Grammophon production team. The set's discs are also available as individual volumes.

CARLOS MONTOYA

FLAMENCO FINGERPICKING HERO

Spanish guitar legend Carlos Montoya (1903–93) helped propel the flamenco style of music from accompaniment for gypsy folk dances and songs to a serious and internationally popular form of guitar music. Montoya was born into a gypsy family in Spain. He studied guitar with his mother and a local barber, eventually learning from professionals and becoming an expert on the history of flamenco. His uncle, Ramon Montoya, was a successful flamenco guitarist, and Carlos started playing professionally at the age of 14 for singers and dancers in Madrid cafes.

Montoya began touring in the Twenties and Thirties, giving performances in Europe, Asia and North America as a dance accompanist. At the beginning of the Second World War Montoya was on tour in the United States with a touring Spanish dancer, La Argentinita. He settled in New York City and eventually became a US citizen. Montoya became popular enough to tour as a solo artist, and added blues, jazz and folk music to his flamenco repertoire.

In 1948 Montoya began touring with symphonies and orchestras and performing guitar recitals. He became the first flamenco guitarist to tour the world as a guest performer with orchestras. His appearances expanded to television and recording, with more than 40 albums, some with symphonies and orchestras, completed. His reissued albums on CD include *The Art Of Flamenco* (1993), *Flamenco* (1996) and *Flamenco Direct* (1990).

As have other performers who gain wide fame as crowd-pleasing instrumental soloists, Montoya had many critics and detractors among purists and serious scholars of Spanish guitar. Because flamenco is grounded traditionally as an accompaniment for dancers, maintaining a solid rhythm, or compas, on guitar is fundamental. Montoya's excursions into varying dynamics and time changes on classics like 'Malagueña', which Montoya filled with rapid-fire hammer-ons and pull-offs, sometimes at the expense of precise fingering, got him categorized as a flashy showman. But fans around the world fell in love with the emotion and fiery romance suggested by his playing. Montoya died at the age of 89 in Wainscott, NY.

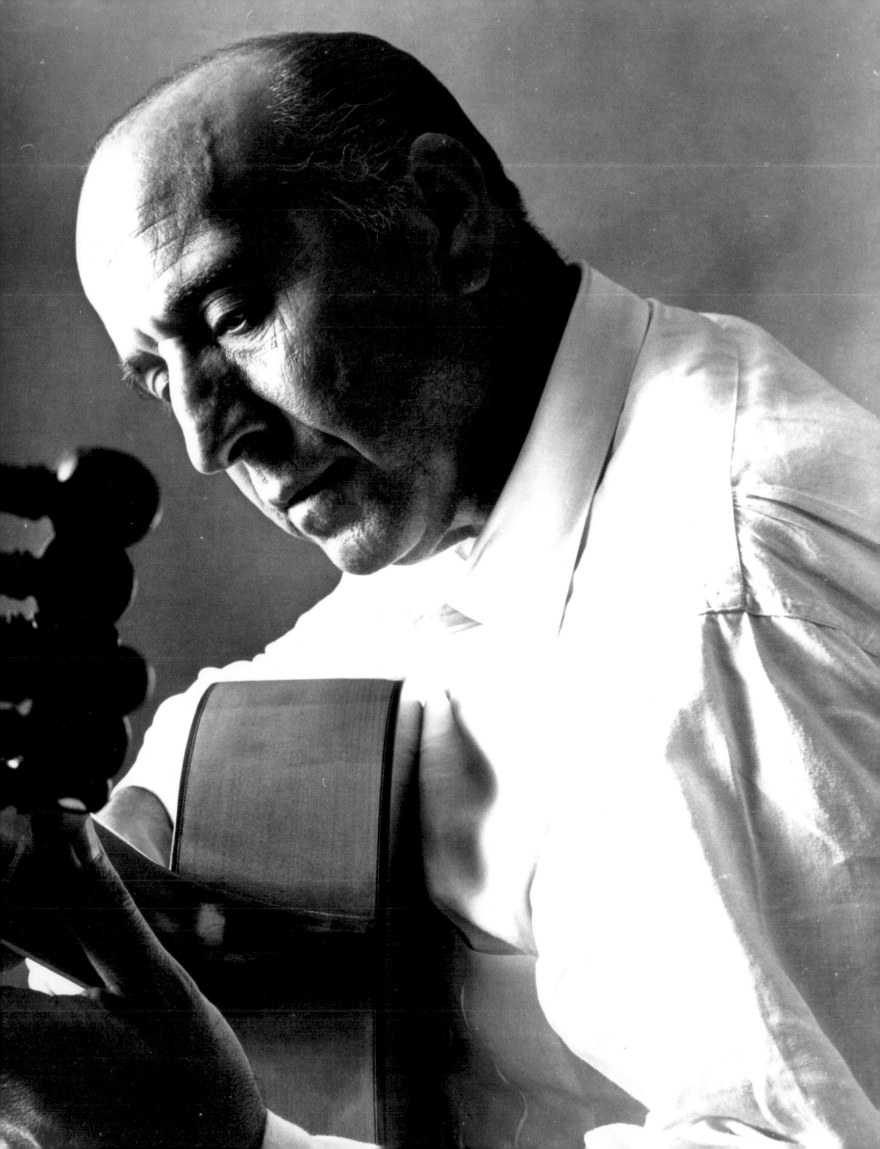

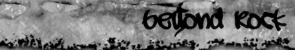

MAYBELLE CARTER

THE CARTER SCRATCH

As a member of the first family of country music, Maybelle Carter (1909–78) distinguished herself far beyond her role as accompanist to her brother-in-law A.P. Carter and his wife Sara (Maybelle's cousin) in the Carter Family (pictured right), the first recording stars of country music.

Maybelle (seen on the left) was born Maybelle Addington in Nickelsville, Virginia. In 1926 she married Ezra J. Carter. The Carter Family was formed in 1927 by her brother-in-law A.P. and his wife Sara. Maybelle was the guitarist and doubled on autoharp and banjo. Maybelle's unique style involved using her thumb (with thumb-pick) to play bass and melody while her index finger filled out the rhythm on the higher strings. The technique, now known as the 'Carter scratch', is identifiable on any of the Carters' recordings of the nineteenth-century folk classic 'Wildwood Flower'.

In 1927, A.P. convinced Sara and a pregnant Maybelle to travel from Virginia to Tennessee, where they would audition for Ralph Peer, a record producer who was looking for new talent. In fall of that year, the Victor recording company released a 78-RPM record of the group performing 'Wandering Boy' and 'Poor Orphan Child'. But it was 1928's release of 'The Storms Are On The Ocean' and 'Single Girl, Married Girl' that boosted the family's popularity.

The Carter Family performed together on radio shows and records until the breakup of A.P. and Sara's marriage in 1942. Many of the Carters' recordings, such as 'Can The Circle Be Unbroken', 'Cannonball Blues' and 'Keep On The Sunny Side', became country music standards. After the breakup, Maybelle continued to perform with her daughters Anita, June and Helen as Mother Maybelle & the Carter Sisters. Daughter June would eventually marry country legend Johnny Cash, and Mother Maybelle & the Carter Sisters would be regulars on Cash's Seventies television show.

The Carter Family was elected to the Country Music Hall Of Fame in 1970. In 1988, they were inducted into the Grammy Hall Of Fame. In 1993, they were honoured on a US postage stamp. In 2001 Maybelle was initiated into the International Bluegrass Music Hall Of Honor. Mother Maybelle died in October 1978, in Nashville.

DJANGO REINHARDT

GYPSY GUITAR GIANT

Django Reinhardt (1910–53) overcame physical disabilities to create a unique playing style and one of the most highly influential sounds in jazz. He was born in Belgium to gypsy parents. At the age of eight his mother's tribe settled near Paris. The French Gypsies, or Manouches, were medieval in their beliefs, and distrustful of modern science. But Django grew up exposed to Paris while living the life of the nomadic gypsy.

When he was 12 he received his first instrument, a banjo/guitar that was given to him by a neighbour. He learned to play by mimicking the fingerings of musicians he watched, and was soon impressing adults with his ability. Before he was 13 he began his musical career playing in dance halls. He made his first recordings with accordionist Jean Vaissade for the Ideal Company. Django could not read or write at the time, and his name appeared as Jiango Renard.

In November 1928 the 18-year-old Django returned from a performance at a new club to the caravan in which he lived with his new wife. The caravan was filled with celluloid flowers his wife had made to sell at market. Django thought he heard a mouse and bent down with a candle to look. The wick from the candle fell into the highly flammable celluloid flowers,

and in a matter of seconds the caravan was engulfed in flames. Django wrapped himself in a blanket, and he and his wife barely made it outside, but his left hand and his right side were badly burned from knee to waist.

Django was bedridden for 18 months. Given a guitar, he created a whole new fingering system built around the two fingers on his left hand that had full mobility. His fourth and fifth digits of the left hand were permanently curled towards the palm due to the tendons shrinking from the heat of the fire. He could use them on the first two strings of the guitar for chords and octaves, but could not extend the fingers. His soloing was accomplished with only the index and middle fingers.

Django was influenced by jazz recordings of guitarist Eddie Lang and violinist Joe Venuti, and by Louis Armstrong and Duke Ellington. In 1934 the Quintet Of The Hot Club Of France was formed by a chance meeting of Django and violinist Stéphane Grappelli (pictured below). A band of 14 musicians, including Django, were commissioned to play at the Hotel Cambridge. During intermission, Django would play in a corner, and one day Grappelli joined in. Both were so pleased with the exchange that they played regularly and filled out with Roger Chaput (guitar), Louis Vola (bass) and eventually Django's brother Joseph (guitar).

A small record company Ultraphone recorded the Hot Club's first sides, 'Dinah', 'Tiger Rag', 'Oh Lady Be Good' and 'I Saw Stars'. These first records made a big impression, and the Quintet went on to record hundreds of sides, building a following on both sides of the ocean. The concept of 'lead guitar' (Django) and backing 'rhythm guitar' (Joseph Reinhardt, Roger Chaput or Pierre Ferret) was born. They also used their guitars for percussive sounds, as they had no true percussion section.

Django played and recorded also with many American jazz legends such as Coleman Hawkins, Benny Carter, Rex Stewart and Louis Armstrong. Reinhardt could neither read nor write music, and was barely literate. Grappelli helped him learn musical notation.

In 1939 the Quintet was touring in England when war broke out. Django returned to Paris while Grappelli remained in England. Django played and recorded throughout the war years, with Hubert Rostaing on clarinet. Django narrowly avoided the fate of kin who died in Nazi concentration camps. After the war he rejoined Grappelli, and they again played and recorded. He toured briefly with Duke Ellington in America and returned to Paris, where he continued his career until 1951 when he retired to the small village of Samois sur Seine.

In May 1953 Django suffered a massive brain haemorrhage and died. Today he is well represented on CD with *The Classic Early Recordings In Chronological Order* (2000), *Quintette Du Hot Club De France: 25 Classics 1934–1940* (1998), the remastered *Djangology* (2002) and others.

LES PAUL

INNOVATOR AND ICON

Les Paul (1915–2009) developed a reputation in modern music beyond his status as a successful performer and guitar innovator through his pioneering work with multitrack recording. Born Lester Polsfuss in Waukesha, Wisconsin, the nine-year-old Paul first picked up harmonica from a street musician. Soon he was playing for money in the streets. He was attracted to electronics, and about the same time began conducting his own experiments with sound. He started playing guitar at the age of 11 and, by the time he was 18, played country music under the name Rhubarb Red. After hearing Django Reinhardt, he switched over to jazz and changed his name to Les Paul.

In 1943, after a successful stint on New York radio, Paul (pictured below with B.B. King) moved to Hollywood, formed a trio, and soon was appearing with stars like Nat 'King' Cole and Bing Crosby, with whom he recorded a hit version of 'It's Been A Long, Long Time'. Crosby would help finance Paul's experiments, which resulted in the Gibson Guitar Company adopting Paul's suggestions for a guitar that in the Fifties became the Les Paul model. But Paul almost had to leave guitar behind forever. His right arm was shattered in a 1948 car crash. The doctors could not restore mobility to the arm, but set it at a right angle so that Paul could continue to play.

In 1947, Capitol Records released a recording that had begun as an experiment in Paul's garage. It featured Paul playing eight different parts on electric guitar. His experiments initiated the process of multitrack recording, which he used to successful effect when he teamed with singer Mary Ford for a string of Fifties hits like 'How High The Moon', which featured overdubbed

guitars playing in harmony. Paul's fame helped his namesake guitar gain fans, ultimately exploding in popularity in the rock era. When Gibson changed the design without telling him, he demanded his name be removed from the headstock. That guitar, renamed the SG, also became a popular guitar with rockers. Paul continued to innovate and perform, and in the twenty-first century he still held down a long-running weekly gig at New York's Iridium jazz club. Les Paul succumbed to complications from pneumonia in 2009.

CHARLIE CHRISTIAN

THE FIRST GREAT SOLOIST

Charlie Christian (1916–42) pushed guitar to the forefront of the big-band era, furthering the instrument's evolution from a provider of acoustic accompaniment to an electrified foreground instrument that could pound out rhythm like a drum set or solo out front like a horn. His playing, in fact, was likened to jazz horn players who were leading the evolution of traditional jazz into a new, modern jazz during the Thirties and Forties.

Christian was born in Texas but soon moved to Oklahoma with his family. The family was musical and young Charlie and his brothers would sometimes perform live for donations to help support the family. Christian picked up guitar from his father, inheriting his father's instruments when he died. He began playing around Oklahoma City around 1931, learning

from guitarist 'Bigfoot' Ralph Hamilton. Christian was a natural, however, and soon was gigging around the Midwest. By 1936, he was playing electric guitar and had become a regional attraction. He would jam with stars travelling through Oklahoma City, among them Teddy Wilson and Art Tatum. It was jazz pianist Mary Lou Williams who told producer John Hammond about Christian.

Christian auditioned for Hammond, who became convinced that Christian would be a perfect fit for Benny Goodman, who in 1939 was forming a new sextet. Goodman was not pleased when Hammond arranged for Christian to travel to California for an onstage tryout with Goodman, but after trying to stump Christian by calling the tune 'Rose Room', Goodman was astounded by Christian's command of the tune (he had been playing it for years), and the quality and originality of Christian's solos. Christian was hired on the spot and became a star of the Benny Goodman Sextet, winning accolades and awards from jazz fans and critics.

In the spring of 1940, Goodman reorganized his sextet, retaining Christian and filling the group out with Count Basie, former Duke Ellington trumpeter Cootie Williams and former Artie Shaw tenor-saxophonist Georgie Auld. The Goodman Sextet was in 1940 an all-star band that dominated the jazz polls in 1941.

Christian was influenced more by horn players such as Lester Young and Herschel Evans than by early acoustic guitarists like Eddie Lang and jazz-bluesman Lonnie Johnson, although they both had contributed to the expansion of the guitar's role from 'rhythm section' instrument to a solo instrument. Christian admitted he wanted his guitar to sound like a tenor saxophone. By 1939 several players had adopted electric guitar, but Christian was the first great soloist on the amplified instrument.

Christian's frequent participation in after-hours jam sessions helped spur the developing form of bebop, while he performed more accessible swing during his 'day job' with Goodman. Often jamming late-night at Minton's Playhouse in Harlem in New York City, Christian created flights of improvisational fancy on extended solos, some of which were recorded by students on primitive tape recorders. There are also recordings of the partial Goodman Sextet made in March of 1941. With Goodman and bassist Artie Bernstein absent, Christian and the rest of the Sextet recorded for nearly 20 minutes as the engineers tested equipment. Two recordings from that session, 'Blues In B' and 'Waiting For Benny', were released years later. These foreshadow the bop-jam sessions of the late Forties and contrast with the more formal swing music recorded after Goodman had arrived at the studio. Other Goodman Sextet records that foretell bop are *Seven Come Eleven* (1939) and *Air Mail Special* (1940 and 1941).

Christian was a habitual drinker and marijuana user. In the late Thirties he had contracted tuberculosis and in early 1940 was hospitalized for a short period. In early 1941 Christian resumed his hectic lifestyle, heading to Harlem for late-night jam sessions after finishing gigs with the Goodman Sextet and Orchestra in New York City. In June of 1941 he was admitted to Seaview, a sanitarium on Staten Island in New York City. He was reported to be making progress, but he declined in health and died in March 1942.

Most of Christian's recorded works, with Benny Goodman and others, are available on CD, including *Selected Broadcasts & Jam Sessions* (2002), *The Genius Of The Electric Guitar* (1989) and *Featuring Charlie Christian 1939–41* (1989).

TAL FARLOW
FAST AND FIERCE SOLOIST

Jazz icon Tal Farlow (1921–98) wowed fans and other guitarists with his blazing speed and physical ability, facilitated by his large hands, to create unique, extended voicings. Farlow was equally well known for his semi-reclusiveness. Trained as a sign painter, he frequently dropped out of the music scene for long periods, living a quiet life on the New Jersey shore until a rare appearance for a recording session or performance.

Farlow was born in 1921 in Greensboro, North Carolina. When he was eight years old his father gave him a mandolin, the strings of which were tuned like the upper strings of a guitar. When he later was given a six-string guitar he retained his four-string fingerings, using his thumb on the low strings. Farlow heard Charlie Christian around 1941 and learned many of Christian's solos note for note. Farlow's first serious work was in 1944. He worked with East-Coast bands, and in late 1949 was recruited by Red Norvo for a trio that featured Charles Mingus on bass. Farlow developed his speed in an effort to keep up with Norvo's blistering tempos.

In 1953 Farlow returned to the East Coast, where he recorded as a sideman and played in Artie Shaw's Gramercy Five. He recorded as a leader for Blue Note. In early 1956 Farlow formed a trio with pianist Eddie Costa and bassist Vinnie Burke. Over the next three years this trio made a number of successful records. *The Complete Verve Tal Farlow Sessions* (2004) include these recordings.

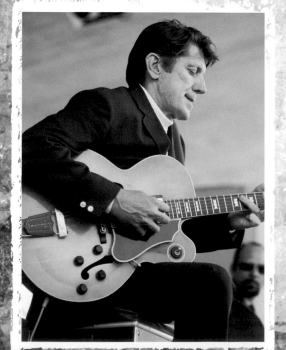

In 1958 Farlow married and moved to the quiet New Jersey coastal town of Sea Bright, where he worked as a sign painter and teacher. He re-emerged when he recorded *The Return Of Tal Farlow* (1969), after which he returned to his life at the shore.

In the Eighties Tal became much more visible. He made half a dozen recordings for the Concord label and performed in Europe and Japan. He toured with Barney Kessel, Herb Ellis and Charlie Byrd as Great Guitars. Farlow worked steadily until the mid-Nineties. In 1997 he was diagnosed with oesophageal cancer. He died in 1998.

CHET ATKINS

MR GUITAR

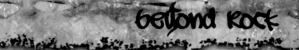

As the first superstar instrumentalist to emerge from the modern Nashville recording scene, Chet Atkins (1924–2001) was a living legend for most of his life, but the Nashville-based guitarist was also a producer, engineer, label executive and A&R man without peer.

Chester Burton 'Chet' Atkins was born on in June 1924 in Luttrell, Tennessee. He started out on ukulele, later adopting fiddle, and traded his brother Lowell an old pistol for a guitar when he was nine. Self-taught, he became an accomplished guitarist while still in high school.

Atkins heard Merle Travis on WLW Radio in 1939. He developed his legendary right-hand fingerpicking style – using his thumb for bass notes and three fingers for melody and harmonies – because he couldn't believe Travis accomplished all he did with just his thumb and index finger.

After dropping out of high school in 1942, Atkins landed several jobs performing on radio and touring the South and Midwest with regional stars. He was sometimes fired because his increasingly sophisticated style was deemed 'not country enough'. Atkins made his first appearance at the Grand Ole Opry in 1946 as a member of Red Foley's band, but was soon back on the road with touring acts. In 1947 Atkins was signed by RCA, but his early recordings didn't sell. He finally was able to settle down in Nashville as guitarist with Mother Maybelle & the Carter Sisters. He began doing more session work as a leader for RCA and finally had his first hit single in 1954 with 'Mr. Sandman'. His albums became more popular, and he became a design consultant for Gretsch, who manufactured a popular Chet Atkins line of electric guitars from 1955–80.

When Atkins' producer Steve Sholes took over pop production in 1957 (a result of his success with Elvis Presley), he put Atkins in charge of RCA's Nashville division. With country music record sales slumping in the wake of rock'n'roll, Atkins and others eliminated fiddles and steel guitar from productions in an attempt to appeal to pop fans. The result became known as the

Nashville Sound, a label Atkins rejected and blamed on the media. But Atkins' arrangements produced big hits for Jim Reeves ('Four Walls' and 'He'll Have To Go') and Don Gibson ('Oh Lonesome Me' and 'Blue Blue Day'). The country 'crossover hit' became more common.

Atkins himself recorded in a sophisticated home studio, where he spent much time creating unique musical and sonic ideas. His records and television appearances earned him the moniker Mister Guitar. By 1968 Atkins had become vice-president of RCA's country division. He had brought Waylon Jennings, Willie Nelson, Connie Smith, Bobby Bare, Dolly Parton, Jerry Reed and John Hartford to the label in the Sixties. In the mid-Sixties, he signed country music's first African-American singer, Charley Pride, whose records helped to move country back to an earthier sound and away from the pop stylings Atkins had ushered in.

Atkins' own biggest hit single came in 1965, with 'Yakety Axe', an adaptation of his friend saxophonist Boots Randolph's 'Yakety Sax'. In the Seventies, Atkins was tiring of his executive duties. He produced fewer records but still had successes, like Perry Como's pop hit 'And I Love You So'. He recorded extensively with close friend and fellow picker Jerry Reed and Les Paul, with whom Atkins won one of his many Grammies for Best Country Instrumental Performance on the album *Chester And Lester* (1976).

By the end of the Seventies, Atkins left RCA and, dissatisfied with the new regime at Gretsch, withdrew his authorization for them to use his name. He signed with Columbia Records, for whom he produced a debut album in 1983 and designed guitars for Gibson.

In the Nineties he continued to release albums, including duo projects with Suzy Bogguss and Mark Knopfler, and performed with orchestras and with friends. Ultimately he suffered a recurrence of colon cancer and died in June 2001.

Atkins received numerous awards, including eleven Grammy Awards (including a Lifetime Achievement Award in 1993) and nine Country Music Association Instrumentalist of the Year awards. *Billboard* magazine awarded him their Century Award, their 'highest honor for distinguished creative achievement', in December 1997. In 2002, Atkins was posthumously inducted into the Rock And Roll Hall Of Fame.

WES MONTGOMERY
THE BOSS GUITAR

Wes Montgomery (1925–68) emerged in the Fifties and gained a wide following in the cool jazz movement before turning to pop-jazz in the Sixties. With his unique use of lead lines played in octaves with his left hand and strummed by his right-hand thumb, Montgomery mixed jazz harmonies with R&B rhythms to gain a pop following and exert broad influence on later pop-jazz guitarists like George Benson.

Montgomery was born in Indianapolis. His brothers, Monk (bass) and Buddy (vibraphone, piano), were also jazz performers. Wes was not skilled at reading music, but he could learn complex melodies and riffs by ear. He started learning guitar at the age of 19, emulating his idol, Charlie Christian. He was known for his ability to play Christian solos note for note.

Montgomery toured and recorded with Lionel Hampton from 1948 to 1950. Cannonball Adderley helped to sign Montgomery to a recording contract and recorded with him on his *Poll Winners* (1960) album. John Coltrane asked Montgomery to join his band, but Montgomery continued to lead his own band, thus earning his nickname Boss Guitar.

From 1959–63 Montgomery recorded for Riverside Records, creating some of his most influential work. *The Incredible Jazz Guitar Of Wes Montgomery* (1960) featured one of Montgomery's best-

known compositions, 'Four On Six'. In 1964 he moved to Verve Records, and his music started to shift towards pop. He didn't abandon jazz entirely, however, and the pair of albums he made with jazz-organ titan Jimmy Smith, *The Dynamic Duo* (1966) and *The Further Adventures Of Jimmy And Wes* (1966) show his ability to blend R&B and pop elements with jazz. In the late Sixties, Montgomery turned to jazzy versions of pop-rock tunes with orchestral arrangements and enjoyed the greatest success of his career. However, he was felled by a heart attack at home in 1968.

Montgomery generally played a Gibson L-5CES guitar with a Fender tube amp and later a Standel solid-state amp with 15-inch speaker. Montgomery stroked the strings with the fleshy part of his thumb, using downstrokes for single notes and a combination of upstrokes and downstrokes for chords and octaves.

JOE PASS

JAZZ VIRTUOSO

California native Joe Pass (1929–94) developed a thoroughly precise jazz technique that propelled him to virtuoso status alongside pianist Oscar Peterson and vocalist Ella Fitzgerald, with whom he made a series of essential recordings for the Pablo label in the Seventies.

Pass was raised in Johnstown, Pennsylvania. He took up guitar after being inspired by singing cowboy Gene Autry. He received his first guitar, a $17 Harmony model on his ninth birthday. Pass's father encouraged him to develop his skills, and by the age of 14, Pass was playing with bands. He began travelling with small jazz groups and moved to New York. He began to abuse drugs, however, and spent much of the Fifties in obscurity. After two years in a drug rehabilitation programme, he slowly returned to playing and emerged in the Sixties.

Pass recorded a series of albums for the Pacific Jazz label and in 1963 received *Downbeat* magazine's New Star Award. He played on Pacific Jazz recordings by various artists, and he toured with George Shearing. But his main gig in the Sixties was TV and recording-session work in Los Angeles. He was a sideman with Frank Sinatra, Sarah Vaughan and others, and worked in many of the bands of late-night TV talk shows. In the early Seventies, Pass collaborated on a series of music books, including *Joe Pass Guitar Style*.

Producer Norman Granz signed Pass to Pablo Records in 1970. In 1974 Pass released his landmark solo album (later expanded to a four-volume set) *Virtuoso*. Also in 1974, Pablo released the album *The Trio*, which featured Pass, Oscar Peterson and Niels-Henning Ørsted Pedersen. *The Trio* won a Grammy for best jazz performance. Pass also recorded Pablo albums with Benny Carter, Zoot Sims, Duke Ellington, and four albums with Ella Fitzgerald towards the end of her career.

Pass used an amazing jazz vocabulary and a command of dynamics and tempo, combined with a sophisticated harmonic sense and a knack for creating counterpoint between improvised lead lines. Pass played a Gibson ES-175 guitar and later a guitar made for him by master crafter Jimmy D'Aquisto.

JOHN FAHEY

FANTASTIC FINGERSTYLIST

John Fahey (1939–2001) was an American fingerstyle guitarist, composer, folklorist, intellectual and eccentric. Influenced by the folk and blues traditions of America, he incorporated classical, Brazilian, Indian and abstract music into his works. His moody instrumentals foreshadowed new-age music, but Fahey's intensity makes him more closely aligned with rock. His eclectic approach won him a cult following that grew with a string of reissues after his death in the Nineties.

Fahey was born in Takoma Park, MD, into a musical household. Hearing Bill Monroe's version of Jimmie Rodgers' 'Blue Yodel No. 7' on the radio ignited his passion for music. In 1952 he purchased his first guitar for $17 from the Sears-Roebuck catalogue. Fahey became an accomplished guitarist in his teens. Already a collector of rare early blues and country music, he made his first album in 1959 on his own Tacoma label, calling himself Blind Joe Death. Fahey did not perform publicly for money until the mid-Sixties, after his third album.

Fahey's early albums were haunting and original. Some of his material even foreshadowed psychedelia, with lengthy improvisations sometimes lasting 20 minutes and the use of Indian modes, unpredictable stylistic shifts and overall strangeness. He also employed odd guitar tunings. His reputation as an eccentric was amplified by his bizarre and lengthy liner notes and

song titles like 'When The Catfish Is In Bloom' and 'Stomping Tonight On The Pennsylvania/Alabama Border'. Fahey maintained his following through the mid-Eighties. With his Takoma label, he was instrumental in starting the career of Leo Kottke. Fahey sold Takoma to Chrysalis in the mid-Seventies, but continued to record and tour regularly.

In 1986 he contracted Epstein-Barr syndrome, a long-lasting viral infection that, combined with other health problems, sapped his energy and resources. The mid-Nineties found him living in poverty. But a major career retrospective on Rhino, *Return Of The Repressed* (1994), boosted his profile to its highest level in years. In 1997, he returned to active recording with *City Of Refuge* (1997) and was planning more recordings when he died following sextuple-bypass surgery at the age of 61.

ALI FARKA TOURÉ

WORLDS APART

Sometimes called 'the African John Lee Hooker', Ali 'Farka' Touré (1939–2006) was a Malian singer and guitarist, and one of Africa's most renowned musicians. Many consider his music to be a bridge between traditional Malian music and its presumed descendant, the blues. The interplay of rhythm and sound in Touré's music was similar to John Lee Hooker's hypnotic blues style. Both singers combined a deep-voice delivery with mid-tempo, foot-stomping rhythms, often with minimal accompaniment.

Ali Ibrahim 'Farka' Touré was born in 1939 in the Muslim village of Kanau on the banks of the Niger River. His nickname, 'Farka', chosen by his parents, means 'donkey', an animal admired for its tenacity and stubbornness. He was ethnically tied to the Songrai (Songhai) and Peul peoples of northern Mali. Touré only occasionally sang in English and usually performed in one of several African languages, mostly Songhay, Fulfulde, Tamasheq or Bambara, as on his breakthrough album, *Ali Farka Touré* (1989), which established his reputation in the world-music community. After its release he toured often in North America and Europe, and recorded frequently, sometimes with contributions from Taj Mahal and members of the Chieftains.

After retreating to his homeland to tend his farm, he was persuaded to record 1994's *Talking Timbuktu*, a popular collaboration with Ry Cooder. Touré found success taxing and again retreated to his homeland. He did not release a record in America for five years afterwards. Finally, in 1999 Touré released *Niafunké*, an album of more traditional African rhythms. Then, once again, Touré went on hiatus, becoming mayor of Niafunké and spending his own money to improve the impoverished town. In 2005 Nonesuch issued *Red & Green*, two albums Touré recorded in the early Eighties, packaged as a two-disc set. Also in 2005, he released the album *In The Heart Of The Moon*, a collaboration with Toumani Diabaté, for which he received a second Grammy Award.

Touré's last album, *Savane*, was released posthumously in 2006. It topped the chart for three consecutive months and was nominated for a Grammy Award in the category Best Contemporary World Music Album. In 2006 Touré died at the age of 66 from bone cancer.

DAVEY GRAHAM

TAKING FOLK TO ROCK

Davey Graham (b. 1940) (originally Davy Graham) is a guitarist who is credited with sparking the folk-rock revolution in the UK in the Sixties. He inspired many of the famous fingerstyle guitarists, such as Bert Jansch, John Renbourn, Martin Carthy, Paul Simon and even Jimmy Page, who heavily based his solo 'White Summer' on Graham's 'She Moved Thru' The Bizarre/Blue Raga'.

Graham was born to a Guyanese mother and a Scottish father and he took up the guitar at the age of 12. As a teenager, he was strongly influenced by Steve Benbow, who played a guitar style influenced by Moroccan music. At the age of 19, Graham wrote what is probably his most famous piece, the acoustic solo tune 'Anji'. Jansch included it on his 1965 debut album as 'Angie'. But the spelling 'Anji' became the most popular after it appeared in this way on Simon & Garfunkel's best-selling album *Sounds Of Silence* (1966).

Graham introduced the DADGAD guitar tuning to British guitarists. The tuning allowed the guitarist more freedom to improvise in the treble while maintaining a solid underlying harmony and rhythm in the bass.

During the Sixties Graham released a string of eclectic albums with music from all around the world in all kinds of genres. His continuous touring of the world and adaptation of foreign styles resulted in many crediting him with founding world music. He was the subject of a 2005 BBC Radio documentary 'Whatever Happened To Davy Graham?'. He also was featured in the BBC Four documentary 'Folk Britannia'. Graham recorded only sporadically after the Sixties, although he performed with the renowned acoustic guitar wizards Stefan Grossman and Duck Baker.

In the twenty-first century, Graham worked closely and consistently with singer-songwriter Mark Pavey. Graham has also worked with familiar guitarists and friends, including Bert Jansch, Duck Baker and Martin Carthy. Graham's final album *Broken Biscuits*, featured originals and new arrangements of traditional songs from around the world. In 2008, Graham was diagnosed with lung cancer. He died in December of that year.

JOHN WILLIAMS

THE SKY'S THE LIMIT

Classical guitarist-composer John Christopher Williams (b. 1941) is a Grammy-Award winning Australian classical guitarist who has explored many styles beyond the classical tradition. John's father Leonard (Len) Williams was an accomplished guitarist who emigrated from Britain to Australia and was best known there for his jazz playing. He taught John to play guitar, and it soon became apparent that the boy was gifted. At the age of 12 he went to Italy to study under Andrés Segovia. Later, he attended the Royal College of Music in London, studying piano because the school did not have a guitar department at the time. Upon graduation, he created one and ran it for two years.

Williams has explored many different musical traditions. He was a member of the fusion group Sky. He is also a composer and arranger. He enjoyed a worldwide hit single with his recording of 'Cavatina' by Stanley Myers, used as the theme music to the Oscar-winning film *The Deer Hunter* (1979). In 1973, Cleo Laine wrote lyrics and recorded the song 'He Was Beautiful' accompanied by Williams. A year later, it was a Top 5 UK hit single for Iris Williams (no relation).

Williams created a highly acclaimed classical-rock fusion duet with Pete Townshend of the Who for Townshend's 'Won't Get Fooled Again', which was performed at the 1979 Amnesty International benefit show 'The Secret Policeman's Ball'. The duet was featured on the resulting album and the film version of the show. Williams' classical-rock fusion band Sky gave the first-ever rock concert at Westminster Abbey. Williams has appeared on over 100 albums (including compilations). He has performed and recorded nearly the entire standard guitar repertory, plus a large quantity of transcriptions, many of which he created. He was a professor of guitar at the Royal College of Music in London from 1960 to 1973. Besides film soundtracks, Williams has arranged Beatles songs and formed his own ensembles (John Williams & Friends, Attacca) to explore other music. On *The Guitarist* (1998) he used Turkish and Greek rhythms and harmonies to support medieval music. *The Magic Box* (2002) examines African music. His most recent collection, *From a Bird* (2008), includes Irish traditionals and music inspired by birdsongs.

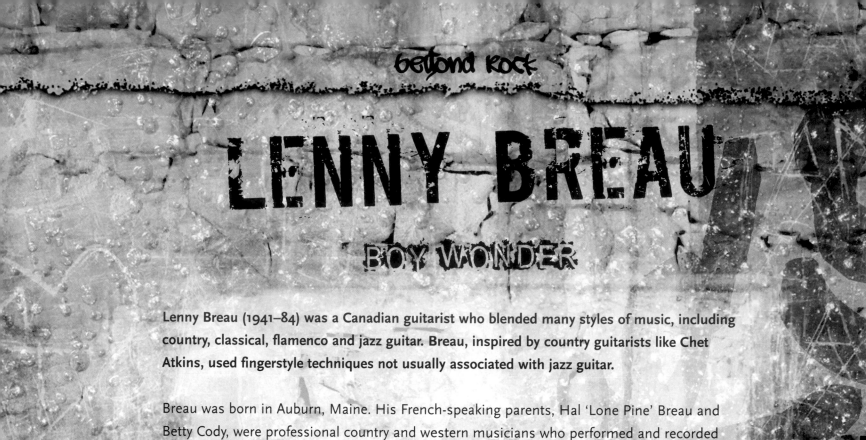

LENNY BREAU

BOY WONDER

Lenny Breau (1941–84) was a Canadian guitarist who blended many styles of music, including country, classical, flamenco and jazz guitar. Breau, inspired by country guitarists like Chet Atkins, used fingerstyle techniques not usually associated with jazz guitar.

Breau was born in Auburn, Maine. His French-speaking parents, Hal 'Lone Pine' Breau and Betty Cody, were professional country and western musicians who performed and recorded in the late Forties and Fifties. Their son began playing guitar at the age of eight, and by the age of 12 he was the lead guitarist for his parents' band, billed as Lone Pine Junior, playing Merle Travis and Chet Atkins instrumentals and occasionally singing. Breau made his first professional recording at the age of 15, billed as Boy Wonder.

Around 1959 Breau left his parents' band and sought out local jazz musicians, performing at Winnipeg venues and learning more jazz technique. In 1961 Breau left for Toronto and created the jazz group Three with singer/actor Don Francks and Don Henstridge on acoustic bass. The Three made appearances on US television as well as in Canadian and New York clubs. Returning to Winnipeg, Breau became a regular session guitarist for radio and television.

Breau's technique combined elements of Chet Atkins- and Merle Travis-style fingerpicking with flamenco. Harmonically he incorporated country, classical, modal, Indian and jazz influences.

By the late Sixties home recordings of Lenny's playing had found their way into the hands of Chet Atkins, who signed Lenny to RCA and released *The Guitar Sounds Of Lenny Breau* (1968) and *The Velvet Touch Of Lenny Breau* (1969). Breau spent most of the Seventies in the United States and settled in Los Angeles in the early Eighties. Only a few more solo albums and a few sessions recorded with steel guitarist Buddy Emmons were issued during his lifetime.

Breau had developed drug problems in the mid-Sixties and struggled with addiction until his death. In August 1984 Breau's body was found in a swimming pool at his apartment complex in Los Angeles, California. His death was ruled a homicide. He had been strangled and his murder is still unsolved.

STEVE CROPPER

THE COLONEL

Steve 'The Colonel' Cropper (b. 1941) is an American guitarist, songwriter, producer and soul musician best known for his work creating the trailblazing soul records produced by Memphis's Stax label as a member of its studio band, which became Booker T & the MGs, in the mid-Sixties.

Stephen Lee Cropper was born on a farm outside Dora, Missouri. In 1950, his family moved to Memphis. Cropper received his first guitar at the age of 14, and started playing with local musicians.

Cropper (pictured below with the Memphis Horns) and guitarist Charlie Freeman formed the Royal Spades, who eventually became the Mar-Keys, named for the marquee outside the Stax (at the time called Satellite Records) offices. The Mar-Keys began playing on sessions there and eventually had a hit single of their own with 1961's 'Last Night'. Also in the band were future legends bassist Donald 'Duck' Dunn and trumpeter Wayne Jackson. Cropper eventually became an A&R man for the label. Along with Booker T. Jones on organ and piano, bassist Dunn and drummer Al Jackson, Jr., Cropper went on to record several hits. As a house guitarist, he played on hundreds of records, from '(Sittin' On) The Dock Of The Bay', co-written with Otis Redding, to Sam and Dave's 'Soul Man', on which Sam Moore shouts, 'Play it, Steve!' Cropper also co-wrote 'Knock On Wood' with Eddie Floyd and 'In The Midnight Hour' with Wilson Pickett.

Cropper left Stax in 1970 and played on or produced records by Jeff Beck, Tower Of Power, John Prine and Jose Feliciano. He played on Ringo Starr's 1973 album *Ringo* and John Lennon's *Rock'n'Roll* (1974). In the late Seventies, Cropper and Duck Dunn became leaders of the Blues Brothers Band. In 1998, he released *Play It, Steve!*, on which he described the inspirations behind his creation of some of soul music's most enduring songs.

In 1996, *Mojo* named Cropper the greatest living guitar player (second all-time behind Jimi Hendrix). In June 2005, Cropper was inducted into the Songwriters Hall Of Fame alongside Bill Withers, John Fogerty, David Porter and Isaac Hayes. He has continued to perform and record with other artists in the 2000s, including the Rascals' Felix Cavaliere for 2008's *Nudge It Up a Notch*.

JOHN McLAUGHLIN

INSPIRATION AND DEVOTION

John McLaughlin (b. 1942) led the Mahavishnu Orchestra and a series of other bands that stretched the boundaries of jazz-rock fusion and world music, as he inspired guitarists worldwide with his inventiveness and devotion to exotic sounds and spirituality.

McLaughlin started on guitar when he was 11 and was initially inspired by blues and swing players. McLaughlin worked with Alexis Korner, Graham Bond, Ginger Baker and others in the Sixties and played free jazz with Gunter Hampel for six months. His first album was *Extrapolation* (1969). He recorded *My Goals Beyond* (1970), an album of acoustic solos and jams with Indian musicians.

My Goals Beyond was inspired by McLaughlin's decision to follow the Indian spiritual leader Sri Chinmoy, to whom he had been introduced in 1970. The album was dedicated to Chinmoy and included one of the guru's poems printed on the liner notes. It was on this album that McLaughlin took the name Mahavishnu.

In 1969 McLaughlin moved to New York to play with Tony Williams' Lifetime, and he became a member of Miles Davis' band, appearing on the records *In A Silent Way* (1969), *Bitches Brew* (1969), *On The Corner* (1972), *Big Fun* (1969), on which he is featured soloist on 'Go Ahead John', and *A Tribute To Jack Johnson* (1970). Davis paid tribute to McLaughlin in the liner notes to *Jack Johnson*, calling McLaughlin's playing 'far in'.

In 1971 McLaughlin formed the Mahavishnu Orchestra, a group with a rock image but with the sophisticated vocabulary of jazz. After three influential albums (*The Inner Mounting Flame*, *Birds Of Fire* and *Between Nothingness And Eternity*), the group disbanded in 1973. McLaughlin, who recorded a powerful spiritual album with Carlos Santana that was influenced by John Coltrane, put together a new Mahavishnu Orchestra in 1974 that, despite the inclusion of Jean-Luc Ponty, failed to catch on and broke up by 1975.

McLaughlin then surprised the music world by radically shifting directions, switching to acoustic guitar and playing Indian music with his group Shakti (pictured below). They made a strong impact on the nascent world-music scene during their three years. In Shakti McLaughlin played a custom steel-string acoustic guitar (made by luthier Abe Wechter and the Gibson guitar company), which featured two tiers of strings over the soundhole: a conventional six-string configuration with an additional seven strings strung underneath at a 45-degree angle. The two string groups were independently tunable and were played as sympathetic strings, much like a sitar or veena. The instrument also featured a scalloped fretboard along the full length of the neck, which enabled McLaughlin to play bends far beyond the reach of a conventional fretboard.

In 1979 McLaughlin teamed up with Jaco Pastorius (bass) and Tony Williams (drums) for the short-lived Trio Of Doom. They only played one concert, at the Karl Marx Theatre in Havana, Cuba on 3 March 1979. They recorded three of the tracks at CBS Studios in New York in 8 March 1979.

McLaughlin then recorded and performed alternating between electric- and acoustic-guitar projects. He led the One Truth Band; played in trios with Al Di Meola and Paco De Lucía; popped up on some mid-Eighties Miles Davis records; and formed a short-lived third version of the Mahavishnu Orchestra (with saxophonist Bill Evans). McLaughlin also recorded a tribute to pianist Bill Evans, and, in 1993, toured with a jazz trio featuring organist Joey DeFrancesco and drummer Dennis Chambers. Throughout his career McLaughlin's modus operandi has been to assemble groups built around a concept or recording project, explore the possibilities of the association fully, and then move on to a new interest or concept.

In recent years McLaughlin created a ballet score, 'Thieves And Poets', released in 2003, and created arrangements of jazz standards for classical guitar ensembles. In 2007, he left Universal Records and joined the small Internet-based Abstract Logix label. He also began touring with a new jazz-fusion quartet, the 4th Dimension. McLaughlin toured in 2008 with Chick Corea, Vinnie Colaiuta, Kenny Garrett and Christian McBride as Five Peace Band. A live album of the tour was released in 2009.

McLaughlin has played many guitars in his varied career, including a Gibson EDS-1275 doubleneck (1971–73), the Double Rainbow doubleneck guitar made by Rex Bogue, (1973–75), the 'Shakti' guitar (with seven additional drone strings) and the 'Marielle' acoustic guitar with cutaway.

ANDY SUMMERS

AUTHORITY OF THE POLICE

One of the greatest achievements any guitar player can attain is an immediately recognizable signature tone and style. And though many of the guitarists in this book have realized this goal, few have done it as emphatically as Police guitarist Andy Summers (b. 1942). From the chord stabs of 'Roxanne' and 'Don't Stand So Close To Me' to the arpeggios of 'Message In A Bottle' and 'Every Breath You Take', Summers's chiming, shimmering Telecaster tones are like no other, and no other guitarist has ever matched them.

Andrew James Somers was born in Poulton-Fylde, Lancashire, England. His family later moved to Bournemouth, where Summers took up the guitar at the age of 14. He soon immersed himself in the local jazz scene, and by the age 16 was regularly playing local venues.

The young guitarist soon joined Zoot Money's Big Roll Band, a jazzy soul and R&B outfit that became a regular fixture on London's Soho scene. In 1967 the band changed its name to Dantalion's Chariot, and its sound to a more psychedelic one, in accord with the changing musical landscape of the era. He would also play with Soft Machine and in a revamped version of the Animals during this time.

Summers then decided to leave the London scene and go to America, where he enrolled at the University of California at Los Angeles to study classical guitar and composition. Upon graduation in 1973 the hungry guitarist returned to his native England, where he worked as a session guitarist for such cult favorites as Kevin Ayers and Kevin Coyne, before landing a job as sideman for, of all people, Neil Sedaka, a gig he got through guitarist Robert Fripp.

In 1977, while travelling on the London Underground one day, Summers had a chance meeting with drummer Stewart Copeland, which led to him joining the short-lived Strontium 90 with Copeland, vocalist Mike Howlett and bassist Sting. Copeland and Sting then invited Summers to join their full-time project the Police. The trio clicked and, despite a slow start,

their debut album *Outlandos d'Amour* (1978), with its hit singles 'Roxanne' and 'Can't Stand Losing You', soon brought the band's unique brand of jazz- and reggae-influenced punk-pop to worldwide prominence.

Over the next three albums the Police would amass numerous hit singles as well as Grammy awards for two instrumental album tracks. In 1983 the trio released *Synchronicity*, which would top the *Billboard* album charts and spawn the No. 1 smash 'Every Breath You Take'. But just as the band reached the pinnacle of pop music, it imploded.

Over the course of those six years with the Police, Summers developed an enduring signature guitar tone. Relying most frequently on his treasured 1963 Fender Telecaster modified with a Gibson PAF pickup in the neck position, Summers used an arsenal of analog chorus and delay effects to craft texturally rich and sophisticated rhythm parts. His preference for suspended

chords and complex jazz voicings, stemming from his fascination with music ranging from twentieth-century composers like Ravel and Bartòk to jazz luminaries Wes Montgomery and Thelonious Monk, was crucial to his singular harmonic approach to rock guitar.

After the breakup of the Police, Summers embarked on a solo career, including two instrumental progressive-rock albums, *I Advance Masked* (1982; recorded prior to *Synchronicity*) and *Bewitched* (1984), with his old friend Robert Fripp. He followed with 1989's Grammy nominated *The Golden Wire* and 1997's acclaimed *The Last Dance Of Mr. X* (1997). Additionally, Summers flexed his compositional chops working on Hollywood film scores, including *Down And Out In Beverly Hills* and *Weekend At Bernie's*.

In 2003, the Police were inducted into the Rock and Roll Hall of Fame, an event that saw Summers reunite with Sting and Copeland to perform three tunes. The trio performed again for the 2007 Grammy Awards and subsequently announced a world tour. The 2007–2008 reunion tour became the third biggest money-making tour of all time. *Certifiable: Live in Buenos Aires*, was released in various configurations, including a two-DVD, two-CD set.

In addition to his music, Summers is also a published author and photographer. Most notable are his critically acclaimed autobiography *One Train Later* and his photo book *I'll Be Watching You: Inside The Police, 1980–83*.

GEORGE BENSON

SMOOTH JAZZ SUPERSTAR

Jazz and R&B star George Benson (b. 1943) seemed destined for a respected but low-key career in cool jazz until he adopted a funky hybrid of jazz and soul for the 1976 album *Breezin'*. Driven by accessible instrumentals and a smash reworking of Leon Russell's 'This Masquerade', the album made Benson the biggest star to cross over from jazz to pop since Stan Getz in 1962 with 'The Girl From Ipanema'. Benson followed up with successful albums that helped create the smooth jazz genre.

Benson was born and raised in Pittsburgh. He started out playing straight-ahead instrumental jazz with organist Jack McDuff. At 21, Benson recorded his first album as leader, *The New Boss Guitar* (1964), with McDuff on organ. Benson's next recording was *It's Uptown With The George Benson Quartet* (1965), with Lonnie Smith on organ and Ronnie Cuber on baritone sax. This album showcases Benson's talent in constructing swinging bebop lines at blistering tempos. Benson followed it up with *The George Benson Cookbook* (1966), also with Smith and Cuber. Benson recorded with Miles Davis in the mid-Sixties, and for Verve, A&M and CTI. He made several albums with guest artists and attempted to follow in his idol Wes Montgomery's footsteps by recording jazz versions of pop albums like *Abbey Road* and *White Rabbit*. In 1975 he signed with Warner Brothers, and then came *Breezin'*.

On the strength of 'This Masquerade', which was the first single to top the pop, R&B and jazz charts simultaneously, Benson became a star. He followed up with the hits 'On Broadway', 'Turn Your Love Around' and others. Benson accumulated three other platinum LPs and two gold albums at Warner. In the ensuing 30 years he travelled the world and recorded and performed with orchestras and a host of music stars. In 2009, Benson was recognized by the National Endowment of the Arts as a Jazz Master, the highest honour awarded in the US for jazz. During 2009, he recorded the album *Songs and Stories*, with bassist Marcus Miller and David Paich and Steve Lukather of Toto.

Benson originally played a Gibson L5 and later developed an association with Ibanez, playing one of the signature models (GB10 or GB200) which they developed for him.

LARRY CORYELL

FATHER OF FUSION

Larry Coryell (b. 1943), a father of jazz-rock fusion, has recorded more than 70 albums over the past 35 years. Born in Galveston, Texas, Coryell tried his hand at a number of instruments before settling on the guitar. Chet Atkins, Chuck Berry and Wes Montgomery were major influences.

As a child Coryell studied piano, switching to guitar in his teens. After studying at the University of Washington, he moved to New York City in 1965, where he played behind guitarist Gabor Szabo in drummer Chico Hamilton's jazz quintet. By 1966, he had replaced Szabo, and later that year made his vinyl debut with Hamilton's band.

Also in 1966 he co-founded an early jazz-rock band, the Free Spirits, with whom he recorded one album, *Free Spirit: Out Of Sight And Sound* (1966). Soon after his stint with the Free Spirits he joined vibraphonist Gary Burton's band, recording three albums. In 1969 he recorded *Memphis Underground* with flautist Herbie Mann. Coryell gained national fame with the Gary Burton Quartet in 1967 and became a highly sought session guitarist in rock, jazz and pop. He toured with Jack Bruce, and recorded with artists as diverse as the Fifth Dimension, Charles Mingus and Chick Corea.

In 1974 Coryell formed the Eleventh House, the most popular and successful fusion band of its time, which included Randy Brecker, Mike Mandel, Danny Trifan and Alphonse Mouzon. After the Eleventh House disbanded, Coryell made a series of solo albums, followed by a direct-to-disc recording with the Brecker Brothers. In 1979 Coryell formed the Guitar Trio with jazz-fusion guitarist John McLaughlin and flamenco guitarist Paco de Lucía. In early 1980 Coryell was replaced by Al Di Meola. In the Nineties Coryell made an admittedly calculated attempt at smooth jazz for the adult contemporary market, a move he has said he ultimately found too limiting. He returned to form with *Spaces Revisited* (1997), reuniting with Billy Cobham, his partner for *Spaces* (1974). Recent albums include *Monk, 'Trane, Miles And Me* (1999), *Cedars Of Avalon* (2002) and *Tricycles* (2004) as well as *Electric* (2005) and *Traffic* (2006) with Lenny White and Victor Bailey. In 2007, he released an autobiography, *Improvising: My Life in Music*.

JOHN RENBOURN

FATHER OF MODERN FOLK

John Renbourn (b. 1944) is a father of contemporary British folk music and an acknowledged master of fingerstyle guitar. He is best known for his collaboration with guitarist Bert Jansch and his work with the folk group Pentangle. Renbourn created music that fused British and Celtic folk with blues, jazz, British early music, classical guitar and Eastern forms.

Renbourn began playing guitar as a teen in his native Torquay, England. At first he was into skiffle, a style that became popular as the folk-music revival was beginning. An instructional book introduced Renbourn to the music of many American folk artists, and he began to research them. In 1964 he began studying classical guitar at the George Abbot School in Guildford. Two years later he was playing folk music in Soho where he met many other musicians, including Paul Simon, Davey Graham and Bert Jansch. Renbourn and Jansch were roommates for a while, and they developed a rapport when jamming together. Both men had fledgling recording careers at the time. Renbourn performed on Jansch's second album and afterwards they teamed up formally to record *Bert And John* (1966). They developed an intricate duet style that became known as 'folk baroque'.

In 1967 the two founded Pentangle and remained together through to 1978. Renbourn, as with the other group members, continued to release such solo albums as *The Hermit* (1976) and *The Black Balloon* (1979). He formed the John Renbourn Group in the Eighties and began adding East Indian percussion and jazz woodwinds to his music. Around the mid-Eighties, he teamed up with guitarist Stefan Grossman and embarked upon a series of world tours. The two also recorded a few albums before Renbourn went on to found the ensemble Ship Of Fools and play music with a stronger Celtic influence.

He continues to tour alone and with other guitarists including Grossman, Larry Coryell and Isaac Guillory. He also occasionally reunites with Jansch and sometimes tours with Scottish storyteller Robin Williamson. In 2005 he toured Japan and collaborated with Clive Carroll on the score for the film *Driving Lessons*. He continues to perform and give guitar workshops.

Early on, Renbourn played the English-made Scarth guitar. In the mid-Sixties, he acquired a Gibson J-50 and later played a Guild D-55.

PETER TOSH

A WAILING WAILER

Peter Tosh (1944–87), born Winston Hubert McIntosh, was the guitarist in the original Wailing Wailers. His mercurial temperament, provocative advocacy of the Rastafari movement and untimely death drew attention from his role in the most important band in the history of reggae. Tosh grew up in Kingston, Jamaica. His height (6ft 5in/2m) and temperament earned him the nickname Stepping Razor. Tosh began to sing and play guitar at a young age, inspired by the music his radio could get from distant American stations.

In the early Sixties Tosh met Bob Marley and Bunny Wailer, and the trio began harmonizing and playing guitars together. In 1962 they formed the Wailing Wailers. The band recorded several successful ska singles before splitting in late 1965. After immersion in the Rastafari movement, the original trio reunited and renamed the group the Wailers.

The band left ska behind, and added socially conscious lyrics to their down-tempo grooves. The Wailers teamed with production wizard Lee Perry to record the early reggae hits 'Soul Rebel', 'Duppy Conqueror' and 'Small Axe'. Adding bassist Aston 'Family Man' Barrett and his brother, drummer Carlton, in 1970, the Wailers became Caribbean superstars and signed a recording contract with Island Records. Their debut, *Catch A Fire* (1973), was followed by *Burnin'* the same year.

In 1973, Tosh's skull was fractured in a car accident that killed his girlfriend. Tosh clashed with Island Records president Chris Blackwell, and when the label refused to issue his solo album in 1974, Tosh and Bunny Wailer left the band.

Tosh's post-Wailers career was characterized by the rebellious title track from his solo debut, *Legalize It* (1976). As Marley became an icon with the positive message of 'One Love', Tosh railed against the establishment. He released *Equal Rights* (1977), *Bush Doctor* (1978), *Mystic Man* (1979) and *Wanted Dread And Alive* (1981). After the release of 1983's *Mama Africa*, Tosh withdrew, only to return and win a Grammy for Best Reggae Performance in 1987 for *No Nuclear War*. However, in September 1987 a three-man gang came to Tosh's house demanding money, and when Tosh could not produce any, he was shot dead.

JOHN ABERCROMBIE

FREE JAZZ AND COLLABORATIONS

John Abercrombie (b. 1944) is a stylist who has managed to incorporate flavours of folk and rock along with world-music influences into his jazz-based repertoire. He was a highly influential fusion guitarist in the late Sixties and Seventies and has had an abundant career, working solo and with a multitude of collaborators, including Billy Cobham, Ralph Towner, Jack DeJohnette and the Brecker Brothers.

Abercrombie was born in Port Chester, New York, and attended Boston's Berklee College of Music from 1962 to 1967. While at Berklee, he toured with bluesman Johnny Hammond. After relocating to New York in 1969, Abercrombie worked in groups led by drummers Chico Hamilton and Billy Cobham. Abercrombie first received widespread attention in Cobham's Spectrum group. He also recorded two albums with the jazz-rock band Dreams in 1970.

Abercrombie's first album as leader was *Timeless* (1974), a trio album with drummer Jack DeJohnette and keyboardist Jan Hammer. Abercrombie and DeJohnette reunited for *Gateway* (1975) and *Gateway 2* (1977), with bassist Dave Holland replacing Hammer. He began his association with Towner on *Sargasso Sea* (1976); the duo again teamed for *Five Years Later* (1981). In 1987, Abercrombie began a five-album collaboration with organist Jeff Palmer.

Most recently, Abercrombie has broadened his circle of collaborators, appearing on *Three Guitars* (2003) with Badi Assad and Larry Coryell; *Speak Easy* (2004) with Jarek Smietana, Harvie S and Adam Czerwinski; *As We Speak* (2006), with the Mark Egan trio and Danny Gottlieb; and *Baseline: The Guitar Album* (2007) with Hein Van De Geyn.

Abercrombie's twenty-first century work includes *Cat 'N' Mouse* (2002), *Class Trip* (2004), *A Nice Idea* (with pianist Andy LaVerne) (2005), *Structures* (recorded with a single microphone) (2006), *Third Quartet* (2007) and *Wait Till You See Her* (2009). Abercrombie has augmented his playing and recording with contributions as clinician and teacher. Explaining his approach to standards, he said, 'As much as I've played those tunes over the years, I still enjoy playing them. And because I know them so well, I'm very free with them. I'm just as free with them as when I'm playing no chords at all. That, to me, is free jazz.'

ADRIAN LEGG

DEFYING CATEGORIZATION

Fingerstyle master Adrian Legg (b. 1948) defies categorization. But though his music combines British folk, Celtic, rock, classical, blues, jazz and country sounds, Legg's warm, soulful playing is the thread that unites the styles.

Born in Hackney, London, England, Legg took the first steps of his musical journey playing the oboe as a lad. As many teenage boys are wont to do, however, he eventually became interested in the guitar. His father, who was a choirmaster, organist and Anglican priest, provided young Adrian with a firm grounding in the European harmonic tradition. Indeed, Legg has cited those ancient and modern hymns as being among his biggest musical influences. These were especially evident on his introspective 2004 album, *Inheritance*.

As a fingerstylist, Legg has few peers. But as an innovative and inventive guitarist, he stands alone at the genre's acme. Aside from being a master of such traditional fingerstyle techniques as Travis picking and banjo rolls, Legg has introduced entirely new techniques to the vernacular. His use of banjo tuners with carefully placed stops to enable mid-phrase pitch modulations is downright revolutionary. And while capo use is common in fingerstyle guitar, Legg's employment of custom-made partial capos, slotted capos and half capos is as singular as it is mesmerizing. Finally, his pitch modulation via string bending on chord voicings – borrowed from country music's pedal-steel guitarists – gives his phrases a vocal quality often lacking in even the most notable fingerstylists.

Over the course of his career, Legg has been as involved in music technology nearly as much as he has on the fretboard itself. Legg's intense passion for music-making tools was first demonstrated in the form of his 1981 book, *Customizing Your Electric Guitar*, and is still evident in his use of looping devices and synth pads to fill out his live solo performances. But perhaps it is no more evident than in his custom electric guitar, which features a two-piece swamp ash body with a cavity hollowed out and then vented on the treble side cutaway, a Graph-Tech piezo pickup and a specially made Waffair Theene DiMarzio magnetic pickup, Bill Keith banjo tuners with fixed stops and, perhaps most interesting, an overall scale and shape designed to fit inside the overhead compartments of commercial airliners.

JOHN MARTYN

GRACE AND GLORY

British singer-songwriter and guitarist John Martyn (1948–2009) was born Iain David McGeachy in England. In his 40-year career he has released 20 studio albums. Martyn's parents divorced when he was five, and he spent his childhood in England and Scotland.

Martyn's musical career began when he was 17. He blended blues and folk into a unique style, working in the London folk scene of the mid-Sixties. He signed to Chris Blackwell's Island Records in 1967 and released his first album, *London Conversation* (1968). By 1970 Martyn had incorporated jazz into his work and developed a unique acoustic guitar sound using effects boxes. This sound was first apparent on *Stormbringer* in 1970, which featured Martyn's then wife, Beverley Kutner. She also appeared on *The Road To Ruin* in 1970.

In 1973 Martyn released *Solid Air*, the title song a tribute to the singer-songwriter Nick Drake, a close friend and label mate. Martyn developed his signature slurred and guttural vocal style. *Solid Air* includes 'May You Never', perhaps Martyn's best-known song, which was recorded by Eric Clapton and many others. Following the success of *Solid Air*, Martyn became experimental with *Inside Out* (1974), pensive with *Sunday's Child* (1975) and a naturalist with *One World* (1977).

Martyn's breakup with Beverley resulted in the heart-wrenching *Grace And Danger* (1980), the rawness of which has made the album Martyn's most discussed work. In the late Eighties Martyn cited *Grace And Danger* as his favourite album. 'Some people keep diaries', he said. 'I make records'. A deluxe double-disc re-master of the album was released in 2007. Phil Collins played drums and sang backing vocals on *Grace And Danger* and produced Martyn's next album, *Glorious Fool* (1981). Martyn left Island records in 1981 and has recorded sporadically since then. In 2006 the documentary 'Johnny Too Bad' documented the period surrounding the operation to amputate John's right leg below the knee (the result of a burst cyst) and the writing and recording of *On The Cobbles* (2004). In 2008 Martyn received the lifetime achievement award at the BBC Radio 2 Folk Awards. He died from pneumonia in 2009.

JUAN MARTÍN

USING THE GUITAR TO PAINT

Juan Cristóbal Martín (b. 1948) was born in Málaga, Spain, and started learning the guitar at the age of six. In his early twenties he moved to Madrid to study under Nino Ricardo and Paco de Lucía. Martín was influenced by classic flamenco and the Spanish classical guitar tradition. His major influences included de Lucía, Tomatito and Andrés Segovia. But Martín's work evokes jazz guitarists like Joe Pass as well, and even the style of the late Brazilian guitar virtuoso Laurindo Almeida, one of the first guitarists to combine samba with cool jazz and a major influence on Martín.

One of Martín's early recordings was *Picasso Portraits* (1981). Each section is an audio depiction of a painting by Pablo Picasso. Martin composed the pieces, and the album included guest appearances by Simon Phillips (session musician for Mike Oldfield and many others), most of the Gordon Giltrap Band and some members of the Jeff Beck Band.

Although it was not released until the Nineties, he recorded a track with Rory Gallagher in 1984 (on the album *Wheels Within Wheels*). The same track has Richard Thompson and David Lindley on it. Martín recorded with Herbie Hancock in 1987 and played on stage with Miles Davis.

Martín began his record career in the Eighties, when he recorded a few albums for RCA's Novus label, including *Through The Moving Window* and *Painter In Sound* (both 1990). Martín crossed paths with jazz greats ranging from tenor and soprano saxophonist Wayne Shorter to Brazilian singer Flora Purim and her percussionist husband, Airto Moreira. Martín recorded for the Alex label in the early to mid-Nineties, and in the late Nineties and early Noughties recorded extensively for the independent Flamenco Vision label. By early 2005 Martín had recorded at least 16 albums.

Martín released a successful instructional book *Juan Martín's Guitar Method El Arte Flamenco De La Guitarra*, which was printed in both English and Spanish.

Martín has been voted in the top three guitarists in the world in the magazine *Guitar Player*. His latest albums have flamenco dancers on the soundtrack, adding the sounds of flamenco zapateado dancing to the music.

RICHARD THOMPSON

LAUDED BY THE CRITICS

In his 40-year career as an award-winning songwriter, guitarist and musician's musician, Richard Thompson (b. 1949) has won fans for his work as an original member of Fairport Convention (pictured below), as part of a duo with former wife Linda Thompson and as a solo artist. His songs have been recorded by Bonnie Raitt, Elvis Costello, Emmylou Harris, David Gilmour, the Corrs, Norma Waterson, the Blind Boys Of Alabama and many others.

Thompson was born in West London, England. His father was a Scotland Yard detective and an amateur guitar player. Several other family members played music professionally. Thompson embraced rock'n'roll music at an early age, but also absorbed his father's collection of jazz and traditional Scottish music.

While still in school, he formed his first band Emil & the Detectives with classmate Hugh Cornwell on bass. By the age of 18 Thompson was playing with the newly formed Fairport Convention. Thompson's guitar playing caught the ear of American producer Joe Boyd. Largely on the strength of Thompson's playing Boyd signed them to his management company.

Soon Thompson developed a reputation as an outstanding guitar player and began writing songs seriously. By the time of Fairport Convention's first album in 1969, Thompson was already crafting thoughtful songs with unconventional lyrics like 'Meet On The Ledge', 'Genesis Hall' and 'Crazy Man Michael'.

In January 1971 Thompson left Fairport Convention and released his first solo album, *Henry The Human Fly* (1972). The album was not well received, but Thompson had begun a relationship with one of the album's singers, Linda Peters, and they were married in October 1972. Linda would now be the primary interpreter of his songs.

The first Richard and Linda Thompson album, *I Want To See The Bright Lights Tonight* was released in April of 1974. The album impressed critics but

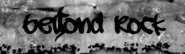

ADRIAN BELEW

AN UNDERRATED SIX-STRINGER

Master of guitar-generated sound effects, Adrian Belew (b. 1949) makes his Parker Deluxe guitar not only sing but also scream, squawk, roar, tweet and talk in elephant tongue. Best known for his time in King Crimson during the early Eighties as comic foil to Robert Fripp's relatively nerdy straight man, Belew is one of the most underrated six-stringers in the world today.

Adrian was born Robert Steven Belew in Covington, Kentucky. He began his musical career as a drummer, playing in his high-school marching band. But after discovering the Beatles, he picked up a guitar and taught himself how to play. After honing his skills, he joined a popular Nashville-area cover band called Sweetheart in 1975. Two years later, while on a Nashville tour stop, Frank Zappa caught a show and immediately recruited Belew to join his own band, which he did.

As Zappa's 1978 world tour was winding down, David Bowie saw Belew's performance and invited him to join his band after his Zappa stint was finished. Belew took the gig and accompanied Bowie on his 1978 world tour as well as on his 1978 live album, *Stage*, and 1979's studio effort, *Lodger*.

As good fortune would have it, Belew soon met Talking Heads producer Jerry Harrison, who invited him to contribute guitar tracks to their 1980 album *Remain In Light* and then continue

on as a touring guitarist. On the first day of the Talking Heads tour, Belew met guitarist Robert Fripp, who invited him to join a reconstructed King Crimson. Abandoning their prog-rock roots for a more modern, Talking Heads-style sound for which Belew's quirky guitar style was well-suited, Crimson recorded three acclaimed albums – *Discipline* (1981), *Beat* (1982) and *Three Of A Perfect Pair* (1984) – before disbanding once more. Belew spent the remainder of the Eighties and the first half of the Nineties recording as both a solo artist and a member of the Bears, as well as a session guitarist, notably on Paul Simon's 1986 masterpiece, *Graceland*, and Nine Inch Nails' *The Downward Spiral* (1994). In 1995 he reunited with his Crimson mates to record *THRAK*, and has since recorded two more King Crimson albums. Belew continues to explore new musical frontiers in his Power Trio. He released *A Cup Of Coffee And A Slice of Time* (2009) with pianist Michael Clay.

BiLL FRISELL

SENSATIONAL SESSION STAR

Bill Frisell (b. 1951) is a North American guitarist and composer who built an eclectic career creating guitar music in several disciplines and genres. He was born William Richard 'Bill' Frisell in Baltimore, Maryland, but spent most of his youth in the Denver area. He went to the University of Northern Colorado, where he studied guitar with Johnny Smith. After graduation, he went to the Berklee School of Music in Boston and studied with jazz legend Jim Hall.

Frisell's major break came when Pat Metheny recommended him to drummer Paul Motian for a session. Motian's label, ECM Records, made Frisell its in-house guitar player, and he worked on several albums. Frisell's first solo release was *In Line* (1983), a solo guitar album, with contributions from bassist Arild Andersen. In the Eighties Frisell worked with saxophonist-composer John Zorn and worked with many others in New York. He again worked with Motian's trio, along with saxophonist Joe Lovano. In 1988 Frisell left New York City and moved to Seattle.

In the early Nineties Frisell made two of his best-known albums: *Have A Little Faith* (1992), an ambitious album tackling Charles Ives and Aaron Copland ('Billy The Kid'), John Hiatt (the title song), Bob Dylan ('Just Like A Woman'), and Madonna ('Live To Tell'); and *This Land* 1992), a complementary set of originals. He also performed soundtracks to the silent films of Buster Keaton with his trio, and contributed to Ryuichi Sakamoto's album *Heartbeat*. In the mid-

Nineties, Frisell provided music for the TV version of 'The Far Side'. It was released on the album *Quartet* (1996) along with music written for Keaton's 'Convict'. Some of Frisell's songs, including 'Over The Rainbow' and 'Coffaro's Theme', were featured in the movie *Finding Forrester* (2000). In 2003, Frisell's *The Intercontinentals* was nominated for a Grammy Award. He won the 2005 Grammy Award for Best Contemporary Jazz Album for *Unspeakable*. Recent releases include *Floratone* (2007), *History, Mystery* (2008), *Hemispheres* (2008), and *Disfarmer* (2009).

Frisell's eclectic work, though rooted in jazz, has touched on progressive folk, classical music, country music, noise and more. He uses an array of effects, including delay, distortion, reverb, octave shifters and volume pedals to create unique textures.

JOHN SCOFIELD

A JAZZ GUITAR GREAT

Considered one of modern jazz guitar's 'big three' guitarists – along with Pat Metheny and Bill Frisell – John Scofield (b. 1951) is also one of the most versatile players of his generation. Conversant in fusion and hard bop as well as in the heady grooves of the jam-band scene, his stew of blues and jazz mixed with post-bop and funk-edged jazz and delivered in angular yet fluid phrases is one of jazz's most distinctive sounds.

Born in Dayton, Ohio, and raised in suburban Connecticut, Scofield took up the guitar at the age of 11, inspired by both rock and blues players. He attended Berklee College of Music in Boston. After making his recording debut with Gerry Mulligan and Chet Baker, Scofield would become a member of the Billy Cobham/George Duke band for two years. In 1977 he recorded with Charles Mingus and then joined Gary Burton's quartet, replacing Pat Metheny. That same year, Scofield released his debut solo album titled simply *John Scofield*, thus beginning his career as a bandleader. In 1979 the guitarist teamed up with his mentor Steve Swallow and drummer Andy Nussbaum (later replaced by Bill Stewart) to form the John Scofield Trio, a group that would be central to Scofield's career. From 1982 to 1985, Scofield toured and recorded with Miles Davis, his work on the 1983 album *Decoy* being particularly striking.

Since that time, Scofield has prominently led his trio and other groups in the international jazz scene, recording over 30 albums as a leader, including collaborations with Pat Metheny, Charlie Haden, Medeski, Martin & Wood, Bill Frisell, Brad Mehldau, Gov't Mule, Joe Lovano and Phil Lesh. Further, he has played and recorded with Jim Hall, Ron Carter, Herbie Hancock and Joe Henderson,

among many jazz legends. Recent highlights include his excursions into the drum and bass electronic music world on 2002's *Überjam*, as well as the more traditional sounds of *Saudades* (2006), recorded as Trio Beyond, with drummer Jack DeJohnette and keyboardist Larry Goldings. For nearly 20 years Scofield has plied his lines on an Ibanez AS-200, and more recently on his signature-model Ibanez JSM100, through a Mesa/Boogie Mark I reissue and an arsenal of modulation effects. One trademark of Scofield's style is his use of portable looping effects, particularly the Boomerang Phrase Sampler, to create multi-layered guitar parts in a live setting. Scofield moved to EmArCy for *This Meets That* (2007) and *Piety Street* (2009).

LEE RITENOUR

CAPTAIN FINGERS

Lee Ritenour (b. 1952) began his career as a session player at 16 and grew into an internationally respected guitarist, composer and producer. He has appeared on over 3,000 sessions and recorded 40 solo and collaboration albums. He had a worldwide hit with 'Is It You' in 1981. As for his guitar playing, his nickname, Captain Fingers, says it all.

Lee Mack Ritenour was born in Los Angeles, California. He played his first recording session with the Mamas & the Papas in 1968 and by the mid-Seventies was a much sought-after session guitarist. A major influence was jazz guitarist Wes Montgomery. In 1976 Ritenour released his first solo album, *First Course*. This was followed up by his fusion work *Captain Fingers* in 1976. Since *First Course* he has released over 30 albums, including *Rit's House* in 2002. One of his most notable works is his pop album *Rit* (1981), which featured vocalist Eric Tagg and contained the chart hits 'Is It You' and 'Mr. Briefcase'. In the Nineties, he was one of the founding members of group Fourplay. He has been nominated for 17 Grammies, has won one and won (or held a high ranking in) countless fan polls.

Throughout his career Ritenour has experimented with different styles of music. He has often incorporated elements of funk, pop, rock, blues and Brazilian music into his jazz releases. In

the early Eighties Ritenour was given his own Ibanez signature-model guitar, the LR-10, which was produced from 1981 to 1987. It can be heard exclusively on his album *Rit*. Currently Ritenour plays the Gibson ES-335 and L5 that he first played in the Seventies, and also plays his signature Lee Ritenour Model archtop made by Gibson.

In February 2004 Ritenour completed a project looking back on his career called *Overtime*. Featuring musicians he has worked with, including Dave Grusin, Patrice Rushen, Harvey Mason and many others, the CD and DVD were recorded in front of a small audience. His latest album, entitled *Smoke N' Mirrors*, was released in August 2006. It featured on drums Ritenour's 13-year-old son Wesley, a namesake of his dad's idol, Wes Montgomery. He teamed with Dave Grusin for 2008's *Amparo*.

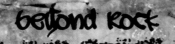

AL DI MEOLA
A TECHNICAL MAESTRO

Al Di Meola (b. 1954) rose to the top tier of contemporary jazz guitarists through his work with Chick Corea's Return To Forever in the Seventies. In addition to a prolific solo career, he has collaborated on projects with bassist Stanley Clarke, keyboardist Jan Hammer, violinist Jean-Luc Ponty and guitarists John McLaughlin and Paco de Lucía.

Al Laurence Dimeola was born in Jersey City, New Jersey, and grew up in nearby Bergenfield. In 1971 he enrolled in the Berklee College of Music in Boston. In 1974 he joined Chick Corea's band, Return To Forever, remaining until 1976. In RTF Di Meola was first noted for his technical mastery and fast, complex guitar solos and compositions. Di Meola built on his reputation with his first solo album *Land Of The Midnight Sun* (1976). He branched out to explore Mediterranean cultures and acoustic genres like flamenco on cuts like 'Mediterranean Sundance' and 'Lady Of Rome, Sister Of Brazil' from *Elegant Gypsy* (1977).

Di Meola continued to explore Latin motifs on albums like *Casino* (1978) and *Splendido Hotel* (1980). He showed his range on acoustic numbers like 'Fantasia Suite For Two Guitars' from the *Casino* album, and on the best-selling live album with McLaughlin and de Lucía, *Friday Night In San Francisco* (1980). Also in 1980 he toured with fellow Latin rocker, Carlos Santana.

With *Scenario* (1983), he explored the electronic side of jazz in a collaboration with Jan Hammer. He broadened his acoustic sensibilities on *Cielo E Terra* (1985) and incorporated guitar/synthesizers on albums such as *Soaring Through A Dream* (1985).

In the Nineties, Di Meola moved into ethnic and world music and explored modern Latin styles. He mixed acoustic and guitar-synthesizer pieces with a selection of electric guitar numbers from earlier albums, such as the blistering 'Race With Devil On Spanish Highway' from *Elegant Gypsy*.

Di Meola has been more active on acoustic guitar in recent years because of tinnitus from years of playing at excessive volumes. He played a series of dates with Return To Forever's mid-Seventies line-up of Chick Corea, Stanley Clarke and Lenny White in 2008.

VINCE GILL

COUNTRY CROSSOVER STAR

Vince Gill (b. 1957) broke out of a respected but static 10-year career as a bandmember and solo act and into country stardom with the 1990 hit 'When I Call Your Name'. Gill was in the forefront of the neotraditional country movement and became one of the biggest crossover singing stars in Nashville. It helped that he was an excellent country guitar player, capable of blistering solos in styles from hard rock to chicken pickin'.

Vincent Grant Gill was born in Norman, Oklahoma. At the encouragement of his father, a part-time country musician, Gill learned to play banjo and guitar before he started high school. By graduation he had advanced enough to get work in Ricky Skagg's Boone Creek and later Rodney Crowell's road band, the Cherry Bombs. In 1979 he became a member of the country rock band Pure Prairie League and gained national exposure as lead singer of the hit 'Let Me Love You Tonight'.

Gill signed with RCA Records in 1983, but had only a few charted hits. In 1989, he switched to MCA Records, where he recorded his breakthrough hit 'When I Call Your Name'. He followed with *Pocket Full Of Gold* (1991), *I Still Believe In You* (1993) and *When Love Finds You* (1995). Eleven singles from those albums made the Top 3 on the US country charts, with four hitting No. 1, along with a No. 1 duet with Reba McEntire, 'The Heart Won't Lie'.

From there the accolades and awards poured in for Gill. Gill hosted the televised CMA Awards every year from 1992 to 2003. In 2004 he received a Grammy Award for Best Male Country Vocal Performance. In 1997 he was inducted into the Western Performers Hall Of Fame in Oklahoma City. In 2007, Gill was inducted into the Country Music Hall Of Fame, and in 2008, Gill won his nineteenth Grammy for Best Country Album, *These Days*, a four-CD set of 43 new recordings performed in a range of musical styles. Guest performers included Sheryl Crow, Emmylou Harris, Diana Krall, Trisha Yearwood, Michael McDonald, Bonnie Raitt, Leann Rimes, Gretchen Wilson and Gill's wife Amy Grant, among others.

PRINCE

A TALENTED SHOWMAN

Prince (b. 1958) has used guitar as a stage prop that exudes flash on a par with his wardrobe, enigmatic persona and overall showmanship, but his talent on the instrument was a crucial element in bringing his unique blend of rock and soul to a worldwide audience.

Prince Rogers Nelson, also known as the Artist Formerly Known As Prince, also known as an unpronounceable symbol, was born in Minneapolis, Minnesota, to John L. Nelson and Mattie Shaw. John was a pianist and songwriter, and Mattie was a singer. He is named after the Prince Rogers Trio, his father's jazz band. Prince's parents divorced, and he had a troubled relationship with his stepfather. Prince lived briefly with his father, who bought him his first guitar, and later moved in with a neighbourhood family, the Andersons, befriending their son, André Anderson, later André Cymone.

The friends played in local party bands together and, as Prince's talents developed, he grew from background instrumentalist to front man. He began to do more studio work for local musicians and producers, and a demo tape he made in 1976 led to a contract with Warner Bros., which allowed him creative control over his songs.

Prince's first two albums were standard late-Seventies funk-pop. The single 'Soft And Wet', from *For You* (1978), reached No. 12 on the US R&B charts. 'I Wanna Be Your Lover', from *Prince* (1979), reached No. 1. With 1980's *Dirty Mind* Prince began to catch fire, on the strength of the album's musical versatility and stark treatment of sex. The follow-up, *Controversy* (1981), made an international splash with its title song. Then came *1999*, a monster hit that sold over three million copies and gave the world a party song that would last way beyond the date in its title.

And then Prince became a movie star with 1985's *Purple Rain*. The soundtrack eventually sold over ten million copies in the US and spent 24 weeks at No. 1. Partially recorded with his

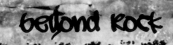

touring band, the Revolution, the record featured the most pop-oriented music Prince ever made, including the title song and the international smash 'When Doves Cry'.

Not content to repeat himself, Prince experimented with psycho-psychedelia on *Around The World In A Day* (1985), which nevertheless sold over two million copies. In 1986 he released *Parade*, which spawned the sparse funk of 'Kiss' and served as the soundtrack to Prince's second film, *Under The Cherry Moon*. 'Kiss' would top the Billboard Hot 100, while 'Manic Monday', written by Prince for the Bangles, reached No. 2. In 1987 Prince continued his roll with the sprawling masterpiece *Sign 'O' The Times*.

Prince was set to release the hard funk of *The Black Album* by the end of the year, but, judging the album too dark in tone, withdrew it before its release. Instead, he released *Lovesexy*, a commercial disaster, in 1988. With the soundtrack to 1989's *Batman*, Prince returned to the top of the charts. But then *Graffiti Bridge* (1990), the sequel to *Purple Rain*, turned out to be a commercial disappointment. In 1991 Prince formed the New Power Generation. With their first album, *Diamonds And Pearls* (1991), Prince had his biggest hit since 1985.

The following year, Prince released his twelfth album, which was titled with a cryptic, unpronounceable symbol (later copyrighted as 'Love Symbol #2'). The album reached the Top 10 of the US album charts. In 1993, he also changed his stage name to the Love Symbol, which is a combination of the symbols for male (♂) and female (♀). Because the symbol was/is unpronounceable, he was often referred to as Symbol, the Artist Formerly Known As Prince, or simply the Artist.

In 1994 he released the single 'The Most Beautiful Girl In The World' independently, and the song became his biggest hit in years. Later that summer, Warner released *Come* under the name of Prince; the record went gold. In subsequent years Prince completed his obligation to his long-time adversary Warner Bros., set up his own label, NPG, and released the albums *Crystal Ball*, *New Power Soul* and jazzy albums that didn't excite long-time fans. He resurged, however, with *Musicology* (2003), and garnered a Grammy nomination for Best Male Pop Vocal Performance. Prince was inducted into the Rock And Roll Hall Of Fame in 2004. His latest release was the triple-album set containing *LOtUSFLOW3R*, *MPLSoUND* and *Elixer* (by protege Bria Valente) in 2009.

STANLEY JORDAN

THE TWO-HANDED TAPPER

Jazz and fusion guitarist Stanley Jordan (b. 1959) caught listeners' attention with his touch technique, an advanced form of two-handed tapping, for playing guitar. By quickly tapping (or 'hammering') his finger down behind the appropriate fret with varying force, Jordan produced a unique legato sound not usually associated with tapping.

Jordan was born in Chicago, Illinois. He received a degree in music from Princeton University in 1981. He was a classically trained pianist before playing guitar, and his desire for piano-like voicing of chords on guitar led to the tapping technique. He was the first artist to be signed by the reborn Blue Note Records in 1985. Jordan's *Magic Touch* (1985) was the first new release of the label. Smooth-jazz radio embraced his versions of 'The Lady In My Life' (first recorded by Michael Jackson) and the Beatles' 'Eleanor Rigby', helping *Magic Touch* top *Billboard*'s jazz chart for a stunning 51 weeks. The album went gold, a rare achievement for an instrumental CD.

On subsequent albums Jordan tried to stretch out as his label sought more radio-friendly material. On Blue Note he was marketed as a smooth-jazz hero, confining Jordan to an increasingly restrictive radio format. Subsequent albums included a solo-guitar project titled *Standards Volume 1* (1986), on which Jordan rightfully assigned the category to pop songs by Stevie Wonder and Simon & Garfunkel as well as standards by Henry Mancini ('Moon River') and Hoagy Carmichael ('Georgia On My Mind'). He followed that with the band album *Flying Home* (1988) and *Cornucopia* (1990), which mixed jazz recorded live with studio originals. After moving to Arista Records in 1994, he recorded *Bolero*, which featured a 17-minute arrangement of Ravel's 'Bolero' broken up into multiple stylistic sections.

Jordan's main guitar at the time was built by Vigier Guitars in 1982. Vigier modified one of its models with a flat fingerboard, creating a very low action that facilitated the tapping technique.

Jordan left the mainstream record business and took up residence in Sedona, Arizona, where he owns a book and music store and studies music therapy. He continues to tour.

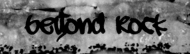

BRAD PAISLEY

TAKING CENTRE STAGE

Brad Paisley (b. 1972) is that rare country music star whose guitar-playing prowess equals his singing and songwriting talent. Paisley recorded five gold or platinum albums between 1999 and 2008 and had ten No. 1 singles on the country charts. His guitar playing on those records proved him to be one of the most accomplished pickers in Nashville.

Brad Douglas Paisley was born in Glen Dale, West Virginia. His maternal grandfather gave Paisley his first guitar at the age of eight and taught him how to play. At the age of 12 Paisley wrote his first song, and by age of 13, he was an opening act for country singers such as Ricky Skaggs and George Jones in West Virginia. Paisley later was awarded a music scholarship to Belmont University in Nashville. After graduating from Belmont, Paisley signed a songwriting contract with EMI Music Publishing. He wrote David Kersh's Top 5 hit, 'Another You', as well as cuts by Tracy Byrd and David Ball.

In 1999 he had his first No. 1 hit, 'He Didn't Have To Be'. In 2000 Paisley won the Country Music Association's (CMA) Horizon Award and the Academy Of Country Music's Best New Male Vocalist trophy. He received his first Grammy Award nomination a year later for Best New Artist. In February 2001 Paisley was inducted into the Grand Ole Opry.

In 2002 he won the CMA Music Video Of The Year for 'I'm Gonna Miss Her (The Fishin' Song)'. After his debut, *Who Needs Pictures* (1999), and *Part II* (2001), Paisley released his third album, *Mud On The Tires* (2003). The title track reached No. 1 in 2004. In 2005 he released *Time Well Wasted*, which contained the hit 'Alcohol'.

In 2006, the album *Time Well Wasted* won the Country Music Association Award for Best Album, and it won Album Of The Year at the 2006 ACM Awards. Paisley's guitar playing finally took centre stage in 2008, when he won his first Grammy Award for Best Country Instrumental for 'Throttleneck'. His album *American Saturday Night* was released in 2009. The album's lead-off single, 'Then' became Paisley's fourteenth No. 1 hit.

JOHNNY HILAND

NASHVILLE'S RECENT BEST

Johnny Hiland (b. 1975) is one of the top guitarists to emerge from the Nashville music scene in recent years. His playing combines country chicken pickin' with elements of blues, metal and jazz. Often compared to Danny Gatton, Hiland displays an amazing vocabulary as he plays seemingly effortlessly onstage. His skill is also noteworthy because he is legally blind as a result of nystagmus, an ocular condition causing involuntary eye movement.

Hiland was born in Woodland, Maine. He grew up in a trailer home and took to the guitar at a young age. At eight, he joined his family's band, the Three Js, which toured New England under the auspices of the Down East Country Music Association. At the age of 10, Hiland won the Talent America contest, entitling him to a performance in New York City. In high school his musical tastes extended beyond bluegrass to the guitar rock of players like Joe Satriani and Eddie Van Halen. After high school, he attended the University of Southern Maine as a history major, but ultimately dropped out to become a professional musician.

In 1996 he moved to Nashville, where he quickly attracted attention at local clubs, earning a residency at the World-Famous Turf and, when that club was destroyed by a tornado, at Robert's Western Wear with Don Kelly's band. He backed Gary Chapman at the Ryman Auditorium, home of the Grand Ole Opry, and became the first unsigned artist in Nashville to receive an endorsement deal with Fender musical instruments. Steve Vai signed Hiland to his Favored Nations label after hearing his demo. Hiland's first album of original guitar instrumentals, *Johnny Hiland*, was released in 2004. Meanwhile, Hiland (pictured left with Mac Wilson) had become a busy session musician in Nashville, recording with the likes of Ricky Skaggs, Randy Travis and Janie Fricke.

Hiland played a Fender Telecaster until the mid-Noughties, when he switched to Paul Reed Smith guitars. PRS made a Johnny Hiland signature model. In 2010 Hiland joined the Ernie Ball/Music Man company as an endorsee. Hiland prefers the Music Man Silhouette guitar.

OTHER GREAT GUITARISTS

Ackerman, William	Solo	1970s–00s
Ade, King Sunny	Solo	1960s–00s
Akkerman, Jan	Focus, solo	1970s–00s
Aldrich, Doug	Burning Rain, Dio, Whitesnake, solo	1980s–00s
Aleman, Oscar	Solo	1930s–70s
Alexander, Charles David	Solo	1970s–00s
Allison, Luther	Solo	1960s–90s
Almeida, Laurindo	Session guitarist, LA Four	1950s–90s
Amigo, Vicente	Manolo Sanlucar	1980s–00s
Anderson, Muriel	Solo	1980s–00s
Anderson, Scotty	Solo	1980s–00s
Andress, Tuck	Tuck & Patti	1980s–90s
Antoine, Marc	Session guitarist, solo	1970s–00s
Asheton, Ron	Iggy Pop, the Stooges	1960s–00s
Auten, D.R.	Solo	1960s–00s
Bachmann, Randy	Guess Who, Bachman-Turner Overdrive	1960s–00s
Bailey, Derek	Session guitarist, Spontaneous Music Ensemble	1960s–00s
Baker, Mickey 'Guitar'	Session guitarist, Mickey & Sylvia	1950s–90s
Barbosa-Lima, Carlos	Solo	1970s–00s
Barnes, George	Session guitarist, solo	1930s–70s
Barre, Martin	Jethro Tull	1960s–00s
Barrueco, Manuel	Solo	1970s–00s
Basho, Robbie	Solo	1960s–80s
Batio, Michael Angelo	Nitro, solo	1980s–00s
Batten, Jennifer	Jeff Beck, Michael Jackson, Solo	1980s–00s
Baty, Little Charlie	Little Charley & the Nightcaps, solo	1970s–00s
Bauer, Billy	Session guitarist	1940s–50s
Baughman, Steve	The Owner's Daughter, Solo	1990s–00s
Bautista, Roland	Earth, Wind & Fire, Tom Waits	1970s–00s
Beach, Reb	Winger, Dokken, Whitesnake	1980s–00s
Beamer, Keola	Solo	1970s–00s
Bean, Billy	Solo, session guitarist	1950s–60s
Bell, Eric	Thin Lizzy	1960s–00s
Bellas, George	UFO, solo	1990s–00s
Bennett, Stephen	Solo	1980s–00s
Bennett, Wayne	Bobby 'Blue' Band, session guitarist	1970s–90s
Bensusan, Pierre	Solo	1970s–00s
Bhatt, Vishwa Mohan	Solo	1970s–00s
Bhattacharya, Debashish	Solo	1980s–00s
Bickert, Ed	Session guitarist	1950s–90s
Bishop, Elvin	Solo, Elvin Bishop Group	1960s–00s
Blackwell, Scrapper	Solo, Duo with Leroy Carr	1920s–60s
Blake, Norman	June Carter, Bob Dylan	1950s–00s
Blind Blake	Session guitarist, solo	1920s–30s
Boggs, Noel	Bob Wills & the Texas Playboys	1950s–60s
Bolin, Tommy	James Gang, Deep Purple	1960s–70s
Bonamassa, Joe	Solo	1990s–00s
Bonfa, Luiz	Solo	1950s–90s
Boon, D.	The Minutemen	1970s–80s
Box, Mick	Uriah Heep	1970s–00s
Boyd, Liona	Solo	1980s–00s
Bream, Julian	Solo, Julian Bream Consort	1950s–90s
Bresch, Thom	Solo	1970s–00s
Bromberg, David	Solo, Bob Dylan, Jerry Garcia, George Harrison	1960s–80s
Brooks, Lonnie	Session guitarist, solo	1950s–90s
Broonzy, Big Bill	Solo	1920s–50s
Brown, 'Gatemouth'	Solo	1940s–00s
Brown, Junior	Solo	1960s–00s
Brown, Norman	Solo, Boyz II Men, Stevie Wonder	1990s–00s
Brozman, Bob	Solo, the Cheap Suit Serenaders	1980s–00s
Bruce, Jack	Cream, Manfred Mann, West, Bruce & Laing	1960s–00s
Bruno, Jimmy	Frank Sinatra, Buddy Rish, Solo	1960s–00s
Bryant, Jimmy	West	1950s–70s
Buchanan, Roy	Solo	1950s–80s
Buckethead	Guns N' Roses, Praxis, C2B3, solo	1980s–00s
Buckingham, Lindsey	Fleetwood Mac	1960s–00s
Bull, Sandy	Solo	1960s–80s
Bullock, Hiram	Solo, Pete Townshend, Eric Clapton, Miles Davis	1970s–00s
Burrell, Kenny	Stan Getz, Billie Holiday, Johnny Coltrane	1950s–00s
Buxton, Glen	Alice Cooper	1960s–90s
Byrd, Charlie	Stan Getz	1950s–90s
Byrd, Jerry	Country All Stars	1940s–90s
California, Randy	Spirit, solo	1970s–90s
Campbell, Mike	Tom Petty & the Heartbreakers	1970s–00s
Campbell, Glenn	Solo	1960s–00s
Campbell, Vivian	Dio, Whitesnake, Def Leppard	1970s–00s
Cantrell, Jerry	Alice In Chains, solo	1990s–00s
Carmichael, Greg	Acoustic Alchemy	1970s–90s
Carthy, Martin	Steeleye Span, The Albion Band	1960s–00s
Chad, Dominick	Mansun, solo	1980s–00s
Chadbourne, Eugene	Shockabilly	1970s–00s
Chaquico, Craig	Jefferson Starship, Starship, Solo	1960s–00s
Christ, John	Danzig, solo	1980s–00s
Cipollina, John	Quicksilver Messenger Service	1960s–80s
Clark, Roy	Solo	1950s–00s
Clark, Steve	Def Leppard	1970s–80s
Clarke, Stanley	Return To Forever, Chick Corea	1970s–00s
Cody, Harry	Shotgun Messiah	1980s–00s
Coleman, Fitzroy	Solo	1940s–70s
Collen, Phil	Def Leppard	1970s–00s
Collins, Albert	Solo	1950s–90s
Collins, Allen	Lynyrd Skynyrd	1960s–80s
Connors, Bill	Solo, Return Of Forever	1970s–00s
Conti, Robert	Solo	1960s–00s
Copeland, Johnny	Solo	1950s–80s
Corgan, Billy	Smashing Pumpkins, solo	1980s–00s
Coulter, William	Solo, Orison	1980s–00s
Cray, Robert	Solo	1980s–00s
Crayton, Pee Wee	Solo	1940s–80s
D'Agostino, Peppino	Solo	1980s–00s
Dadi, Marcel	Solo	1970s–90s
Davis, Rev. Gary	Solo	1930s–70s
DeGarmo, Chris	Queensryche, Jerry Cantrell	1980s–00s
DeGrassi, Alex	Solo	1970s–00s
DeMarchena, Melchor	Solo	1940s–80s
DeMartini, Warren	Ratt	1980s–00s
Dharma, Buck	Blue Oyster Cult	1960s–00s
Diaz, Alirio	Solo	1950s–00s
Dibala, Diblo	Loketo, Matchatcha	1970s–00s
Diorio, Joe	Solo	1960s–00s
Dominguez, Juanjo	Solo	1970s–00s
Donelly, Tanya	Solo, Throwing Muses, The Breeders	1980s–00s
Donohue, Pat	Solo	1980s–00s
Dowling, Mike	Solo	1970s–00s
Downing, K.K.	Judas Priest	1960s–00s
Drake, Nick	Solo	1960s–70s
Duarte, Chris	The Chris Duarte Group, session guitarist	1990s–00s
Duffy, Billy	The Cult	1970s–00s
Dunn, Michael	Solo	1960s–00s
Dykes, Doyle	Solo	1990s–00s
Dylan, Bob	Solo	1950s–00s
Eaglin, Snooks	Solo	1950s–00s
Earl, Ronnie	Roomful Of Blues	1970s–00s
Einziger, Mike	Incubus	1990s–00s
Eklundh, Mattias 'I.A.'	Freak Kitchen	1980s–00s
Elliot, Mike	Solo	1970s–00s
Ellis, Herb	Oscar Peterson Trio, Ella Fitzgerald	1940s–90s
Ellis, Tinsley	Solo	1980s–00s
Embrey, Danny	Solo	1980s–00s
Emmanuel, Tommy	Solo, Goldrush, Tina Turner	1960s–00s
Emmitt, Rik	Triumph	1970s–00s
Emmons, Buddy	The Everly Brothers	1950s–90s
Entwistle, John	The Who	1960s–00s
Escudero, Mario	Concert guitarist	1940s–80s
Eubanks, Kevin	Solo, Tonight Show Band	1970s–00s
Farrell, Tim	Solo	1980s–00s
Feiten, Buzz	The Rascals, Laren-Feiten Band	1960s–00s
Felder, Don	The Eagles	1970s–00s
Fernandez, Julio	Spyro Gyra	1980s–00s
Finger, Peter	Solo	1970s–90s
Fisk, Eliot	Solo	1980s–00s
Flatt, Lester	Flatt & Scruggs	1940s–70s
Fogerty, John	Creedence Clearwater Revival, solo	1950s–00s
Ford, Lita	The Runaways, solo	1970s–00s
Ford, Robben	Charles Ford Blues Band, Solo	1960s–00s
Forte, Stephan	Adagio, solo	1990s–00s
Frame, Roddy	Aztec Camera, solo	1980s–00s
Freeman, Russ	The Rippingtons, Mariah Carey	1950s–00s
Frehley, Ace	Kiss	1960s–00s
Freymuth, Dirk	Solo	2000s
Frith, Fred	Henry Crow, solo	1960s–00s
Fulson, Lowell	Solo	1940s–90s
Funderburgh, Anson	The Rockets, the Fabulous Thunderbirds	1970s–00s
Gaines, Steve	Lynyrd Skynyrd	1970s
Galbraith, Paul	Solo	1980s–00s
Gallup, Cliff	Gene Vincent's Blue Caps, Solo	1950s–60s
Gambale, Frank	Chick Corea, Vital Information, solo	1980s–00s
Garland, Hank	Solo, Elvis Presley	1940s–60s
Garrett, Amos	Stony Plain, solo	1970s–00s
Gatton, Danny	Liz Meyer & Friends, solo	1960s–90s
Gaughan, Dick	Solo	1970s–00s
Geissman, Grant	Solo	1970s–00s
George, Lowell	Little Feat, solo	1960s–70s
Geremia, Paul	Solo	1960s–00s
Gerhard, Edward	Solo	1980s–00s
Gers, Janick	Iron Maiden	1980s–00s
Gilderdale, Miles	Acoustic Alchemy, Zoots & Roots	1980s–00s
Gilewitz, Richard	Solo	1990s–00s
Gill, Andy	Gang Of Four	1970s–00s
Gillis, Brad	Night Ranger, Ozzy Osbourne	1980s–00s
Ginn, Greg	Black Flag	1970s–00s
Golub, Jeff	Solo	1990s–00s
Goodrick, Mick	Solo	1970s–00s
Goodsall, John	Brand X, session guitarist	1970s–00s
Gorham, Scott	Thin Lizzy	1970s–00s
Gossard, Stone	Pearl Jam, Temple Of The Dog	1980s–00s
Graham, Jonny	Earth, Wind & Fire, Al McKay's LA All Stars	1970s–00s
Green, Freddie	Count Basie	1930s–80s
Green, Grant	Blue Note Records, solo	1950s–70s
Green, Mick	The Pirates, Van Morrison	1970s–00s
Greenwich, Sonny	Charles Lloyd, Hank Mobley	1960s–90s
Grela, Roberto	Solo	1930s–80s
Grier, David	Solo, Psychograss	1990s
Grossman, Stefan	Solo, Even Dozen Jug Band	1960s–90s
Guitar Shorty	Walter Johnson Band, solo	1950s–00s
Guns, Tracii	Guns N' Roses, LA Guns	1980s–90s
Guthrie, Woody	Solo	1930s–60s
Hall, Jim	Bill Evans, Pat Metheny	1950s–00s
Hammond, John	Solo	1960s–00s
Hanneman, Jeff	Slayer	1980s–00s
Hannon, Frank	Tesla	1980s–00s
Harkness, Sean	Solo	1980s–00s
Harper, Nick	Roy Harper	1990s–00s
Harper, Roy	Nick Harper, Dave Gilmour	1960s–00s
Harris, Corey	Solo	1990s–00s
Hart, Alvin 'Youngblood'	Solo	1990s–00s
Harvey, P.J.	Solo	1990s–00s
Haynes, Warren	Allman Brothers Band, Gov't Mule, solo	1980s–00s
Hayward, Justin	Moody Blues, solo	1960s–00s
Healey, Jeff	Solo	1980s–00s
Hedges, Michael	Solo	1980s–90s
Henderson, Scott	Tribal Tech, solo	1980s–00s
Hetfield, James	Metallica	1970s–00s
Hicks, Tony	The Hollies	1960s–00s
Hoey, Gary	Solo, Vinnie	1990s–00s
Hole, Dave	Solo	1970s–00s
Holly, Buddy	The Crickets	1950s
Hollywood Fats	James Harman	1970s–80s
Hooker, Earl	Solo, Muddy Waters	1940s–70s
Hoopii, Sol	Solo	1920s–50s
Hopkins, Lightnin'	Solo, Wilson Smith	1940s–70s
House, Son	Solo	1930s–70s
Howe, Greg	Planet X, solo	1980s–00s
Hughes, Brian	Solo, Loreena McKennit	1990s–00s
Hunter, Charlie	Solo, Disposable Heroes Of Hiphoprisy	1990s–00s
Huttlinger, Peter	Solo, John Denver, LeAnn Rhymes	1990s–00s
Isbin, Sharon	Solo	1970s–00s
Isley, Ernie	The Isley Brothers, solo	1970s–00s
Izmailov, Enver	Solo	1990s–00s
Jabs, Matthias	Scorpions	1970s–00s
James, Skip	Solo	1930s–60s
Jett, Joan	The Runaways, the Blackhearts, solo	1970s–00s
Johns, Daniel	Silverchair, the Dissociatives	1990s–00s
Johnson, Alphonso	Weather Report, session guitarist	1970s–00s
Johnson, Blind Willie	Solo	1920s–30s
Johnson, Henry	Solo	1970s–00s
Johnson, Lonnie	Solo	1920s–60s
Johnson, Orville	Solo, session guitarist	1970s–00s
Johnson, Richard	Solo	1970s–00s
Johnston, Randy	Solo	1990s–00s

other great guitarists

Jones, Buster B.	Solo	1990s–00s
Jones, Mick	Foreigner	1960s–00s
Jones, Steve	The Sex Pistols	1970s–00s
Jones, Tommy	Solo	1980s–00s
Jordan, Ronny	The Flaming Lips	1990s–00s
Juber, Laurence	Wings, session guitarist	1970s–00s
Kaapana, Ledward	Hui 'Ohana, solo	1980s–00s
Kaiser, Henry	Solo	1970s–00s
Kane, Raymond	Solo	1950s–00s
Kaukonen, Jorma	Jefferson Airplane, Hot Tuna	1960s–00s
Kendall, Mark	Great White	1980s–00s
Keneally, Mike	Frank Zappa, the Mike Keneally Band, solo	1980s–00s
Kessel, Barney	Solo, session guitarist	1940s–70s
Khan, Steve	Solo, Steely Dan, Bill Joel	1970s–00s
King, Earl	Solo	1950s–00s
King, Kaki	Solo	2000s
King, Kerry	Slayer	1980s–00s
Kirtley, Pat	Solo	1990s–00s
Klugh, Earl	Solo	1970s–00s
Konadu, Alex	Solo	1990s–00s
Kottke, Leo	Solo	1960s–00s
Kotzen, Ritchie	Poison, Mr Big, solo	1980s–00s
Kraft, Norbert	Solo	1970s–00s
Kramer, Wayne	The MC5	1960s–00s
Kress, Carl	Solo, session guitarist	1930s–60s
Kubek, Smokin' Joe	Solo	1990s–00s
Lagoya, Alexandre	Solo	1950s–90s
Lagrene, Bireli	Solo	1980s–00s
Lalonde, Larry 'Ler'	Primus	1980s–00s
Lane, Shawn	Black Oak Arkansas, Willy, Solo	1970s–00s
Lang, Eddie	Solo, session guitarist	1910s–30s
Lang, Peter	Solo	1970s–00s
Lanham, Roy	Sons Of The Pioneers, solo	1940s–80s
Latimer, Andy	Camel	1960s–00s
Lenoir, J.B.	Solo	1950s–60s
Levene, Kieth	Public Image Ltd	1970s–00s
Lister, Ainsley	Solo	1990s–00s
Little Milton	Solo	1950s–00s
Lockwood Jr, Robert	Solo, King Biscuit Time	1930s–00s
Lofgren, Nils	E Street Band	1970s–00s
Lofsky, Lorne	Solo, Oscar Peterson Quartet	1980s–00s
Loomis, Jeff	Nevermore	1990s–00s
MacAlpine, Tony	Solo, Planet X, Ring Of Fire	1980s–00s
Mack, Lonnie	Solo	1950s–00s
Magic Sam	Solo	1950s–60s
Mahal, Taj	Solo	1960s–00s
Malakian, Daron	System Of A Down	1990s–00s
Malone, Russell	Solo, session guitarist	1980s–00s
Mandel, Harvey	Solo, Canned Heat	1960s–00s
Mangore, Agustin Barrios	Solo	1910s–40s
Manzanera, Phil	Roxy Music, solo	1970s–00s
Maphis, Joe	Solo	1940s–80s
Marino, Frank	Mahogany Rush	1970s–00s
Marley, Bob	Solo, the Wailers	1960s–80s
Mars, Mick	Mötley Crüe	1980s–00s
Martin, Grady	Session guitarist, solo	1940s–90s
Martino, Pat	Solo	1960s–00s
Martyn, John	Solo	1970s–90s
Mascis, J.	Dinosaur Junior, the Fog	1990s–00s
Mason, Brent	Session guitarist, solo	1980s–00s
Mayfield, Curtis	The Impressions	1950s–90s
McCartney, Paul	The Quarrymen, the Beatles, Wings	1950s–00s
McDowell, Mississippi Fred	Solo	1950s–70s
McGeoch, John	Magazine, Visage	1970s–90s
McKay, Al	Earth, Wind & Fire, LA All Stars	1960s–00s
McLaughlin, Billy	Solo	1990s–00s
McManus, Tony	Solo	1990s–00s
McMeen, El	Solo	1970s–00s
McTell, Blind Willie	Solo, session guitarist	1920s–50s
Messer, Michael	The Michael Messer Band, Solo	1980s–00s
Messina, Jim	Buffalo Springfield, Poco, Loggins and Messina	1960s–00s
Messina, Joe	The Funk Brothers, Motown sessions	1960s–00s
Michael, Dorian	Solo	1970s–00s
Miller, Jerry	Moby Grape	1950s–00s
Mitchell, Joni	Solo	1960s–00s
Mitchell, Kim	Max Webster, solo	1970s–00s
Mize, Bill	Solo	1950s–00s
Mo, Keb	Solo	1980s–00s
Montgomery, Monte	Solo	1990s–00s
Montoya, Coco	Solo, Bluesbreakers	1970s–00s
Montoya, Ramon	Solo	1920s–40s
Montrose, Ronnie	Montrose, Edgar Winter Group	1970s–00s
Moore, Oscar	Nat King Cole Trio	1930s–60s
Moore, Tracy	Solo	1980s–00s
Moore, Vinnie	Alice Cooper, solo	1970s–00s
Mottola, Tony	Solo, Frank Sinatra, Perry Como	1940s–90s
Murphey, Matt 'Guitar'	Howlin' Wolf, Blues Brothers	1950s–00s
Mustaine, Dave	Metallica, Megadeth	1980s–00s
Muthspiel, Wolfgang	Solo	1980s–00s
Naumov, Yuri	Solo	1980s–00s
Navarro, Ken	Solo	1990s–00s
Nawahi, King Bennie	Solo	1920s–70s
Neaga, Greg	Solo	1990s–00s

Nichols, Roy	Merle Haggard	1960s–90s
Nico, Doctor	Grand Kalle & l'African Jazz	1960s–70s
Niedt, Douglas	Solo	1980s–00s
Nighthawk, Robert	Solo	1930s–60s
Nimo, Koo	Solo	1960s–00s
Nocentelli, Leo	The Meters	1980s–00s
Nogueira, Paulinho	Solo	1960s–90s
Nolen, Jimmy	The J.B.'s, James Brown	1950s–80s
Nyame, E.K.	Solo	1990s–00s
O'Brien, Ed	Radiohead	1980s–00s
Ostroushko, Peter	Solo	1970s–00s
Otis, Shuggie	Solo	1960s–00s
Pacetti, Sam	Solo	1990s–00s
Pahinui, Gabby	Session guitarist, solo	1940s–70s
Paredes, Carlos	Solo	1960s–70s
Pareja, Alex	The Number Twelve Looks Like You	2000s
Parfitt, Rick	Status Quo	1960s–00s
Parkening, Christopher	Solo	1960s–00s
Parks, Dean	Solo	1980s–00s
Pastorius, Jaco	Weather Report	1960s–80s
Paul, Gayla Drake	Solo	1980s–00s
Pauling, Lowman	The 5" Royales	1950s–60s
Peña, Paco	Solo	1950s–00s
Perkins, Carl	Solo	1950s–90s
Petteway, Al	Solo	1990s–00s
Phelps, Kelly Joe	Solo	1990s–00s
Phillips, Steve	Notting Hillbillies, solo	1960s–00s
Pisano, John	Session guitarist	1970s–00s
Pitrelli, Al	Trans-Siberian Orchestra, Savatage, Megadeth	1980s–00s
Pizzarelli, Bucky	Solo, the Three Sounds Trio	1940s–00s
Pizzarelli, John	Solo, Buck Pizzarelli	1980s–00s
Platino, Franco	Solo	1990s–00s
Powell, Andy	Wishbone Ash	1970s–00s
Powell, Baden	Solo	1960s–00s
Presti, Ida	Alexandre Lagoya	1950s–60s
Price, Rod	Foghat, solo	1960s–00s
Quine, Robert	The Voidoids	1960s–00s
Rabin, Trevor	Yes	1970s–00s
Ralphs, Mick	Bad Company	1980s–00s
Ramone, Johnny	The Ramones	1970s–90s
Ramos, Kid	The Fabulous Thunderbirds	1980s–00s
Ranaldo, Lee	Sonic Youth	1980s–00s
Randolph, Robert	Robert Randolph & the Family Band, Santana	2000s
Raney, Jimmy	Solo, Red Norvo Trio	1950s–90s
Ranglin, Ernest	Solo, session guitarist	1960s–00s
Reed, Jerry	Session guitarist	1960s–00s
Reed, Lou	The Velvet Underground	1950s–00s
Reed, Preston	Solo	1970s–00s
Reid, Vernon	Living Colour	1980s–00s
Remler, Emily	Solo	1980s
Reynolds, Tim	TR3, Dave Matthews Band	1980s–00s
Rhodes, Red	Solo, session guitarist	1960s–90s
Ricardo, Nino	Solo	1940s–70s
Rice, Tony	Solo	1970s–00s
Richrath, Gary	REO Speedwagon, solo	1970s–00s
Rintour, Lee	Solo, session guitarist	1990s–00s
Roberts, Howard	Solo, session guitarist	1940s–70s
Robertson, Brian	Thin Lizzy, Motorhead	1970s–00s
Robertson, Robbie	The Band, solo	1950s–00s
Robillard, Duke	Fabulous Thunderbirds, session guitarist	1960s–90s
Robinson, Fenton	Session guitarist	1950s–00s
Rogers, Roy	Solo	1970s–00s
Roller, Peter	Rhythm Method	1980s–00s
Rollo, Zoot Horn	The Magic Band	1960s–00s
Romeo, Michael	Symphony X, solo	1990s–00s
Romero, Angel	Los Romeros, solo	1960s–00s
Romero, Pepe	Los Romeros, solo	1960s–00s
Rosenwinkel, Kurt	Solo	1990s–00s
Ross, Don	Solo	1980s–00s
Rossi, Francis	Status Quo	1960s–00s
Rossington, Gary	Lynyrd Skynyrd, Rossington Band	1970s–00s
Rotella, Thom	Solo	1980s–00s
Roth, Arlen	Solo	1970s–00s
Rowan, Peter	Earth Opera, Seatrain, solo	1960s–00s
Rush, Otis	Solo	1950s–00s
Ruskin, Rick	Session guitarist, solo	1960s–70s
Russell, David	Solo	1990s–00s
Rypdal, Terje	George Russell, Jan Garbarek	1970s–00s
Sabicas	Solo	1920s–70s
Sanlucar, Manolo	Solo	1960s–00s
Saraceno, Blues	Poison, solo	1980s–00s
Schaffer, Rob	Into The Moat	2000s
Scholz, Tom	Boston	1970s–00s
Schwartz, Dan	Solo	1990s–00s
Seals, Son	Solo	1970s–00s
Seeger, Pete	The Weavers, Solo	1940s–00s
Sergeant, Will	Echo & the Bunnymen, solo	1970s–00s
Serranito	Solo	1960s–00s
Sete, Bola	Solo, A Tribe Called Quest	1960s–00s
Setzer, Brian	The Stray Cats, the Brian Setzer Orchestra	1980s–00s
Shamblin, Eldon	Bob Wills & his Texas Playboys	1930s–80s
Sharrock, Sonny	Solo	1960s–90s
Shepherd, Kenny Wayne	Kenny Wayne Shepherd Band	1990s–00s

Simmonds, Kim	Solo, Savoy Brown Blues Band	1960s–00s
Simon, Paul	Simon & Garfunkel, solo	1950s–00s
Simpson, Martin	Solo, Jessica Radcliffe	1970s–00s
Skeoch, Tommy	Tesla	1980s–00s
Smith, Doug	Solo	1980s–00s
Smith, Fred 'Sonic'	The MC5	1960s–90s
Smith, Johnny	Solo	1930s–60s
Smith, Richard	Solo	1980s–00s
Smith, Robert	The Cure	1970s–00s
Smither, Chris	Solo	1970s–00s
Sollscher, Goran	Solo	1970s–00s
Sor, Fernando	Solo	1900s–30s
Sparks, Tim	Solo	1970s–00s
Squire, John	The Stone Roses	1980s–00s
Staples, Roebuck 'Pops'	The Staple Singers	1940s–90s
Stefani, Mark	Solo	1970s–00s
Stephens, Leigh	Blue Cheer	1960s–00s
Steurmer, Darryl	Solo, Phil Collins	1970s–00s
Stinson, G.E.	Shadowfax	1970s–00s
Stockdale, Andrew	Wolfmother	2000s
Stuermer, Daryl	Genesis, Phil Collins, solo	1970s–00s
Sultan, Kenny	Solo, Tom Ball	1980s–00s
Sumlin, Hubert	Solo, Howlin' Wolf	1950s–00s
Sweet, Michael	Stryper	1980s–00s
Sykes, John	Blue Murder, Whitesnake, Thin Lizzy	1980s–00s
Szabo, Gabor	Solo, Chico Hamilton Quintet	1950s–80s
Tabor, Ty	Kings X, Jelly Bean, Poundhound, Jughead, Platypus	1980s–00s
Takasaki, Akira	Lazy, Loudness, Ji-Zo, solo	1980s–00s
Tarplin, Marv	The Miracles	1960s–00s
Tárrega, Francisco	Solo	1870s–00s
Taylor, Andy	Duran Duran	1980s–00s
Taylor, Eddie	Solo	1950s–80s
Taylor, Hound Dog	Solo	1950s–70s
Taylor, James	Solo	1960s–00s
Taylor, Martin	Solo	1960s–00s
Tedesco, Tommy	Session guitarist	1960s–90s
Thackery, Jimmy	Solo, the Nighthawks	1970s–00s
Thal, Ron 'Bumblefoot'	Guns N' Roses, Bumblefoot, Solo	1990s–00s
Tharpe, Sister Rosetta	Solo	1930s–40s
Thordendal, Fredrik	Meshuggah	1980s–00s
Thorogood, George	Solo, the Delaware Destroyers	1970s–00s
Tibbetts, Steve	Solo	1970s–00s
Timmons, Andy	Danger Danger, Ceili Rain	1980s–00s
Tingstad, Eric	Nancy Rumbel	1980s–00s
Tolkki, Timo	Stratovarius	1980s–00s
Towner, Ralph	Oregon, Consort	1970s–00s
Traum, Artie	Solo, Happy Traum	1960s–00s
Travers, Pat	Pat Travers Band	1970s–00s
Travis, Merle	Solo	1930s–80s
Trower, Robin	Procal Harum, solo	1960s–00s
Trucks, Derek	Derek Trucks Band, Allman Brothers Band	1990s–00s
Tucker, Luther	Luther Tucker Band	1970s–90s
Turner, Ike	The Kings Of Rhythm, The Ike & Tina Turner Revue, solo	1950s–00s
Ulmer, James Blood	Solo, Odyssey	1970s–00s
Upchurch, Phil	The Phil Upchurch Combo	1960s–90s
Vachon, Chris	Roomful Of Blues	1970s–00s
Van Eps, George	Solo, session guitarist	1950s–90s
Vaughan, Jimmy	The Fabulous Thunderbirds	1960s–00s
Vega, Suzanne	Solo	1980s–00s
Vestine, Henry	Canned Heat	1960s–90s
Volpe, Harry	Solo	1920s–90s
Wakenius, Ulf	Solo	1990s–00s
Walker, Joe Louis	Solo	1960s–00s
Ward, Robert	Ohio Untouchables	1960s–00s
Watson, 'Wah Wah'	Session guitarist	1960s–80s
Watson, Doc	Solo	1960s–00s
Webb, Nick	Acoustic Alchemy	1980s–90s
Webb, Stan	Chicken Shack	1960s–00s
West, Speedy	Jimmy Bryant, session guitarist	1940s–00s
White, Robert	The Funk Brothers, Motown sessions	1950s–70s
Whitfield, Mark	Session guitarist, solo	1990s–00s
Wilcox, David	Solo	1980s–00s
Williams, Brooks	Solo	1990s–00s
Williams, John	Solo	1950s–00s
Williams, Robert 'Pete'	Solo	1960s–70s
Willis, Eddie	The Funk Brothers, Motown sessions	1960s–70s
Wilton, Michael	Queensryche	1980s–00s
Wisefield, Laurie	Wishbone Ash, Roger Chapman	1970s–00s
Womack, Bobby	Solo, the Valentinos	1960s–00s
Wood, Ron	Faces, the Rolling Stones	1960s–00s
Woolman, Benjamin	Solo	1990s–00s
Wray, Link	Lucky Wray & the Palomino Ranch Hands (& his Ace-Men)	1950s–90s
Wyatt, Keith	The Blasters	1950s–00s
Yamashita, Kazuhito	Solo	1980s–00s
Yepes, Narciso	Solo	1940s–90s
York, Andrew	Solo, Los Angeles Guitar Quartet	1980s–00s
Young, Reggie	Session guitarist	1960s–70s

ACKNOWLEDGEMENTS

picture credits

Jason Becker (www.jasonbeckerguitar.com): 234, 235. **Corbis:** 332; Gene Ambo/Retna Ltd: 220; Sayre Berman: 239; Joe Giron: 224, 225; Hulton-Deutsch Collection: 329; Harvey L. Silver: 249; Scott D. Smith/Retna Ltd: 238. **FlamencoVision** (www.juanmartin.com): 403; **Foundry Arts:** 208, 410. **Getty Images:** Baron: 330; Michael Ochs Archives: 88, 89, 95, 115, 214, 333, 387; Michael Ochs Archives/Michael Dobo: 150; Michael Ochs Archives/Larry Hulst: 192; Michael Ochs Archives/Jon Sievert: 365; Redferns/Gilles Petard: 411; Redferns/Gai Terell: 253; Rusty Russell: 441; Wire Image/Tom Hill 166; WireImage/Paul Natkin: 209. **Steve Hackett** (www.stevehackett.com): 46. **LFI:** Robin Kaplan: 197; Larry Marano: 221; Ron Wolfson: 196. With grateful thanks to **Redferns** and the following photographers: 112, 134; Richard E. Aaron: 14, 26, 48, 54, 87, 110, 125, 156, 158, 165, 174, 175, 186, 205, 250, 259, 282, 368, 375, 389, 390, 435; Jorgen Angel: 32, 43, 163, 204; Roberta Bayley: 283; BBC Photo Library: 84, 118, 162; Paul Bergen: 42, 132, 268, 322, 325, 416; Carey Brandon: 60, 65, 72; Colin Burgess: 392; Henrietta Butler: 359; Clayton Call: 37, 154, 274, 393; Mike Cameron: 287; Sandy Caspers: 67, 313; Charlie Gillet Archive: 96, 142; Stephanie Chernikowski: 104; Rogan Coles: 413; David Corio: 202; Fin Costello: 29, 38, 39, 55, 62, 63, 128, 136, 172, 178, 179, 180, 181, 190, 191, 194, 195, 198, 199, 262, 378, 394, 395, 407; Pete Cronin: 201, 398; Rico D'Rozario: 433; David Warner Ellis Photography: 36; Deltahaze Corporation: 77, 82, 83; Phil Dent: 265; Ian Dickson: 40, 49, 85, 168, 255, 260, 263, 296, 319; Alain Dister: 35, 103, 105; James Dittiger 218, 293, 415; Erica Echenberg: 44, 161; Echoes Archives: 376, 385, 396, 426; Alison Eliott: 438; Tabatha Fireman: 316, 323, 421; Patrick Ford: 289, 312, 431; Fotex Agentur Gmbh: 47, 131; GAB Archives: 78, 79, 119, 120, 129, 155, 248, 251, 334, 335, 348, 356, 371; Ramerez Gant: 318; GEMS: 98, 121, 144, 151, 244, 258, 404, 406; Suzie Gibbons: 297; Giles Petard Collection: 80, 81, 90, 108; Mick Gold: 126; Harry Goodwin: 148, 254; William Gottlieb: 337, 341; Beth Gwinn: 350, 430; Dimitrie Hakke: 291; Tim Hall: 423, 432; Harry Herd: 321; Ron Howard: 16, 264; Mick Hutson: 50, 143, 184, 187, 188, 207, 212, 213, 216, 219, 223, 226, 227, 228, 230, 231, 233, 237, 286, 292, 311, 324, 429; JP Jazz Archive: 342, 344, 345; Jens Jurgensen: 232; Bob King: 68, 193, 203, 266, 267; John Lynn Kirk: 414; Robert Knight: 23, 24, 53, 102, 167, 222, 236, 315, 439, 440; Bo Landy: 229; Elliott Landy: 86, 101, 127, 146; Andrew Lepley: 377, 397, 405, 417, 436, 437; Barry Levine: 138; Michel Linssen: 215, 308, 310, 428; Graham Lowe: 169; Neil Lupin: 61; Jon Lusk: 358; Susie MacDonald: 30; Andrew Maclear: 147; Hayley Madden: 70, 171, 273, 290, 402; Stefanie Mainey: 301; Max Jones Files: 336, 338, 339, 343; Steve Morley: 242, 247, 288; Keith Morris: 92, 93, 401; Leon Morris: 243; Stuart Mostyn: 317; Brend Muller: 217; Ilpo Musto: 139; Vitaliano Napolitano: 422; New Eyes: 113; Petra Niemeier: 17, 153; Peter Pakvis: 58, 73, 130, 302, 320; PALM/RSCH: 328, 331; Ed Perlstein: 20, 31; Jan Persson: 18, 28, 124, 140, 149, 182, 366, 380, 388, 424; Martin Philbey: 64, 271, 307, 314; Stefan M. Prager: 269, 306, 427; Mike Prior: 189; Andrew Putler: 25, 27, 157, 370, 400; Christina Radish: 276; RB: 21, 34, 117; David Redfern: 19, 33, 91, 97, 100, 109, 122, 135, 137, 141, 152, 159, 173, 246, 252, 346, 347, 349, 352, 353, 354, 355, 362, 369, 379, 383, 386, 412, 418, 419; Lorne Resnick: 15, 45, 57; Adam Ritchie: 145; Simon Ritter: 277; Ebet Roberts: 52, 56, 59, 66, 114, 116, 170, 185, 200, 206, 211, 245, 257, 270, 275, 278, 279, 303, 304, 309, 340, 351, 357, 367, 372, 373, 374, 391, 408, 409, 420, 434; Donna Santisi: 256; Jim Sharpe: 284; Brian Shuel: 360, 361, 382; Nicky J. Sims: 363, 381; Kevin Statham: 305; Barbara Steinwehe: 111, 123, 272; Peter Still: 425; Stockpop.com: 51; Jon Super: 71, 299; Virginia Turbett: 99, 210; Richard Upper: 133, 160; Lex Van Rossen: 164, 384; Rob Verhorst: 22, 41; Leslie West: 183; Gary Wolstenholme: 69; Stephen Wright: 285, 298, 300; Yani Yordanova: 294, 295; Charlyn Zlotnik: 261. **Topham Picturepoint:** Arena Images/Jan Kilby: 399.

author biographies

Rusty Cutchin (Consultant Editor and Author)
Rusty Cutchin has been a guitarist, recording engineer, producer and journalist for over 25 years. He has been technical editor of *Guitar One* magazine, as well as editor-in-chief of *Home Recording* magazine and an associate editor of *Electronic Musician* magazine. He has been a contributor and consultant editor to 10 books on music, guitar, and recording. As a recording engineer, he worked on records by Richie Sambora, Mariah Carey, Yoko Ono, and many others. His articles have appeared in *Billboard*, *Hits*, *Musician*, *Country Fever*, *Cashbox*, and *International Musician and Recording World*.

Hugh Fielder (Author)
Hugh Fielder can remember the 1960s even though he was there. He can remember the 1970s and 1980s because he was at *Sounds* magazine (RIP) and the 1990s because he was editor of Tower Records' *TOP* magazine. He has shared a spliff with Bob Marley, a glass of wine with David Gilmour, a pint with Robert Plant, a cup of tea with Keith Richards and a frosty stare with Axl Rose. He has watched Mike Oldfield strip naked in front of him and Bobby Womack fall asleep while he was interviewing him.

Mike Gent (Author)
Nurturing an obsession with pop music which dates back to first hearing Slade's 'Gudbuy T'Jane' in 1972, Mike Gent remains fixated, despite failing to master any musical instrument, with the possible exception of the recorder. A freelance writer since 2001, he has contributed to *Writers' Forum*, *Book and Magazine Collector*, *Record Buyer*, *When Saturday Comes*, *Inside David Bowie and the Spiders* (DVD), *The Kinks 1964–1978* (DVD), *The Beatles 1962–1970* (DVD), *Remember the Eighties*, *Where Were You When? – Music That Changed Our Lives*, *The Definitive Illustrated Encyclopaedia of Rock* and *The Little Book of the World Cup*. His personal guitar hero is Johnny Marr.

Michael Mueller (Author)
Michael Mueller is a New York-based guitarist, author, editor, and journalist. He is the former editor-in-chief of *Guitar One* magazine, where he interviewed such legendary guitarists as Angus Young, Joe Satriani, John Petrucci, Steve Vai, Zakk Wylde, Eric Johnson, Mark Tremonti, and Frank Gambale, among many others. Currently, he is a contributor to *Guitar Edge* magazine and *GuitarInstructor.com*. He has also written for *Guitar World*, *Women Who Rock*, and *Home Recording*.

As an author, Mueller has written several instructional books, including the *Hal Leonard Rock Guitar Method*, *Jazz For the Rock Guitarist* (Hal Leonard), and *Sight Reading for the Rock Guitarist* (Cherry Lane). Additionally, he has worked behind the scenes to produce several instructional guitar videos for the Hal Leonard Corporation, including the *Hal Leonard Guitar Method*, *Best of Lennon & McCartney* (for electric, acoustic, and bass guitar), and *Guitar Soloing*.

Dave Simons (Author)
Dave Simons is a musician and journalist, and has covered the recording arts, past and present, for a variety of publications including *Home Recording*, *Guitar One* and *Musician*. His recent books include *Studio Stories: How the Great New York Records Were Made* (Backbeat) and *Read the Beatles: Classic and New Writings on the Beatles, Their Legacy, and Why They Still Matter* (Penguin).

RESOURCES

further reading

Anderson, P. and Watkinson, M., *Syd Barrett: Crazy Diamond: The Dawn of Pink Floyd*, Omnibus Press, 1991

Assante, E., *Legends of Rock: The Artists, Instruments, Myths and History of 50 Years of Youth Music*, White Star, 2007

Bego, M., *Bonnie Raitt: Still in the Nick of Time*, Cooper Square Press, 2003

Bene, D., *Randy Rhoads: A Life*, Roxx Productions, 2005

Bloom, J., *Black Knight: Ritchie Blackmore*, Omnibus Press, 2006

Bockris, V., *Keith Richards: The Biography*, De Capo Press, 2003

Carcieri, M., *Prince: A Life in Music*, iUniverse Inc., 2004

Carson, A. and Beck, J., *Jeff Beck: Crazy Fingers*, Backbeat Books, 2001

Case, G., *Jimmy Page: Magus, Musician, Man: An Unauthorized Biography*, Hal Leonard, 2007

Chapman, C., *Interviews with the Jazz Greats*, Mel Bay Publications, 2001

Chapman, R. and Clapton, E., *Guitar: Music, History, Players*, DK Publishing, 2003

Charlesworth, C., *A–Z of Rock Guitarists*, Proteus Publishing, 1983

Cherry Lane Music (ed.), *Guitar One Presents Legends of the Lead Guitar: The Best of Interviews: 1995–2000*, Cherry Lane Music, 2001

Christie, I., *Everybody Wants Some: The Van Halen Saga*, Wiley John & Sons, 2007

Clapton, E., *Clapton: The Autobiography*, Broadway Books, 2007

Clarke, S., *Peter Frampton: The Man Who Came Alive*, Castle Books, 1977

Clayson, A., *Legendary Sessions: The Rolling Stones*, Beggars Banquet, Flame Tree Publishing, 2008

Cochran, B. and Van Hecke, S., *Three Steps to Heaven: The Eddie Cochran Story*, Hal Leonard, 2003

Cochran, R. and Atkins, C., *Chet Atkins: Me and My Guitars*, Hal Leonard, 2003

Collis, J., *Ike Turner: King of Rhythm*, Do Not Press, 2004

Crawford, B. and Patoski, J., *Stevie Ray Vaughan: Caught in the Crossfire*, Little Brown & Company, 1994

Cross, C., *Heavier than Heaven: A Biography of Kurt Cobain*, Hyperion, 2002

Cross, C., *Room Full of Mirrors: A Biography of Jimi Hendrix*, Hyperion, 2005

Cyr, M., *A Wished-for Song: A Portrait of Jeff Buckley*, Hal Leonard, 2002

Dann, T., *Darker than the Deepest Sea: The Search for Nick Drake*, De Capo Press, 2006

Davies, D., *Kink: An Autobiography*, Hyperion, 1998

Dome, M. and Fogg, R., *Eddie Van Halen: Know the Man, Play the Music*, Backbeat Books, 2005

Duarte, J., *Andres Segovia As I Knew Him*, Mel Bay Publications, 1999

Forbes-Roberts, R. and Lees, G., *One Long Tune: The Life and Music of Lenny Breau*, University of North Texas Press, 2006

Frame, P., *The Complete Rock Family Trees*, Omnibus Press, 1983

Franz, S., *The Amazing Secret History of Elmore James*, Bluesource Publications, 2003

Freeth, N. and Douse, C., *Icons of Music: Great Guitarists*, Thunder Bay Press, 2002

Gill, C., *Guitar Legends: The Definitive Guide to the World's Greatest Guitar Players*, HarperCollins, 1995

Goins, W.E. and McKinney C.R., *A Biography of Charlie Christian, Jazz Guitar's King of Swing*, Edwin Mellen Press, 2005

Gregory, H., *1000 Great Guitarists*, Backbeat Books, 2002

Grouse, L., *Fancy Fretwork: The Great Jazz Guitarists*, Franklin Watts, 2000

Hal Leonard (ed.), *Guitar World Presents the 100 Greatest Guitarists of All Time*, Hal Leonard, 2002

Harper, C. and Marr, J., *Dazzling Stranger: Bert Jansch and the British Folk and Blues Revival*, Bloomsbury Publishing, 2006

Harrison, G., *I, Me, Mine*, Weidenfeld & Nicolson, 2002

Heatley, M., *Neil Young in His Own Words*, Omnibus Press, 1997

Heatley, M. (ed.), *The Definitive Illustrated Encyclopaedia of Rock*, Flame Tree Publishing, 2006

Hendrix, J. and McDermott, J., *Jimi Hendrix: An Illustrated Experience*, Atria Books, 2007

Hjort, C. and Hinman, D., *Jeff's Book: A Chronology of Jeff Beck's Career 1965–1980*, Rock'n'Roll Research Press, 2000

Ingram, A., *The Gibson 335: Its History and Its Players*, Centerstream Publications, 2006

Jackson, B., *Garcia: An American Life*, Penguin Group, 2000

Jackson, L., *Brian May*, Portrait, 2007

Keenom, B. and Wolkin, J.M., *Michael Bloomfield: If You Love These Blues: An Oral History*, Miller Freeman Books, 2000

Kempster, G., *Guitars: Sounds, Chrome and Stars*, Flame Tree Publishing, 2007

Kienzle, R., *Great Guitarists: The Most Influential Players in Jazz, Country, Blues and Rock*, Facts on File, 1985

King, B.B. and Ritz, D., *Blues All Around Me: The Autobiography of B.B. King*, HarperCollins, 1999

Lawrence, R., *The Les Paul Legacy: The Man, the Sound, and the Gibson Guitar*, Hal Leonard, 2008

Leonard, M. (ed.), *The Illustrated Complete Guitar Handbook*, Flame Tree Publishing, 2005

Leonard, M. (ed.), *Learn to Play Guitar*, Star Fire Books, 2005

Mairants, I., *The Great Jazz Guitarists: Birth of Bebop Part 1*, Sanctuary Publishing, 2002

Mairants, I., *The Great Jazz Guitarists: On From the 1950s Part 2*, Sanctuary Publishing, 2002

Marshall, W., *The Guitar Style of Mark Knopfler*, Hal Leonard, 1999

Marten, N. and Paul, L., *Guitar Heaven*, Collins Design, 2007

Mason, N., *Inside Out: A Personal History of Pink Floyd*, Chronicle Books, 2005

McCulloch, B. and Pearson, B., *Robert Johnson: Lost and Found*, University of Illinois Press, 2003

McDonough, J., *Shakey: Neil Young's Biography*, Anchor Books, 2002

Mead, D., *Talking Guitars*, Sanctuary Publishing, 2004

Mitchell, T., *Sonic Transmission: Television: Tom Verlaine, Richard Hell*, Glitter Books, 2006

Mueller, M., *Sight Reading for the Rock Guitarist*, Cherry Lane, 2005

Mueller, M., *Rock Guitar Method*, Hal Leonard, 2002

Mueller, M., *Jazz for the Rock Guitarist*, Hal Leonard, 2005

Navarro, D. and Strauss, N., *Don't Try This At Home*, HarperCollins, 2004

Newquist, H.P. and Prown, P., *Legends of Rock Guitar*, Hal Leonard, 1997

Nilsen, P., *Dance, Music, Sex, Romance: Prince: The First Decade*, SAF Publishing, 2004

Obrecht, J., *Rollin' and Tumblin': The Postwar Blues Guitarists*, Backbeat Books, 2000

Oldfield, M., *Changeling: The Autobiography*, Virgin Books, 2007

Ophee, M. (ed.), *Dictionary of Guitarists: A Biographical, Bibliographical, Historical, Critical Dictionary of Guitars, Guitarists, Guitar-Makers, Dances and Songs*, Editions Orphee, 1986

Pegg, B., *Brown-eyed Handsome Man: The Life and Hard Times of Chuck Berry*, Routledge, 2002

Poe, R. and Gibbons, B., *Skydog: The Duane Allman Story*, Backbeat Books, 2006

Reddington, H., *The Lost Women of Rock Music: Female Musicians of the Punk Era*, Ashgate Publishing, 2007

Rogan, J., *Morrissey and Marr: The Severed Alliance*, Omnibus Press, 1993

Rolf, J. (ed.), *The Definitive Illustrated Encyclopedia of Jazz and Blues*, Flame Tree Publishing, 2007

Rolling Stone (ed.), *Harrison*, Simon & Schuster, 2002

Rubin, D., *Birth of the Groove: R&B, Soul and Funk Guitar 1945–1965*, Hal Leonard, 2004

Rubin, D., *Inside the Blues, 1942–1982: Four Decades of the Greatest Electric Blues Guitarists*, Hal Leonard, 2007

Salewicz, C., *Reggae Rebel, The Life of Peter Tosh*, Omnibus Press, 2003

Sanchez, A. and May, B., *Van Halen 101*, Author House, 2005

Sandford, C., *Keith Richards: Satisfaction*, Carroll & Graf Publishing, 2004

Schumacher, M., *Crossroads: The Life and Music of Eric Clapton*, Citadel, 2003

Shirley, I., *Led Zeppelin Revealed*, Flame Tree Publishing, 2008

Simons, D., *Studio Stories: How the Great New York Records Were Made*, Backbeat Books, 2004

Simons, D., *Read the Beatles: Classic and New Writings on the Beatles, Their Legacy, and Why They Still Matter*, Penguin, 2006

Slash and Bozza, A., *Slash: The Autobiography*, HarperCollins, 2007

Slaven, N., *Electric Don Quixote: The Definitive Story of Frank Zappa*, Omnibus Press, 2003

Stump, P., *Go Ahead John: The Music of John McLaughlin*, SAF Publishing, 1999

Summers, A. and the Edge, *One Train Later: A Memoir*, St Martin's Press, 2006

Tosone, J., *Classical Guitarists: Conversations*, McFarland & Co., 2000

Vernon, P., *Jean 'Django' Reinhardt: A Contextual Bio-discography 1910–1953*, Ashgate, 2003

Wheeler, T., *The Soul of Tone: Celebrating 60 Years of Fender Amps*, Hal Leonard, 2007

White, G., *Bo Diddley: Living Legend*, Sanctuary Publishing, 1995

Whittaker, S.C., *Unsung Heroes of Rock Guitar: 15 Great Rock Guitarists in Their Own Words*, BookSurge Publishing, 2003

Wilcock, D. and Guy, B., *Damn Right I've Got the Blues: Buddy Guy and the Blues Roots of Rock and Roll*, Hal Leonard, 1993

Wilkerson, M., *Who Are You: The Life of Pete Townshend*, Omnibus Press, 2008

Woog, A., *Carlos Santana: Legendary Guitarist*, Gale Group, 2006

Zappa, F. and Ochiogrosso, P., *The Real Frank Zappa Book*, Simon & Schuster, 1990

websites

www.acguitar.com
www.altpress.com
www.americanbluesmusic.com
www.artistdirect.com
www.aversion.com
www.billboard.com
www.blackmoresnight.com
www.brianmay.com
www.chuckberry.com
www.classicalguitarist.co.uk
www.classicjazzguitar.com
www.clickmusic.com
www.digitaldreamdoor.com
www.downbeat.com
www.dustygroove.com
www.emusician.com
www.ericclapton.com
www.ericjohnson.com
www.famous-guitarists.artemiscrowe.com
www.guitaredgemag.com
www.guitarinstructor.com
www.guitarist.co.uk
www.guitaristheaven.com
www.guitarists.net
www.guitarjamsession.com
www.guitarnotes.com
www.guitarnstuff.com
www.guitarojam.com
www.guitarplayer.com
www.guitarscanada.com/Legends.htm
www.guitarsite.com
www.guitarworld.com
www.hotguitarist.com
www.insound.com
www.jeffbeck.com
www.jimi-hendrix.com
www.jimmypageonline.com
www.jmarr.com
www.johnpetrucci.com
www.keithrichards.com
www.kerrang.com
www.last.fm
www.legendsofjazz.net
www.markknopfler.com
www.modernguitarist.com
www.mojo4music.com
www.musicfirebox.com
www.musicroom.com
www.musicweek.com
www.myspace.com
www.nme.com
www.q4music.com
www.randy-rhoads.com
www.reasontorock.vom
www.recordcollectormag.com
www.rock.com
www.rockdetector.com
www.rockgods.threewayservices.com
www.rockhall.com
www.rocksbackpages.com
www.rollingstone.com
www.santana.com
www.satriani.com
www.stevehackett.com
www.stevehowe.com
www.stevemorse.com
www.thewire.co.uk
www.ultimaterockgods.com
www.van-halen.com
www.vh1.com
www.worldguitarist.com
www.worldsgreatestguitarist.com
www.yngwie.org
www.zappa.com

INDEX